Education

Between Two Worlds

Education
Between
Two Worlds

by

ALEXANDER MEIKLEJOHN

Essay Index Reprint Series

 BOOKS FOR LIBRARIES PRESS
FREEPORT, NEW YORK

Reprinted 1972 by arrangement with
Harper & Row, Publishers, Inc.

Library of Congress Cataloging in Publication Data

Meiklejohn, Alexander, 1872-1964.
    Education between two worlds.

    (Essay index reprint series)
    1. Education--Philosophy. I. Title.
LB875.M33 1972   370.1   71-167385
ISBN 0-8369-2565-3

PRINTED IN THE UNITED STATES OF AMERICA
BY
NEW WORLD BOOK MANUFACTURING CO., INC.
HALLANDALE, FLORIDA 33009

To

HELEN

Contents

Preface

I HAVE tried in this book to write about education. Especially I have wanted to understand the schools and colleges of the United States. But I find myself writing about the World War. Have I then wandered from my theme? I think not. The catastrophe which has come upon humanity is, in its deepest aspect, the collapse of human learning and teaching. We shall escape that catastrophe, shall ensure that it does not come upon us again, only as we succeed in devising better learning and better teaching. Under the conditions of modern life the primary need of mankind is that we have better education.

How long will the Great War last? Its first phase ended in 1918, with nothing permanent accomplished. Millions of men had died in vain. No questions had been answered. No policies had been established. Our minds had failed utterly to understand what our bodies had been doing.

The second phase of the conflict is now raging. Englishmen and Americans are alike hoping that it will soon be over, that it will, again, end in "a victory for the democracies." But if so, will that be the end of the Great War? Or will it be simply the completing of another skirmish, whose real function is to prepare the way for the wider and more fundamental fighting which is to follow? How will the Great War be ended?

The tragic question which I am asking can, I think, be answered, at least in principle. The war will end when the intellectual problem which underlies it has been clearly seen and, relatively speaking, solved. The war means that our Protestant-capitalist civilization has been, for three hundred years, creating for itself a dilemma. The difficulties of that dilemma have been piling up until now the burden of them is intolerable. The body politic of the modern world is writhing and struggling in the attempt to rid itself of that burden. But all our writhings and strugglings are vain unless our minds can clarify the issue, can transform the conflict into a question, can answer that question in the forms of cool, fair, impartial investigation and reflection.

Now it is the first contention of this book that the outlines of the dilemma by which our culture is torn and distracted can be best discovered in the field of education. The basic cleavage which runs through our beliefs and values comes to light when we try to determine what we shall teach and how we shall teach it. The school displays us to ourselves as neither banks nor mills nor roads nor machines can possibly do. It is the interpreter of all of these. The teacher who knows what he is doing has, therefore, a unique opportunity for learning the inner meaning of the community which he serves. There is no better way of finding out what freedom is than to undertake the task of so forming the minds and wills of individuals that they shall be free. There is no better way of discovering what social controls are than to try, while working under those controls, to bring other human beings into right relations of conformity to them and criticism of them. One learns what a state is and does when one teaches as a servant of the state, as an interpreter and critic of the government which one serves. In a word, to study education is to study the society which gives education. To understand a society is to know what and why it teaches.

The schools with which this argument is concerned are those of the Anglo-Saxon democracies of the last three centuries. In the life of England and America as we now know them, three hundred years of cultural change have moved on to a culminating and desperate crisis. That culture, in its religious and moral aspects, we have called Protestantism. On the economic and political side it has appeared as Capitalism. And these two together have established and maintained a way of life which we describe as Democratic. This book is devoted to an attempt to understand the education which is given by the Anglo-Saxon democracies, to study the learning and teaching which have been done by a Protestant-capitalist civilization.

Book I

PROTESTANT-CAPITALIST EDUCATION

Chapter 1. FROM CHURCH
TO STATE

THREE hundred years ago Anglo-Saxon teaching was done chiefly by the church. In early days English and American education was, in the main, created and sustained, inspired and controlled, by religious groups. But, today, in the greater part of the Protestant world at least, education is secular. The school has been, or is being, cut off from the church. With the exception of some "private" schools and colleges it has been taken over by another social institution. What institution is that? As matter of sober fact, who is now in charge of the teaching of our people?

There can be no doubt that, with conscious intention or without it, Anglo-Saxon Protestant civilization has drifted into an answer to that question. It is the state which is replacing the church. It is government, national, provincial, or local, which has control of teaching. Education is not only becoming secular. It is also becoming political. It is not simply Russia, Germany and Italy which have made the state the successful rival of the church. In spite of all our protestations to the contrary, we have been busy for three hundred years effecting the same revolution. We have, in fact, led the way. At the most crucial point in the field of social action we have ousted religion and put government in its place. Our protestations do not mean that we deny the fact. They mean only that, as good Anglo-Saxons, we are reluctant to face it. But the time has come when we must face it. The crucial, the decisive problem of our culture is that of the nature and functions, the powers and limitations, of the political state. That is what England and Germany are fighting about. That is the issue with which America is most deeply concerned. We must see, therefore, how, in the field of teaching, the conflict

3

between democracy and despotism, between reason and violence, has forced itself upon us.

I

From church to state! In three centuries we Protestants have transferred from one of these institutions to the other the task of shaping the minds and characters of our youth. Do we realize what we have done? This is revolution. It is the most fundamental aspect of the social transformation which has brought us from the medieval into the modern world. As compared with it, changes in the gaining and holding of property, the making and enforcing of laws, even the expression of experience in literature and art, are secondary and superficial. In the transition from the medieval to the modern form of human living I doubt if any other change is as significant as the substitution of *political* teaching for *religious*. We have changed our procedure for determining what kind of beings human beings shall be.

The significance of the change from church to state can be measured only if one can measure the difference between the purposes of these two institutions. Traditionally we have regarded them as differing widely in sphere and function. One of them we have called spiritual, the other, prudential. They have, in fact, often been intensely hostile to one another. Churches have tried to lead men in one direction. Governments have been the agents of different motives. And, this being true, it seems to follow that, during the last three hundred years, the intention of education must have radically changed. Has it? What were schools for when the churches controlled them? What are they for now, as our governments support and direct and use them? And, further, can we infer from the fact that political institutions are replacing those of religion, that the two have more in common than we have usually believed? No institution can teach unless it is equipped with the ideas, the appreciations, the wisdom out of which alone teaching can be made. If, at this point,

4

the state is to take the place of the church, then it may be that the state is, or will become, much more like the church than we have commonly thought it to be. What, then, are the human motives to which religious and political teaching have given expression?

The explanation of the fact that it was the church which first created and maintained the school seems fairly clear. In an earlier Europe it was generally recognized that the churches were the guardians of our "way of life." They had convictions about the nature of the world and of man. And from this it followed that they knew how men should live. The churches could define and prescribe the goodness of living and, in large measure, its truth and beauty as well. Speaking with the voice—or the voices —of God, they held authority to mark out the values and customs of our behavior. They were able to teach men and women and children how to live because they knew, as did no other institution, what life should be. They had beliefs and values which could be used for the concrete guidance and control of human behavior. That was their social function. And it was out of those beliefs and values that their control of education came.

If, then, political governments are taking the place of the churches in the making and directing of education it follows that we must ask what are the beliefs and values which those governments express and represent. The city of New York, or San Francisco, or Middletown, has schools whose task it is to prepare young people for living. What do those cities believe about living? What lessons have they to teach? Does New York City believe anything? Has it any values or convictions out of which a scheme of teaching may be made?

Here is, I am sure, the most terrifying question with which present-day education is faced. There may have been a time when the common tastes and beliefs of our American communities were so active, forceful and articulate that they could take cultural dominance over the lives of their individual members, young and old. But times have changed. We are no longer certain what a nation or state or county or town or village believes, if indeed it believes anything. And with that doubt comes the fear that our teaching is likewise lacking in conviction. Culturally a school system cannot rise higher than its source. If a government means little to its citizens then the teaching which is given by its schools will mean just as little to its pupils. We face, therefore, a most urgent question with regard to the public schools and colleges of our contemporary civilization. Are our governments, national, provincial, and local, culturally fitted to do the work which we have assigned them? Have they the wisdom of mind, the strength of character, the sensitiveness of appreciation, which are needed by anyone who is to take charge of the development of the thinking and the attitudes of a people? Can the state replace the church, as we Anglo-Saxons have summoned it to do?

2

As we prepare to deal with this question two explanatory remarks should be made. First, when we speak of the transferring of the school from the church to the state we are describing, not what should have happened, but what has happened. We are not saying, as yet, that the change is good. Nor are we condemning it as bad. We are simply recording a fact. Whether anyone intended it or not, the change has taken place. With some few striking exceptions education in the United States is today politically controlled. And there is no likelihood that it will become private or religious again. We Americans cry out, especially against Russia and Germany, because they have made teaching political, have declared and provided that the churches shall have no part in the training of youth. And yet, in our own different but equally effective Anglo-Saxon way, we have been taking the same action. We do not talk about it as do the Russians and Germans. As already noted, we are unwilling to admit it even to ourselves. And yet we have done

6

it. Educationally, we are revolutionists. We must face the plain and inescapable fact that in our future, so far as we can see, the teaching of our people will be done chiefly by our governments.

And, second, it is a curious feature of this revolutionary transfer of power from church to state that, for the most part, it has happened with the consent, and even on the initiative, of the churches themselves. Slowly, it is true, especially in England, and reluctantly in many cases, these churches have deprived themselves of one of their most cherished prerogatives. We Protestants have torn our teaching loose from its roots. We have broken its connection with the religious beliefs out of which it had grown. The typical Protestant has continued to accept the Bible as, in some sense, the guide of his own living but, in effect, he has wished to exclude the Bible from the teaching of his children. The teacher in the modern school is commissioned to teach many things. But he is not commissioned—he is rather forbidden—to teach that "faith" upon which the community, for which he teaches, has built its own character and intelligence.

3

We have said that our Protestant-capitalist civilization is involved in a dilemma. As we enter upon the attempt to discover the ideas and motives out of which that dilemma arises it may be worth while to note some of the forms which our fears and doubts are taking. They give striking evidence of the inner contradictoriness, the mental distractedness, of the culture to which we belong.

First, it seems to many of us quite possible that our educational revolution has been a colossal blunder. How do we know that governments can teach? The churches, it is true, had not done too well with the task. But they were, at least, in purpose and spirit, suited to the teaching enterprise. They were concerned with beliefs and values. But on what evidence have we based the opinion that the state can take charge of the cultivation of intelligence? Is the state primarily an agency of understanding? Is it the human *mind* in action? It may be that, without clear realization of what we were doing, we have been driven by the pressure of events into ways of teaching which are doomed to failure. There are many critics of current education who would approve that suggestion. They would tell us that the learning which is being created under government direction is pseudo learning, that the teaching which is given by a state is pseudo teaching. They would remind us that the unfitness of the church for a task does not prove the fitness of the state to do it. Are they right? Is education by government inherently false in principle, futile in practice? If so, our predicament is a desperate one. Under present circumstances to say that public education is, of necessity, a failure would seem to be the most unequivocal way of saying that our American culture is doomed. For better or for worse, we have chosen to put the guiding and nurturing and cultivating of the growth of our people into the hands of the state. And we must go through with the experiment. If it succeeds, we succeed. If it fails, we fail. It is, so far as I can see, "our" way of dealing with the problem of the making of a human society and a human education. And we must take its consequences.

If, however, the venture of government education is to have a fair trial, two traditional Anglo-Saxon attitudes toward the state must be seriously questioned. We Protestant-capitalist democrats, in our zest for individual freedom, have been accustomed to think of political controls as hostile to that freedom. As individuals we have feared the encroachments of government upon our rights, our liberties, our independence. That dread in its most extreme form is expressed by the words of H. M. Tomlinson as he defines a human attitude in *All Our Yesterdays*:

My church is down [I hear him saying], My God has been deposed again. There is another God now, the state, the State Almighty. I tell you that God will be worse than Moloch. You had better keep that in mind. It has no vision: it has only expediency. It has no morality, only power. And it will have no arts for it will

8

punish the free spirit with death. It will allow no freedom, only uniformity. Its altar will be the ballot-box, and that will be a lie. Right before us is its pillar of fire. It has a heart of gun metal and its belly is full of wheels. You will have to face the brute, you will have to face it. It is nothing but your worst, nothing but the worst of us, lifted up. The children are being fed to it.

Such words as these reveal a fundamental incoherence and self-contradiction. The state, we say, has no vision, no arts, no morality, no freedom. It is our worst. It is a brute. Its name is Moloch. Therefore, we make it the teacher of our children. Could there be any more convincing evidence of the distractedness of a culture? Is there any wonder that, in planning for our own lives and those of our children, we are obsessed by anxiety and horror and confusion of mind?

A second attitude less extreme in its antagonism toward the state is that of regarding it as merely negative, as merely an agency of regulation and of limitation rather than of active creation.[1] It is one of the curious contradictions of the Protestant era that for three centuries we have both enlarged the powers of government and tried to diminish them. We have been going in two different directions at once. On the one hand, as in the case of education, our corporate interests have inevitably and enormously extended political activities. But, on the other hand, our prevailing political mood has been that of interpreting the state as merely setting limits within which the active behavior of individuals and groups must be kept. In this mood, we think

---

[1] R. M. MacIver in his book *Community* (Macmillan, 1920) says, "Because it can determine only the external forms of conduct, the law of the State must be mainly (though by no means wholly) negative. It must for the most part be content (as the neo-Hegelians themselves are forced to admit, though they do not see the force of the admission) to "hinder hindrances" to social welfare. It can "prevent or punish wrong-doing rather than endorse right-doing" (p. 35). That assertion that the action of government is mainly "negative," our argument will be attacking throughout its course. To regard as merely "hindering hindrances" the institution which is now, for the most part, in charge of learning and of teaching, is to cut the roots of social intelligence, both intellectual and practical.

of government as a necessary evil, called into being, not by any positive values of its own, but only by the unavoidable clashes of those creative agencies by which the real work of the world is done. It has even been said, on high authority, that that is the best government which governs least. But if we are to have state education, such an attitude is no longer possible. Its absurdity becomes unendurable. An institution which teaches a society is not negative. An agency which provides for the advancement of learning, which makes, out of learning, an education for all the people—that institution is not simply preventing something from being done. It is doing something. It is creating a society. It is fashioning human beings. It is directing the course of a civilization. It is—as the church was—a constructive enterprise.

4

Here then, in its educational form, is the crucial problem of our contemporary culture. It is the source of the dilemmas underlying the Great War. What is the relation between government and intelligence? We Anglo-Saxons, when we put the activities of teaching into the hands of the church, were saying, whethe we knew it or not, that the church was the agency of unde standing. Wisdom, we thought, came from God. And the churches, as the representatives of God among men, could therefore take charge of the creating and imparting of that wisdom by which the activities of men are made kind and reasonable. The church could teach.

But it is equally clear that this responsibility has now been, or is now being, transferred by us to the institutions of government. And that can only mean, if we know what we are doing, that the state is now, for us, an institution, the primary institution, of intelligence. Human government is human understanding in action. To know, then, what a state is we must know what intelligence is. And vice versa, to know what intelligence is, we must understand what political agencies are and do. What, then, is the state? Does it speak for reason? Or is it primarily an agency of force, of violence? Any genuine study of education must make its way into—and, one hopes—through, the complications of that network of problems. It is a long road to travel but, so far as I can see, it is the only road which leads, under contemporary conditions, to human peace and freedom.

5

It is the purpose of this argument to deal with educational theory, not merely in the abstract, but also in terms of the immediate cultural crisis in which the modern world is involved. Throughout its course we shall have in mind the successes and failures of our contemporary American schools and colleges. And that means, that we must come to terms with the pragmatic thinking which, under the leadership of John Dewey, has for fifty years, so largely dominated our education and our social theory. It will, however, be of value, as preparation for contemporary discussion, to get some background of historical reflection. I propose therefore that, before considering current arguments we examine the attitudes and ideas of four powerful students of Protestant-capitalist education. First, we shall go back to John Amos Comenius, who, better than anyone else I know, expresses, in its early Protestant form, the Christian view of what schools are and do. Second, we shall speak of John Locke, in whom are found all the self-contradictory social tendencies which have dominated the Protestant-capitalist era. And, third, we shall read Matthew Arnold who, two hundred years after Locke, tells in stinging, desperate words, the futility into which Protestant teaching has fallen, as he sees it in the schools and the culture of England and the United States.

That brief sketch will, I hope, prepare us to formulate the social and educational issue which now torments our Western culture. In the attempt to make that formulation, however, I shall appeal to another thinker who seems to me the most significant student of education in the modern period—Jean Jacques Rousseau. Rousseau combines, as no one else since Plato has done, the study of society and the study of education. Better than anyone else he seems to me to lead the way into the consideration of "modern" problems.

Our discussion of Dewey will be an attempt to see whether or not he and his colleagues have solved the problem which Rousseau stated. My own impression is that the pragmatic attempt has failed at its most essential point. It is significant chiefly because it is so faithfully representative of the inner failure and collapse of the civilization for which it speaks. If that is true, then we must try to go beyond pragmatism. If we can do that we may, perhaps, catch a glimpse of the direction in which our social and educational theory and practice should now proceed.

Chapter 2. JOHN AMOS COMENIUS

John Amos Comenius was born in the last decade of the sixteenth century. At that time the study of educational theory and practice in Europe had risen to one of its highest levels. Both in Protestant and Catholic circles the problems of teaching were being dealt with by keen and powerful minds. One finds in the words of Comenius, therefore, an expression, not only of his own insight, but also of a dominating interest of the Europe to which he belonged.

Comenius was a Czech. He was a preacher as well as a teacher. He became bishop of the small Hussian sect known as the Moravian Brethren, or the Church of the Christian Unity. I often think of him as "The Czech who might have saved England."

In the year 1641-1642, when John Locke was a boy of nine or ten, Comenius, then a man of fifty, was in London. He had come, it is said, by invitation of the Long Parliament, to put into effect plans for a great new institution of learning. He had already won wide fame in Europe because of his theories of knowledge and of teaching. He had written new textbooks, devised new schools, made new and significant suggestions for the organization of the intellectual life of a people. And the English Parliament, at the suggestion of a group of persons who were interested in the New Learning, was seriously considering the granting of funds, the assignment of buildings for the institution which Comenius was to set up and carry on. It was a time when English interest in the advancement of learning was rising to the point of decisive action. Apparently the same impulse which, eighteen years later, led to the founding of the Royal Society, was already gathering force. Comenius found enthusiastic and powerful support awaiting him in London. For a time the outlook was favorable. But in the end nothing was done. Parliament had other more pressing business to attend to. It was harassed by cares more immediate and urgent. It did not act negatively. It simply failed to act. And so Comenius the Czech, after eleven months of waiting for England to do something, went back to the Continent, a sadly disappointed man.

It is interesting to speculate on what might have happened in England, in Western Europe, in the United States, in the British Dominions, in the modern industrial world, if the Parliament had acted favorably. The failure to act was, I think, one of the momentous decisions of modern history. What it meant was that John Locke, rather than John Amos Comenius, became the spokesman, the interpreter, the guide, in words at least, of the course of English and American teaching. The boy of nine, when his time came, took the place which was nearly given to the man of fifty. The *Thoughts Concerning Education* received the hearing which might have been won by the *Great Didactic*. And the tragedy lies in the fact that, in spite of com-mon elements of attitude and idea, the principles of these two men were leading in radically different directions. Between them there was opening up the Great Divide in social and educational theory. And as one sees the outcome of England's characteristic prudence, one cannot help lamenting that Comenius was disappointed. I do not know how much he might have accomplished. I do wish he might have had his chance.

I

But now, putting aside wishing and speculation, what was the essential difference between the two attitudes to which Comenius and Locke gave expression? It is hard to speak of the educational work of Comenius without seeming exaggeration. He is rated by the keen judgment of Professor S. S. Laurie of the University of Edinburgh as "the most eminent (figure) in the history of European education"[1] and, again, as "the most penetrating

[1] S. S. Laurie, *Educational Opinion from the Renaissance*, Cambridge University Press, 1903, p. 157.

writer on method whom the world has ever seen."[2] The memory
of Plato might lead one to question the first of these appraisals.
But of the soundness of the second judgment there can be little
question. His insight into the ways in which teaching may be
done has the clear quality of genius.

Like many another educational reformer, Comenius rebelled
against the scholastic formalism of his own schooling. Early in
his life he became an eager critic of the schools of his time. He
describes them in his *Great Didactic* as "inordinately seeking
knowledge,"[3] as pursuing "nothing but intellectual progress."
And then he asks, "But with what method or with what success
have they done even this? In truth, the only result achieved was
the following. For five, ten, or more years, they detained the
mind over matters that could be mastered in one. What could
have been gently instilled into the intellect was violently impressed upon it, nay rather stuffed and flogged into it. What
might have been placed before the mind plainly and lucidly, was
treated of as obscurely, perplexedly, and intricately as if it were
a complicated riddle. In addition, though for the present we
will pass this over, the intellect was scarcely even nourished by
the actual facts, but was filled with the husks of words, with a
windy and parrotlike loquacity, and with the chaff of opinions. . . . Such a disgraceful waste of time and of labor must
assuredly arise from a faulty method."[4]

In his own lifelong devising of new methods Comenius followed one dominant principle. The pupil was, for him, a living
organism, developing from within in response to influences from
without. The teaching of a child seemed to him analogous to the
cultivation of a plant. The action of education was like that of
the sun. And from this it followed that all learning should be
patterned after the processes of growth as seen in natural objects. From this basic principle he derives, with infinite skill and

[2] *Ibid.*, p. 157.
[3] John Amos Comenius, *The Great Didactic*. Trans. W. M. Keatinge,
A. & C. Black, Ltd., 1923, Part II, p. 230.
[4] *Ibid.*, 230-231.

ingenuity, observations and maxims which apply to every phase of the work of the school and which, taken together, form an amazingly unified, as well as comprehensive, program of teaching. Since the study of "method" is foreign to the purposes of our argument, I can give here, as samples, only a few phrases from the *Great Didactic*:

204, 1. The seeds of knowledge, of virtue, of piety, are as we have seen, naturally implanted in us, but the actual knowledge, virtue, and piety are not so given. These must be acquired by prayer, by education, and by action. He gave no bad definition who said that man was a "teachable animal." And indeed it is only by a proper education that he can become a man.

250, 2. The exact order of instruction must be borrowed from nature.

275, 3. Nature makes no leaps, but proceeds step by step.

264, 4. Nature observes a suitable time.

271, 5. In all the operations of nature, development is from within.

295, 6. Nature produces nothing that is useless.

304, 7. Nature knits everything together in continuous combination.

And dependent on observations such as these are maxims like the following:

307, 1. With every subject of instruction the question of its practical uses must be raised, that nothing useless be learned.

303, 2. All the studies should be so arranged that those which come later may depend on those that have gone before and that those which come first may be fixed in the mind by those that follow.

305, 3. the studies of a lifetime should be so arranged that they form an encyclopedic whole, in which all parts spring from a common source and each is in its right place.

302, 4. men must, as far as possible, be taught to become wise by studying the heavens, the earth, oaks and beeches, but not by studying books: that is to say, they must learn to know and investigate the things themselves and not the observations that other people have made about the things.

16

268, 5. no language (should) be learned from a grammar, but from suitable authors.

333, 6. Knowledge is unsuitable when it is uncongenial to the mind of this or that scholar. For there is as great a difference between the minds of men as exists between the various kinds of plants, of trees, of animals: one must be treated in one way, and another in another, and the same method cannot be applied to all alike.

347, 7. In schools, therefore, let the students learn to write by writing, to talk by talking, to sing by singing, and to reason by reasoning. In this way schools will become work-shops humming with work, and students whose efforts prove successful will experience the truth of the proverb, "We give form to ourselves and to our materials at the same time."

Comenius had no faith in compulsion or punishment as an instrument of education, though he could tolerate their use for the correction of moral iniquity. All his plans provided that learning should be easily, quickly and happily done. If pupils were dull and inattentive we should, first of all, examine the teachers rather than the pupils. Such evidence about pupils suggested to him that, somewhere in their education, teaching had been badly done.

2

But the methods of Comenius, fascinating as they are to a practicing teacher, must not be allowed to distract us from what was for him, and must be for us, of far deeper concern, "Method" is always a secondary fact. Always prior to any "method" is the "content" out of which it springs, by which it is determined. There is, I think, nothing in the world more futile than the attempt to find out how a task should be done when one has not yet decided what the task is, what, under the actual conditions, one wishes to get done. The extent to which, in recent American educational theory and practice, questions of "content" have been thrust aside in favor of problems of "method" is, I think, one of the clearest measures of our educational futility and confusion of mind.

However that may be, it is clear that for Comenius, the procedure of the classroom grows out of convictions which go down deep into the structure of his thought—convictions about the nature of society and the nature of the human mind. He was, as I have said, a bishop of the Church of the Christian Unity. And "unity" was for him always the directing and dominating principle. He believed in the unity of knowledge. He believed also in the unity of mankind. The passion for unification was fundamental to all that he thought or did. In terms of that interest we shall see most clearly his difference from Locke, shall realize what Anglo-Saxon education might have been had his lead been followed.

First, then, as to the unity of knowledge! Professor Laurie has told us that, in the field of education, Comenius was the "most penetrating writer on method whom the world has ever seen." He recognized the need of reforming the habits of teachers. In fact such reform seemed to him necessary for the remaking of Christian civilization. And yet his heart was set on another, a more fundamental, enterprise. In spirit, if not in achievement, he was a follower of Francis Bacon. The New Learning had caught his imagination. As against the mere study of words he believed in the study of sensible, observable things. But, also, he saw a danger threatening the new movement. It was that of the isolation, the logical disconnectedness, of the separate investigations. His teaching mind realized, at a glance, the dangers of specialization. He wanted, therefore, to find some way of bringing all the studies together, of making the many investigations into one investigation. And his solution of the difficulty was a plan for the establishing of an institution of research which should assemble the best men from all the different lines of study, should make them intellectually acquainted with one another, and should thus enable them to unify the new knowledge into a single body of understanding for the guidance of human living.

This was his Pansophic dream in the field of research. It was this institution which he hoped to establish in London, an institution for the unification as well as for the pursuit of knowledge. He was not the only man who dreamed that dream. It had for him, however, a peculiar vividness and power, and he gave to it a very original form. The truth of that statement will be seen in the consequences which he derived from it for the field of education.

The unity which Comenius found binding together all fields of knowledge, is seen in his principle that the content of study is the same from the lowest grade in the school system to the topmost level of university instruction. The pupil, as he advances from grade to grade, does not encounter a succession of separate "subjects." He is pursuing, on ever higher levels, the same subject.

The organization of teaching as Comenius planned it provided for four successive schools, each of which should cover a period of six years. The first learning, beginning at birth, is done at the mother's knee. This is the Mother's school. From seven to thirteen, all children attend the Vernacular school, in which lessons are learned in one's own language and, to some extent, in that of a neighboring country. From thirteen to nineteen, a smaller number of pupils who have shown special aptitude for abstract intellectual work, continue their studies, using the ancient languages, and especially Latin, since that is the customary instrument of communication between scholars. This is the Latin school. From nineteen through twenty-four is the period of the University, in which a special few are trained for technical scholarship, and the best of these for the interpretation of knowledge as a whole. Now the exceedingly significant contention of Comenius is that from the bottom of this ladder to its top the pupils are dealing with the same subject matter. In the Mother's school, in the family contacts of the first six years, the child is learning metaphysics, physics, optics, astronomy, geography, history, arithmetic, geometry, statics, mechanics, reasoning, grammar, rhetoric, poetry, music, economics, politics, ethics, religion, and piety. All these, as studies, find their beginnings in the awakening of the mind of the child, which takes place in the home. And the later progress in learning is not that of a change of intellectual interest. It is a change in the level of understanding of a constant topic—the nature of that world which, throughout his education, the pupil is trying to bring within the grasp of his mind. The unity of knowledge means for Comenius, the unity of the whole scheme of study. Education is, for him, a single enterprise.

And second, Comenius believed in the unity of mankind. He was a thoroughgoing educational democrat. All children, whatever their social status, whatever their sex, are for him to be taught in the same way and to the same end. They must all go to school. They must all go to the same schools. Since they have, all alike, the same fundamental lesson about life to learn, they must all pursue the same course of study. This applies to girls as well as to boys. It applies to the sons of nobles as well as to the sons of peasants. For the purposes of the human fellowship which God has established it is essential that children of different status and of different sex should share, in common schools, a common education. Comenius makes lavish provision for differences of taste, of capacity, of vocational trend. And yet the fundamental purpose of teaching is for him everywhere the same. He takes his Christianity seriously. And the effect of that is to require, throughout the teaching of the community, a single, equal purpose. And he is right. In the making of a democracy, equality in the school is, I am sure, more fundamental, even, than "equality before the law."

This democracy does not mean for Comenius that every pupil who enters the Mother's school is to continue his studies for the twenty-four years which would take him through the university. He recognizes and provides for the "nonintellectuals," as we call them. He insists upon universal attendance only through the Vernacular school. But the selections which are to be made at that point, and again at the time of entrance to the university, are to be based not on social status, or rank, or sex, but on proved capacity and promise. The teachers who know the pupils must help in the planning of their careers. At this point he is not too clear as to ways and means of grappling with the difficulties of a competitive economic order. And yet, in principle, his democracy is steadfast and definite. He knows what a school system must be in order to realize the purposes of a democracy. And he holds to his vision, as giving him direction, even though its full realization is, for the time, beyond his grasp.

3

I have said that Comenius had two basic presuppositions—the unity of knowledge and the unity of mankind. But to say this is not enough. These two ideas are for him only one idea. They are two different sides of his belief in God. Comenius is, first of all, religious. He is important for educational theory because in him Protestant Christian education finds its fullest, its most consistent expression. If one wishes to know what it means to have education planned and carried on by the Christian church I am sure that nowhere else in European literature will he find a truer account of it. The theory of education here given is simply applied Christianity—Christianity taken seriously as the guide of human living. And the genius of Comenius lies in the fact that he makes his Christianity work. It works in the field of knowledge. It works in his dealing with men, and especially with children. He was a follower of John Huss. He had dedicated his mind and his life to the doctrine of Christian unity. And he followed its implications with a clear, unhesitating, unswerving loyalty.

If we should ask Comenius why knowledge is one, his religious answer is clear and unequivocal. Knowledge, as we have it, is knowledge by man of the world. And both man and world are created by God, each with reference to the other. The world which God has made, is made in accordance with the principles of order of His mind. And the men who are trying to know the world are also "made in God's image." When men engage in scientific study, therefore, they are not simply following the drives of their own curiosity and intelligence. They are, by that very act, following after the meaning and intention of the Creator both of themselves and of the objects of their study. In a word, the intellectual standards of the universe are established by a single mind. All that men do, or can hope to do, by their thinking finds its basis, its criteria, its intention, within the creative unity of that mind.

And, in like manner, Comenius holds that all men are, through their kinship with God, members of one social body. If we ask what is the social group whose pattern of culture the teacher must follow, whose outlines he must recognize, the answer of Comenius is very direct. It is the fellowship of humanity. It is the society of mankind, held together as a single society by a common sonship to God. The brotherhood of man is not for Comenius an idle phrase. It is the fundamental fact upon which all education rests. From it all lessons are derived. Toward its realization all teaching is directed. All human beings, whatever their race and country, or status or sex, are members of a single family. And in the last resort, education serves its proper purpose only in so far as it is given by and for and about the purposes of that family. The teaching which Comenius wishes to provide is Christian teaching. And no one else, I think, has so clearly expressed the meaning of that phrase.

4

As we turn now from Comenius toward Locke, it may be worth while to refer again to the great disappointment which was suffered by the older man in London in the year 1642. When he left England, he went to Sweden which had been eagerly calling him. Here again his plans for research and teaching had aroused

great interest in government circles. He discussed them at length
with the highest officials. But again he was doomed to disappointment. His plans for reforming the schools, rewriting the textbooks, met with hearty approval. But the project for the reform
of scientific study was judged visionary and unrealistic. People
could approve his classroom methods, but not the intellectual
and social philosophy from which those methods came. In spite
of his eager and passionate arguments for the Pansophic Institute
his sponsors set him to work, planning courses and devising
teaching materials for the children of Sweden. Years later, as the
end of his life came near, he sadly wrote,

> How badly have I imitated that merchant seeking for good pearls
> who, when he had found a pearl of great price, went away and sold
> all that he had, and bought it! Oh, wretched sons of light, who know
> not how to imitate the wisdom of the children of the world! Would
> that I, having once struck the Pansophic vein, had followed it up,
> neglecting all else! But so it happens when we lend our ear to the
> solicitations clamoring outside us rather than to the light shining
> within us.[5]

We may, perhaps, without abating our admiration for Comenius
as a student of teaching, differ from him as to the planning of his
life. He was a master in the field of educational theory. But he
was not, by habit of mind, an investigator. Probably he would
have been unhappy as the leader of a group of research men.
Undoubtedly he would have made them unhappy too. There is a
large chance that his enterprise would have broken down. He
was at home in a classroom. But his words and attitudes do not
feel like those of a university administrator. One shudders to
think what might have happened to him and to his institution
if hardheaded, closefisted Englishmen had put him in charge of
funds and buildings, and appointments, and public relations.
What a crash there would have been! And yet, it may be that
Comenius was right. His own catastrophe might have meant

[5] Laurie, *John Amos Comenius*, Cambridge University Press, 1887,
p. 157.

success for modern learning and for modern education. England, though she did not know it, was standing at the parting of the ways. She was deciding what should be the intellectual and moral presuppositions underlying the great career of industry and commerce upon which she was preparing to enter. She chose blindly the way of Locke. Her learning and her teaching followed his patterns. What would it have meant to England and to the whole modern industrial and commercial civilization which England has created and so long dominated, if in the forming of her mind and heart and will, education and research, thinking and acting, could have been linked together, unified, as they were in the mind of Comenius rather than sundered and, at times, incoherently hostile, as they have been in fact! I do not mean to suggest that Comenius could have closed the chasm which was, of necessity, opening up between old beliefs and new facts. I do not mean that, single-handed, he could have lashed into submission the wild beasts soon to be let loose by the new competitive industry. But I do mean that his single-minded insight might have saved England, and so England's imitators, from something of the duplicity of mind and of motive which has cursed the rise and growth of modern industry. What would it have meant for the shaping of a new civilization if the boys and girls of England had had the same education, if the children of yeomen, workmen, merchants, and nobles had attended the same schools, if to all of them had been given the same unified scheme of teaching, if that teaching had had organic connection with the life of the society of which they were members! If those conditions had been met England might have had some better understanding of what she was doing. She might have escaped that frightful division of her character into the low cunning of the market place on the one side and the high idealism of her "better nature" on the other. If she had kept or won her spiritual unity, the world might have been saved from something of the brutality, the aggressive exploitation of the weak by the strong, which we call Capitalism. The simple-minded old Czech bishop believed something. And he knew how to teach it. If he had been given his chance he might have profoundly influenced the modern world.[6] But he went sadly to Sweden to do what others told him to do. And John Locke spoke for England. And what the consequences of that were we shall see when we come to the days of Matthew Arnold, and then move on to our own problems in contemporary America.

[6] A similar set of reflections covering American educational and social policy is suggested by Cotton Mather's unsupported statement that Comenius was invited by Winthrop to become president of Harvard. We might have escaped something of the intellectual and moral chaos which we have known as "the elective system." (See *Comenius*, Will S. Monroe, *Scribner's*, 1900, pp. 78 —.)

Chapter 3. JOHN LOCKE

THE difference between Comenius and Locke is the difference between a single-minded person and a double-minded one. If we were to speak unsympathetically, the world "simple-minded" and "muddle-minded" might be substituted. Comenius is a believer who says, "I am a Christian; therefore. . . ." Locke is a believer who says, "I am a Christian; but. . . ." If we could adequately fix the meaning of that "but" which Anglo-Saxon industrialism has attached to the structure of Christian belief and attitude, we should come much nearer to an understanding of the social revolution of the last three centuries, much nearer to knowing why the control of education has gone over from the church to the state.

In terms of religious belief, Comenius and Locke have apparently the same premises. Locke is quite as pious, quite as orthodox, as is Comenius. Whatever may be the implication* of his revolutionary essay, he can demonstrate the existence of God, can know His nature, with calm, untroubled assurance. His proofs on this point are as simple as those of Anselm, as certain as those of Thomas Aquinas. And, further, in the Bible, literally interpreted, he can read God's message to mankind, prescribing how men should live and hence, by implication, how they should be taught. As one follows the "Occasional Thoughts" about teaching, written down by this Fellow of the Royal Society, this inventor of the new way of knowledge which was to run triumphant through the technological world, one seems to be reading—apart from minor details—the shrewd and homely homilies of a Puritan parson. Locke's theory of teaching is, first of all, based upon his faith in God.

And second, Locke is, like Comenius, a follower of Francis Bacon. He, too, is enthusiastic about the New Learning, as against the old. And, for this reason, the attitudes of the two

26

men are on the side of antipathies, apparently the same. Both
were rebels against their own schooling. They shared a common
hatred of the scholastic formalism of the language training to
which they had been subjected. They agreed with strong insist-
ence that only "useful" subjects should be taught. They were
alike certain that progress in wisdom comes, primarily, from
contact with things and persons, and only secondarily from contact with words. They were both—if we may use a contemporary
term—"progressive" in their educational theorizing. They both
wanted change.

And yet, as one gets the feel of the planning which these two
men did for the teaching of youth, the difference between them
is that between a thrill and a shiver, between a day in the sunshine and a day in a London fog. Comenius believes in God.
Therefore he is a democrat. Therefore the unified study of the
world is for him a normal part of the healthy living of every
human being. Locke believes in the same God. But there is also
in his mind something alien, something hostile to that belief. As
against the teaching democracy of Comenius, Locke is a deep-
dyed aristocrat. He thinks of the pursuit of knowledge as a
leisure-class activity to be carried on only by a few gentlemen
who are by taste disposed to amuse themselves in this fashion
rather than through the more rude enjoyments common to their
class. Comenius has a single program of learning for all human
beings. Locke has one scheme of teaching for young gentlemen
of property and another, quite different, for the children of the
working poor. It is dramatic—not to say tragic—to see the intellectual and social unity of the Czech broken into fragments by
the divisive multiplicity of the Englishman.

I

On the intellectual side, both men list "learning" as one of the
aims of teaching. But in what different places! Comenius finds

the school driving at three goals—learning, virtue, and piety. Locke has four purposes—virtue, wisdom, breeding, and learning. It is significant that learning has first place in one of these lists and last place in the other. And the difference is not accidental. It is deliberate and fundamental. For Comenius, to acquire learning is to follow after the mind of God, to try to know the world as it is known by the Mind which made it. Such learning is the means by which virtue and piety are acquired. In fact, each of these three contributes to the development of the others. A young person becomes pious and virtuous by becoming intelligent. These three goals are not to be pursued along three different lines. They are rather three different phases of a single form of behavior—the proper response of a human being to the world with which he has to deal. "It is therefore," says Comenius, "an unhallowed separation if these three elements be not bound together as by an adamantine chain."[1]

How different is the part which learning plays in Locke's plan of teaching! Not only is knowledge secondary in value. It is, for the greater part of the program, irrelevant. There is no "adamantine chain" here, binding together the intellectual and the practical. "Learning must be had," Locke tells us, after he has first made careful provision for physical health, for virtue, for piety, for worldly wisdom, for good breeding, and for reputation, as the essentials of education. But it must be, "in the second place, as subservient to greater qualities."[2] And, again, he says,

The great work of a governor (tutor) is to fashion the carriage and form the mind; to settle in his pupil good habits, and the principles of virtue and wisdom; to give him, by little and little, a view of mankind and work him into a love and imitation of what is excellent and praiseworthy; and, in the possession of it, to give him vigour, activity, and industry. The studies which he sets him upon are but, as it were, the exercises of his faculties, and employment of

[1] *The Great Didactic*, Part II, p. 74.
[2] Adamson, *Educational Writings of John Locke*, Sec. 147, p. 115.

28

his time, to keep him from sauntering and idleness, to teach him application, and accustom him to take pains, and to give him some little taste of what his own industry may perfect. For who expects that, under a tutor a young gentleman should be an accomplished critic, orator, or logician; go to the bottom of metaphysics, natural philosophy, or mathematics; or be a master in history or chronology? Though something of each is to be taught him, but it is only to open the door that he may look in, and, as it were, begin an acquaintance, but not to dwell there; and a governor would be much blamed that should keep his pupil too long and lead him too far in most of them. But of good breeding, knowledge of the world, virtue, industry, and a love of reputation, he cannot have too much; and, if he have these, he will not long want what he needs or desires of the other.[3]

Could anything be further from the educational faith of Comenius? "Don't let a young man take his studies too seriously," Locke seems to be saying. How familiar is the sound of these words today! How Lockian is our own worldly wisdom! "A boy goes to college to make friends, to learn to stand on his own feet, to meet his fellows from other parts of the country, to sharpen his muscles and his wits in the relatively harmless struggles of an undergraduate society. His chief business is to 'make good' in that. It makes little difference what he studies." The Americans who say such words as these today can find strong backing in *Some Thoughts Concerning Education* of the shrewd and cautious English thinker and public servant. Studies may serve the immature young male "to keep him from sauntering and idleness, to teach him application, and accustom him to take pains." But if one takes studying seriously as a primary activity of the human individual, if one regards learning as the normal way of "becoming a man," he will find no comfort or guidance in the worldly wisdom of John Locke. He had better go to Comenius, whose faith in the efficacy of intelligence as a basis for virtue and piety was the cornerstone of his whole structure of education.

[3] *Ibid.*, pp. 75-76, Sec. 94.

2

And further, Locke's sundering of learning from its proper function in relation to the other virtues destroys all the unity which Comenius had found in the intellectual life. Both men are agreed that "only the useful should be taught." But what lessons are useful? Locke finds many of them. And each is directed toward a separate, specific end. He can see that reading, writing, and arithmetic will help anyone who has charge of business affairs. He strongly suggests that a course in the keeping of accounts is desirable for a property owner. He recommends the study of history, law, and politics to those who may be destined for responsibility in public office or for the control of industry. He thinks a young man should learn to "know men," not so much by abstract study as by travel and experience and precept. But in each case his interest is specific and practical even to the limit of being narrowly vocational. His "usefulness" is shrewd and sensible. But in all this he is far from the meaning which Comenius gives to the word "useful." For the latter, all real knowledge is of use. It is only the verbal, the fictitious, the formalistic, which he rejects. It is a man's normal business to know the world, to know it accurately and comprehensively and with well-unified understanding. For Comenius, the hodge-podge collection of scattered information, directed largely toward occupational interests which Locke recommends, is not learning at all. For him learning is the attempt to be intelligent about living. It is "useful" to know God, to know the world which God has made, to know one's fellows, to know one's proper place among them—and all this so that one may live with piety and virtue. "He gave no bad definition who said that man was a 'teachable animal.' And indeed it is only by a proper education that he can become a man."

Second, just as he destroys the unity which Comenius had sought for the school curriculum, so does Locke break down the social unity of the educational program. Comenius plans, as we have said, only one set of schools. Boys and girls, peasants and nobles, are to share the same classrooms. He is a democrat. There is no better definition of democracy than to say that it is a society which has only one set of schools. But what of Locke, the man who so profoundly affected the framing of our own American "democratic" institutions? We do not, I think, understand him unless we place side by side with his *Thoughts Concerning Education*, first published in 1693, the memorandum which he prepared in 1697, dealing with the reform of the Poor Law. In that document he made suggestions for the education of the children of the working poor. It is too commonly forgotten that Locke had two plans for the education of the young people of England.

3

The *Thoughts Concerning Education*, prepared as advice on the bringing up of the son of a friend, has to do with the fitting of young men of family and property for the meeting of the opportunities and duties which belong to their station. Its intent is aristocratic. And, quite naturally, its ruling motive is a prudence which is closely akin to fear. Locke would not send his pupil to a school. That is too dangerous. He would keep him at home, safely isolated under the care of a tutor. That, of course, is dangerous too, for it is hard to find a safe tutor. And yet, the perils of school life are too great to be faced. As we have seen, the primary purpose of all teaching is the inculcation of virtue and worldly wisdom and good breeding. "And the great principle and foundation of all virtue and worth is placed in this, that a man is able to deny himself his own desires, cross his own inclinations and purely follow what reason directs as best, though the appetite bear the other way."[4] At every point, Locke is on his guard against the moral contamination of his pupil by asso-

[4] Adamson, p. 28, Sec. 33.

ciation with other human beings. As already suggested, tutors are dangerous. But even worse are fellow pupils.

Vice, if we may believe the general complaint, ripens so fast now-a-days, and runs up to seed so early in young people, that it is impossible to keep a young lad from the spreading contagion, if you will venture him abroad in the herd, and trust to chance, or his own inclination, for the choice of his company at school. By what fate vice has so thriven amongst us these few years past, and by what hands it has been built up to so uncontrolled a dominion, I shall leave others to inquire.[5]

There are political insinuations as well as educational theory in these last words. But the fact is clear that Locke does not think that parents should take the risk of contamination involved in school association with the sons of other parents like themselves. There are, however, other perils at home as well. The "taint of servants" terrifies him. Over and over again he returns to the theme. Parents must with the most eager care guard their children from the evil influence of those who, living under their own roofs, wait upon them. And even worse than these, though more easily avoided, are the "beggars' boys and the abhorred rascality" of the common people. Young gentlemen should know these only as horrible examples of such vices as lying which "is proper only to them" and is "not tolerable in anyone who would converse with people of condition, or have any esteem or reputation in the world."[6]

So much for the education of the upper classes, as planned by this pious Puritan philosopher and public servant! What has he to say about the education of the poor? Fortunately we have his memorandum on the subject, which was prepared in 1697, but never adopted, and was regarded by himself and his friends as proposing a decided step forward in England's care for the children of her manual workers. In brief, his suggestion is that there be set up in every parish a "working school" for the "children

[5] *Ibid.*, p. 53, Sec. 70.
[6] *Ibid.*, p. 103, Sec. 131.

of the laboring people."[7] Assuming that parents can care for their children who are still under three years of age, Locke proposes that, between the ages of three and fourteen, children of poor parents shall be trained by the working schools in the practice of such industries as the parish is carrying on. That will be their education, their complete course of study. He estimates that, while the labor of the youngest pupils will be of little market value, the output, on the whole, will pay for the cost of the schools, "whereas there is no child now which from its birth is maintained by the parish but, before the age of fourteen, costs the parish 50 or 60 pounds." There can be no doubt that in budgetary calculations of this type, he is a better planner than is Comenius. Meanwhile, he tells us, "the children will be kept in much better order, be better provided for, and from infancy inured to work, which is of no small consequence to the making of them sober and industrious all their lives after." The pupils, who are to live at home, will be given at the school, each day a "bellyfull of bread" and, "to this may be added, without any trouble, in cold weather, if it be thought needful, a little warm water-gruel; for the same fire that warms the room may be made use of to boil a pot of it." The course of study would be spinning or knitting or some other local trade. There are elaborate suggestions for the getting of the pupils securely "placed" in the occupations of the parish before they leave the school. And, further, by being taken to church on Sunday, they are to be "brought into some sense of religion; whereas ordinarily now, in their idle and loose way of breeding up, they are as utter strangers to religion and morality as they are to industry."

4

Comenius and Locke believed in the same God and read the same Bible. They had also both accepted the New Learning of Europe. Why, then, are their teaching plans, at every point of

[7] H. R. Fox Bourne, *Life of John Locke*, Vol. II, pp. 384-385.

essential human significance, so different? For Comenius, mankind is one fellowship, one society, bound together by the common purpose of using intelligence for the making of a common life. For Locke, mankind falls apart into groups, classes, sects, factions, nations, individuals, which, seeking each its own ends, inevitably tend to plunge into hatred and strife, one against another. For Comenius, thinking is a single inquiry. For Locke it is a miscellaneous collection of separate studies which have connection with living only as each serves to guide some specific useful enterprise. Comenius brings men together. Locke tears them apart. It never seems to occur to Locke—he leaves that to someone else to inquire—why "other" boys are so vicious that they threaten contamination for "his" pupil. Nor does he care to inquire whether anything can be done to save them from viciousness. He does not try to discover what, in the social order of England, are the evil influences which make servants such despicable and evil associates for children. He simply accepts the fact. He does not inquire how England has brought it about that her common people are an "abhorred rascality" nor what conditions are at work to keep them in a degradation in which lying is "proper to them." He is a realist. He faces with hard, shrewd common sense the multiplicity, the incoherence of an actual social order. His Puritan individualism justifies him in going about his own business, with the understanding that other people will go about theirs. When he plans for the education of a boy of his own class, his interest is directed solely toward the welfare and prosperity of that boy. But when he proposes arrangements for the training of the children of the poor his interest is not in them, but in the crafts and industries of England, of which they are to be made docile, dependable, industrious, obedient instruments.

Out of the same Bible in which Comenius finds the democracy which would have made England one people Locke derives and establishes the vicious aristocracy which, throughout the technological era, has divided her into two industrial classes, the

34

masters and the servants. He has managed, without realizing what he is doing, to state the gospel of that competitive struggle for wealth and power which has arrayed man against man, class against class, nation against nation, as England has led the way in the creating and maintaining of the industrial activities of the modern world. How shall we explain this fundamental divergence of thought and social attitude between him and the fellow Christian, fellow Baconian, whom he unwittingly supplanted? If we could answer that question we should see far more clearly than we do the basic conflict of forces in our Protestant-capitalist culture which has reached its culmination in the brutal stupidity of the World War. We should see why the church has lost control of teaching. We should be able to judge whether or not the state, which has taken over that control, is fitted to exercise it with sensitiveness and wisdom. We should thus have made a beginning of a study of the American school and the American college. That beginning I hope we may find as we go on from Comenius and Locke to Matthew Arnold, and, then, to Jean Jacques Rousseau and John Dewey.

Chapter 4. MATTHEW ARNOLD

∧∧∧

IN 1849 Matthew Arnold, then twenty-seven years of age, published his first volume of poetry. It was called *A Strayed Reveler and Other Poems*. In the same year Karl Marx, the German-Jewish exile, began his work in London. A year earlier, when he was thirty, the foreigner had joined with Engels in the first edition of the Communist Manifesto. He had been driven out of Prussia because he advised armed resistance to the state. He came to England and spent his life in the study of modern industrial civilization. For thirty-four years these two men—the Strayed Reveler and the exiled revolutionary—lived in the same city. It would be hard to imagine two men with social backgrounds more different. And yet they were curiously alike in fundamental motive. They were both trying desperately to understand an English society. And in curiously different ways they were both arriving at the same conclusion.

In his own way, Arnold was quite as deeply concerned with the contradictions of capitalism as was Marx. He knew little of technical economic or political theory. But he did know literature and teaching. And in both these fields he found human tragedy arising out of human institutions. Throughout his life therefore he struggled to understand the destructive conflict which was running through English industrial life. His answers have none of the clarity, none of the power of popular leadership, of the Marxian gospel. Arnold stumbles and fumbles. The brilliant economic analysis of Marx strikes out in two directions. It startles and challenges his fellow theorists. But it also stirs and gives hope to untutored common people. Arnold can do neither of these. He hates abstractions. He fears untutored popular movements. And yet, fundamentally, the two men are one in purpose. To both of them it is certain that, in English life, forces have been let loose which clash with one another and which, in their

36

conflict, are destroying the human beings whom they should serve. Marx speaks for economic justice. Arnold speaks for culture, for sweetness and light. Marx is the leader of the "proletariat." Arnold is trying to point a way for the "middle class." I am not here raising the question as to which of these two leads is more promising as men struggle with the desperate problems of a chaotic society. In fact, there is no need to choose between them. But the point is that there are two leads. And we do not understand either Marx or Arnold except as we see the basic identity of direction beneath their obvious and manifold differences. And, further, it is worthy of note that, for thirty-four years, these two men, though living in the same city, did their thinking in total disregard of one another. It was from intellectual dislocations such as this that Comenius had wanted to save England.

I

Arnold's active life went on in two fields. He was a poet. But he was also an inspector of schools. For thirty-five years he earned his living by visiting and reporting upon the teaching done in schools which received government financial aid. It was the combination of these two experiences which made him a social critic. He dreamed of what England might be. And he saw what England was. To understand Arnold as a person one must go back to Locke, and especially to the two kinds of teaching for which Locke had planned.

In his own bringing up, Arnold had received the best that England had to give. He had been cared for. He was the son of Arnold of Rugby and was profoundly stimulated, as well as perplexed, by his father and by the cultural influences of the group to which his father belonged. He studied at Oxford, and no one has put into more fitting words what Oxford means at its best. His way was open into everything that England had of appreciation, of understanding and purpose. He became professor of poetry at Oxford. He achieved recognition first as poet and then as literary critic, so that everything of idea and of taste which was active in English life was playing upon him, was giving challenge to his mind. He liked to say that he came out of the middle class. But that was true only in a limited social sense. Culturally, educationally, he was at the top of English life.

But, over against all this, was his lifelong occupation as Her Majesty's Inspector of Schools. The task was, in many respects, a dreary one, involving infinite reading of papers, infinite visiting of classrooms. It took him from home on long trips of inspection of scattered schools, each caught up in its own network of local complications. There was no limit to what might be done in the field. And his high sense of personal integrity drove him on to the point of exhaustion. But, more significant than all this, more disturbing even than the distraction from his writing, was the fact that the elementary schools which Arnold inspected were, in one line at least, the lineal descendants of the parish "working schools" which Locke had tried to improve. They were, of course, far above the level of those of Locke's day. And yet, it is largely true to say that they held the same relative place in English life. The children whose teaching Arnold was supervising were the children of the manual workers and of the lower middle class. They came from families which were caught in the full tide of the English industrial torrent. Contact with them revealed to a sensitive mind, as nothing outside the educational field could have done, the forces which were dragging down the cultural vitality of the English common people. These children would never have the chance to live, which Arnold himself had had. There were—as the forces for which John Locke spoke had arranged there should be—two Englands. Matthew Arnold lived in one of them and inspected the other. If one wishes to see the inevitable human consequences of the ideas and tendencies which found expression in Locke's two plans for education, one cannot do better than to look again at the picture of life which is drawn in *Culture and*

Anarchy, in *Literature and Dogma,* in *Friendship's Garland,* in *Essays in Criticism,* in *Discourses in America,* in the papers on Democracy and Equality, but especially in *A French Eton* and in the *Reports on Elementary Schools.*

2

Matthew Arnold was not an educational reformer. Unlike Comenius and Locke, he was well pleased with his own instruction. What he has to say about methods of teaching is relatively unimportant. For thirty-five years he inspected public elementary schools with a Puritan zeal and diligence. He examined with great care every phase of the educational process both in England and on the Continent. He became, I presume, the most important English-speaking representative of the older tradition of education in the days just before the pragmatic revolt broke out. And for this reason he was a favorite object of attack when the battle began. And yet his critical greatness lies not in his judgment about the devices of the classroom, but in his awareness of the habits of mind of the community, the standards of taste, the customs of social behavior, the religious attitudes, which were shaping both teachers and pupils. He had little faith in scientific studies of education—too little, I should say. But he had a profound sense of the cultural influences which were forming the characters and lives of the English people, old and young. Teaching he understood, not as a collection of classroom tricks, but as the communication of taste and intelligence from one generation to another. And from this it followed that the decisive educational factor in any community was the presence or absence of taste and intelligence in the older generation. He knew that teachers could not give what they did not have. It is this insight which gives to his characterizations of English life such profound educational importance. He began to realize and to make others realize what it means to try to teach for a com-

39

munity which has only two main concerns—"the concern for making money and the concern for saving souls."[1]

3

Arnold's analysis of the education of England takes him back to the Puritanism for which Locke spoke. The record which he finds is one of two centuries of failure, of developing catastrophe. "The great middle class," he tells us, "the kernel of the nation, entered the prison of Puritanism and had the key turned upon its spirit there for two hundred years."[2]

This enslavement of the English mind Arnold finds in two fields, that of religious beliefs and that of social institutions. In both of them he is driven to despair. There can be no doubt of his love for his country. He is English to the core. And yet his castigation is almost incredible. What he called the "Hebraic" elements in the English character, its sturdy independence, its personal integrity, its energy and courage, its fighting spirit— these and like individual virtues—moved him to deep admiration. Those virtues were worth teaching. But they had been bought at a monstrous price. The cultural results of Puritanism filled him with horror. He found the advocates of the "Natural Liberties" of men claiming the right to "do as they pleased," to "like what they pleased," to "think what they pleased." Such claims seemed to him the madness of irresponsible individual license. It was the pushing of those claims which was destroying the "right reason," the "sweetness and light," the "love of humane perfection" which were the values of the second great European tradition—that of Hellenism. Arnold wanted to hold to both these traditions. But he found one of them destroying the other. Individualism was rampant in England. So strong were the competitive, self-assertive forces around him that his voice for the other side was always that of "one crying in the wilderness." He

[1] *Culture and Anarchy,* Macmillan, p. 143.
[2] *Ibid.*

was a prophet who could not save his people. His work is chiefly important, not in making clear the way which the education of the future must take, but in recording with a stark honesty the blunders of the past, the hopeless contradictions of a chaotic present. We must now see the forms which his despair takes in the fields of religious belief and of social theory.

Arnold was, in attitude, quite as religious as were Comenius and Locke. But in belief, two hundred years had brought a most destructive change. Arnold could no longer "prove" the existence of God in intellectual terms. As he examined the traditional dogmas of his people, he was driven to say "there is not a creed which is not shaken; not an accredited dogma which is not shown to be questionable; not a received tradition which does not threaten to dissolve. Our religion has materialized itself in the fact, in the supposed fact, it has attached its emotion to the fact, and now the fact is failing it."[3] The "new knowledge" toward which both Comenius and Locke had been looking, had done its work. Locke's proofs of God were gone, forever.

And, again, the literal interpretation of the Bible, upon which his elders had depended for the guidance of life and education, was no longer possible for him.

The mental habit of him who imagines that Balaam's ass spoke, in no respect differs from the mental habit of him who imagines that a Madonna of wood or stone winked, and the one who says that God's Church makes him believe what he believes, and the other who says that God's Word makes him believe what he believes, are for the philosopher perfectly alike in not really and truly knowing, when they say God's Church and God's word, what it is they say or whereof they affirm.[4]

Religious beliefs and differences of belief, it was clear to him, do not express judgments of fact. They are not intellectual, because they have no intellectual basis on which to build. When men follow different lines of religious faith their relations should

---

[3] *Essays in Criticism*, Second Series, "The Study of Poetry," p. 1.
[4] *Culture and Anarchy*, Macmillan, 1883, p. 123.

be, not like those of disputants who are contradicting one another, but like those of men who prefer one kind of poetry to another. The Bible is not a record of fact. It is the poetry, the highest poetry, of our culture. It can therefore be properly interpreted
only by the poetic imagination, not by the factual mind.

How then had the Protestant sects of England dealt with that
change from fact to poetry? As Arnold saw them they were still
reading their Bibles with literal credulity, still holding fast to
their dogmas, as if the New Learning had never been heard of.
They were so safely immured in the "prison of Puritanism" that
they were unaware of what was going on in the outer world of
the free mind and the free spirit. Their greatest glory was to
believe without having reason for their belief. Their greatest
satisfaction was to be certain, equally without reason, that
other men's beliefs were absurd and sinful. Arnold saw, with
bitter distress, their "spirit of watchful jealousy." It was clear to
him that a large part of the emotion which they called pious or
religious found its most satisfactory expression in attacks upon
the creeds of others. Chapel gloried in its distrust of church,
church in its contempt for chapel. And, even more powerfully,
the Protestants, as a group or a collection of groups, waged hostile
and dogmatic war against the Catholics. "The dissidence of
middle-class Dissent and the Protestantism of the middle-class
Protestant religion"—that slogan Arnold found blazoned on the
banner of the religious sects. It revealed to him an English Protestantism, unacquainted with "right reason," untouched by
"sweetness and light," sinking down into the deepest depths of
stupidity and intolerance.

4

But the same catastrophe had fallen upon the social life as
well. Arnold delighted to quote, as expressing the social philosophy of England, a Mr. Roebuck who said, "I look around me
and I ask what is the state of England. Is not every man able to

say what he likes? I ask you whether, the world over, or in past history, there is anything like it? Nothing. I pray that our un-rivalled happiness may last."[5] There, for Arnold, is the destroyer of "right reason." It is the unbridled, unregulated, irresponsible license of thought and action. Such a man as Mr. Roebuck does not inquire what he ought to say. He says "what he likes." The Puritan individualism, for which Locke had been speaking, had now developed into a fully grown laissez-faire theory of human action.

Our familiar praise of the Constitution under which we live is that it is a system of checks,—a system which stops and paralyses any power in interfering with the free action of individuals. To this effect Mr. Bright, who loves to walk in the old ways of the Constitu-tion, said forcibly in one of his great speeches, what many other people are saying every day less forcibly, that the central idea of English life and politics is the assertion of personal liberty.[6]

The results of this negative, pugnacious, irresponsible insist-ence by the individual upon his own rights, Arnold found about him on every hand. The English community he saw as roughly divided into three social groups, the Barbarians of the upper class, the Philistines of the middle class, and the huge, inert mass of the Populace at the bottom.

The Barbarians are, on the whole, Locke's private pupils. And they are still true to type. They have privilege and they are determined to keep it, as their "right." They have sporting spirit, are fond of games and physical health, are loyal to church and state. In a word, they are "gentlemen." But—or, perhaps, there-fore—their most striking characteristic, as seen by a student of education, is their "idealessness." "One has often wondered whether upon the whole earth there is anything so unintelli-gent, so unapt to perceive how the world is really going, as an ordinary young Englishman of our upper class."[7] And again, "the

[5] *Ibid.*, p. 100.
[6] *Ibid.*, p. 43.
[7] *Ibid.*, p. 55.

peculiar serenity of aristocracies of Teutonic origin appears to come from their never having had any ideas to trouble them."[8] I would like to recommend these words for the consideration of persons who so commonly speak of John Locke as the greatest single mind in the building up of English educational practice and theory.

Of the Populace, Arnold says relatively little. Its place in life has been to do the drudgery, the dull, brutalizing work of industry and of agriculture linked to industry. And the Victorian critic of Victorian England finds in it, in spite of some vague stirrings which suggest future activity, the natural results of the forces which have made it.

And as for the Populace, who, whether he be Barbarian or Philistine, can look at them without sympathy, when he remembers how often—every time that we snatch up a vehement opinion in ignorance and passion, every time that we long to crush an adversary by sheer violence, every time that we are envious, every time that we are brutal, every time that we adore mere power or success, every time that we add our voice to swell a blind clamor against some unpopular personage, every time that we trample savagely on the fallen—he has found in his own bosom the eternal spirit of the Populace, and that there needs only a little help from circumstances to make it triumph in him untamably.[9]

Ignorance, passion, violence, envy, brutality, covetousness, hatred, meanness, cruelty—those are, for Arnold, the qualities of "the eternal spirit of the Populace." Here again is Locke's "abhorred rascality" of the common people. Who made men like that? How has England done it? What shall we say of the schools out of which such pupils have come?

But it is the Philistines—the class from which Arnold himself claims to have come—to whom he chiefly gives his attention. This is the middle class, the Protestants and merchants who have been, slowly but steadily, thrusting themselves up between

[8] *Ibid.*, p. 54.
[9] *Ibid.*, p. 83.

the Barbarians and the Populace, shrewdly and acquisitively taking control of the religious, economic, and political life of England. It is upon this group that Arnold lets loose the full storm of his fury and despair. They have, it is true, certain Puritan, self-centered virtues. They can trade. They can fight, if need be. In business, they are honest. But, with respect to truth and beauty, to the essentials of life, they are not merely uneducated; they are tutored in error, in prejudice, in blindness, in illusions of the most destructive sort. From John Bright down they specialize in superficial, partial, and uncritical views of the world and of society. Their stupidity is equaled only by their self-conceit. In the latter mood they are the backbone of liberalism and reform of every kind. They are eager to refashion everything but themselves. Their aim in life is to bring all other human beings up to their own high standards of enlightenment and virtue. Their leaders, Arnold says, tell the Philistines how "all the world knows that the great middle class of this country supplies the mind, the will, and the power requisite for all the great and good things that have to be done," and congratulate them on their "earnest good sense which penetrates through sophisms, ignores commonplaces, and gives to conventional illusions their true value."[10] And, on the other hand, Arnold finds in them the unmitigated dullness of the stupid.

For Philistine gives the notion of something particularly stiff-necked and perverse in the resistance to light and its children; and therein it especially suits our middle class, who not only do not pursue sweetness and light, but prefer to them that sort of machinery of business, chapels, tea-meetings, and addresses from Mr. Murphy, which makes up the dismal and illiberal life on which I have so often touched.[11]

This is the group which is rising to control over England. What kind of an England will it make? Arnold tells us in bitter, hopeless words:

[10] *Idem,* p. 92.
[11] *Ibid.,* p. 72.

And the work which we collective children of God do, our grand centre of life, our *city*, which we have builded for us to dwell in, is London! London, with its unutterable external hideousness, and with its internal canker of *publicè egestas, privatim opulentia*— to use the words which Sallust puts in Cato's mouth about Rome— unequalled in the world![12]

When a loyal and well-informed critic of a people can make statements like these, does one need further evidence concerning the quality of the teaching by which the mind of that people has been nurtured and formed?

5

We must note at this point what Arnold says of the culture of America. We are, he thought, in especial degree, Philistines, fashioned by the same forces and to the same end. In *A French Eton* he asks,

And what were the old United States but a colossal expression of the English middle class spirit, somewhat more accessible to ideas there than here, because of the democratic air it breathed, much more arrogant and overweening there than here because of the absence of all check and counterpoise to it—but, there as here, full of rawness, hardness, and imperfection; there as here, greatly needing to be liberalized, enlarged, and ennobled, before it could with advantage be suffered to assert itself absolutely. All the energy and success in the world could not have made the United States admirable so long as their spirit had this imperfection. Even if they had overrun the whole earth, their old national style would have still been detestable, and Mr. Beecher would have still been a heated barbarian.[13]

He gave us the same estimate of ourselves when he lectured in America. He hoped that someday we might be educated. But his hope was a very uncertain and tentative one.

[12] *Ibid.*, p. 25.
[13] *A French Eton*, Macmillan, 1864, p. 111.

6

Such then is Arnold's negative account of the England he loved and of the United States which aroused his curiosity and stirred his imagination! How shall we sum it up? The simplest and most adequate statement is that, as Arnold sees it, Anglo-Saxon education has failed, has collapsed. Schools, like apple trees, are known by their fruits. And the fruits of English teaching are, in one field, the Protestant sects, in another field, the Barbarians, the Philistines, and the Populace. The people of England and America have not been educated.

No one felt more deeply than Arnold himself how difficult and equivocal his own position was. He knew that a culture had broken down. But he could not see how to build another to take its place. He could record evils. But he could not explain them. He was not a reformer, a planner, as the Philistines are. His words were rather those of a "prophet of old," preaching Hellenic sweetness and light with phrases of Hebraic violence and wrath. He lashed out with fury against the Puritanism and natural liberty of the English tradition. And yet he could not analyze those ideas and attitudes to find in them the basis for the forming of a new tradition. He criticized Victorianism. But he stands on the record of history as one of the most typical of all Victorians. His own well-known words tell his story with uncanny accuracy.[14]

> For rigorous teachers seized my youth,
> And purged its faith, and trimm'd its fire,
> Show'd me the high, white star of Truth,
> There bade me gaze, and there aspire.
> Even now their whispers pierce the gloom:
> "What dost thou in this living tomb?"
>
> Forgive me, masters of the mind!
> At whose behest I long ago

[14] Stanzas from *The Grand Chartreuse*.

So much unlearnt, so much resign'd—
I come not here to be your foe!
I seek these anchorites, not in ruth,
To curse and to deny your truth;

Not as their friend, or child, I speak!
But as, on some far northern strand,
Thinking of his own Gods, a Greek
In pity and mournful awe might stand
Before some fallen Runic stone—
For both were faiths, and both are gone.

Wandering between two worlds, one dead,
The other powerless to be born,
With nowhere yet to rest my head,
Like these, on earth I wait forlorn.
Their faith, my tears, the world deride—
I come to shed them at their side.

7

When Arnold was thirty-seven, Charles Darwin published the *Origin of Species*. When Arnold was forty-five, Karl Marx gave out the first volume of *Capital*. These were—we now know—the two most decisive expressions of the "new method of thinking" by which the activities of men and their societies were, in the next era, to be interpreted. Darwin established naturalism as the ruling principle for all sciences of human behavior. Marx gave new vigor and new form to the materialistic analysis and description of social action. In the line of the efforts of these two men—if not wholly as a result of them—there have been created in the last seventy-five years, new "sciences" of every phase of human living.

If Arnold were alive again today, the array of these sciences would undoubtedly startle and impress him. Darwin and Marx had both spoken within his hearing. In some sense he must have been aware of them. Yet it is certain that he had no adequate understanding of what they were saying, to what they were leading. He had the conviction that a new world was struggling "to be born." But, in the large, he was himself so much a member of the older order that he could not tell what the new order would be nor by what methods it would take possession of the human scene.

At this point Arnold is, for contemporary discussion, a very significant figure. He challenges our smugness. We who are "modern" and "scientific" are wont to speak of Victorianism as smug and dogmatic and traditional. But where, among the practitioners of our new sciences and technologies, can be found any self-criticism which approaches in severity and honesty that which Arnold gave to the England that he loved? He knew that he did not know how men should live and teach. We do not know either. And yet we are boastful of our "new" methods, our "new" techniques, our "new" efficiencies. We seem incapable of self-assessment. In a world which is rushing to its own destruction because of its own intellectual and moral disorder we glory in our "new" knowledge. We "know" so much that we can no longer "think."

8

Before we leave Arnold we must take account of his suggestions in the direction of positive action. They are too partial and scattered to provide a program. But they do reveal a desperate urge toward social and educational reconstruction.

First, his classification of Englishmen into Barbarians, Philistines, and Populace was not exhaustive. There were also "the remnant" or "the elite." From each of his three social classes there were always emerging a few "aliens." These were rare spirits who rose out of and above the general dullness. These "aliens, if we may so call them," are "persons who are mainly led, not by their class spirit, but by a general humane spirit, by the love of human perfection." They are to be found in England, France, Germany, and other modern countries, as well as in ancient Athens and Rome. Someday they may appear even in America. Their coming, or failing to come, is not, so far as Arnold's explicit argument goes, directly connected with school education. The aliens appear here and there, now and then, as poets do—however that may be.

And further, though English education disappointed him, Arnold never sank into the despair of skepticism. There were lessons for Englishmen to learn. He believed both in Hebraism and Hellenism. The virtues of sturdy independence were worth acquiring as were also the virtues of taste and intelligence. His essential difficulty was not that there was no "good" to the learned but that the first of two great goods had been so badly misconceived that it was destroying both itself and its fellow. He never doubted the validity of the claims upon men of "right reason," of "sweetness and light," of "the humane spirit." These were the materials out of which, by proper education, a culture might be made. Culture, he said, is "the acquainting ourselves with the best that has been known and said in the world and thus with the history of the human spirit." To become educated is to become cultivated. How then shall teaching be carried on? Here, at the crucial point, we find Arnold's basic educational principle. Culture is to be won by contact with the best literature. Great writing is, for him, the expression in words of the most powerful minds, the most lofty spirits of all times and of all countries. The men who do that writing can show us, by their being what they are, what we should be. It is primarily by habitual, responsive, active contact with these great persons that the process of human education should be attempted. Arnold's chief dependence, then, as he estimates the work of the schools, is upon the fellowship of those who love literature, of those who create it and those readers also who find in it the very breath of their own being. He is not—as is commonly said—exclusively devoted to the literatures of the ancient world. All great writing, whatever its period, partakes of perfection and can therefore give it out. As one reads Arnold's Reports on the Elementary Schools there is something pathetic in the eagerness of his longing that out of the grime and stupidity of working-class England there may grow up young people who will be caught by the spirit of the Bible and Homer, Shakespere and Goethe, the French essayists and the German poets. As compared with these all other "subjects" seem to him secondary and even dangerous. He is not hostile to the teaching of the sciences. On the contrary he sees "greatness" in them and wonders how they can be well taught. But he does fear the little-mindedness, the Philistinism, of the scientists. He finds many of them uneducated. How, then, shall they teach?

It is easy to criticize Arnold's content of study. A culture which, for whatever reason, is without effect upon the great body of the people, is subject to deeper and more skeptical questioning than Arnold gave it. If what he says is true, then, so far as general education is concerned, that "culture" might just as well be nonexistent. And yet, at the bottom he is right. The basic principle of all teaching is that of bringing the mind of the pupil into contact with the best minds of the race. It is the first duty of the teacher to establish that contact, and his greatest sin is that, in his attempts to do so, he shall, by his clumsiness, break the circuit. The tragedy of many of our educational methods is that, to so large an extent, our teachers are nonconductors who, by their very intervention, make sure that nothing will happen in the way of genuine transmission of culture. We may, I am sure, quarrel with Arnold's notion of what a great mind is. What he never clearly saw was that the breakdown of English education was at bottom a proof of the breakdown of the culture which that education was intended to express. His own view of "literature" was certainly limited. Perhaps the students of economics and politics and history and natural science had a right to call him, too, a Philistine. And yet, in his own way, he was seeking both breadth and depth in the understanding of life. He wanted to "see life steadily and see it whole." And that idea of his can, by natural development, be made to include the "subjects" of his critics. It has not yet been shown that their ideas can encompass his.

9

In the broader field of social practice, as related to education, Arnold made three suggestions which should also be noted.

First, he mentions now and then a "revolution" which must come in the social order.

We are on our way to what the late Duke of Wellington, with his strong sagacity, foresaw and admirably described as a "revolution by due course of law." This is undoubtedly—if we are still to live and grow and this great nation is not to stagnate and dwindle away, on the one hand, or, on the other, to perish miserably in a mere anarchy and confusion—what we are on the way to.[15]

Our present-day radicals would, I fear, find revolution according to the prescription of the Duke of Wellington, not very revolutionary. And yet, in his own middle-class way, there can be no doubt that Arnold was increasingly aware of the need of radical social change.

And, second, in his public addresses on Democracy and Equality, he becomes more specific. He challenges directly the class division in English social life. The aristocracy of that division, he tells us, must be destroyed. All Englishmen must be on the same social level. His reason for this is characteristically educational. Aristocracy, he says, is the enemy of culture. It is hostile to right reason. Not on grounds of economic justice, but in the interest of poetry and other literature, for the sake of the humane spirit, for the cultivation of taste and understanding, Arnold preaches to England the gospel of social democracy. He challenges aristocracy at the point at which it has always thought itself to be strongest—its fostering of human excellence.

[15] *Ibid.*, p. 70.

That challenge, vague as it still is, goes deeper than any economic analysis. My guess is that, if Anglo-Saxon civilization does ever achieve its needed "revolution," the line which Arnold suggests is the one along which its chief force will go.

And, third, coming closer again to education, Arnold found himself driven to a decision which was, for him, so revolutionary that only with great reluctance could he accept it. He became convinced that the schools of the middle and lower classes should be taken out of the hands of the religious sects and private groups by which many of them had been established, and should be put into the hands of the state. He became a resolute and out-spoken advocate of government education. He would have been unwilling to see the influence of religion taken out of the schools. That would have seemed to him disastrous. And yet his experi-ence with "private" and with "religious" control of teaching forced him to turn to the state as, at least, an escape from evils. It must be said, I think, that "the state" remained for him, in cultural terms, a rather vague entity. He never seems to have asked whether, as it exists in England, the government could serve as an adequate representative of "right reason" and "sweet-ness and light." With such questions of basic political theory his mind did little grappling. And yet he does speak for the most fundamental revolutionary drive in modern society—the placing of education under state control. And as he does so, he notes with shrewd insight the fear, the hatred which all traders and dissenters show toward any plan for increasing the power of a central government.

10

Of all Arnold's discussions of education and social policy *A French Eton* is, I think, the most powerful and significant. In the closing words of that little book his revolutionary impulse comes nearest to finding itself. He has been saying, what he usually said, that if change for the better were to come in England it must come through the middle class. The Barbarians were forever asleep. The Populace was not yet awake. Hope, then, could rest only "in a transformed middle class, in a middle class raised to a higher and more genial culture."[16] But in the final words, he strikes another note which rings sharply as we hear it eighty years later. He suggests that if the middle class could be stirred then, in turn, it might awaken the Populace. And so, at last, the soul of England might be saved.

This obscure embryo, only just beginning to move, travailing in labor and darkness, so much left out of account when we celebrate the glories of our Atlantis . . . might find in a cultured, liberalized, ennobled, transformed middle class, a point toward which it may hopefully work, a goal toward which it may with joy direct its aspiration.[17]

There is tenderness in those words which comes very near to understanding. And in that mood he goes on to speak to the Populace. He claims friendship with them, declares that he has fought for them against the claptrap and fears and prejudices of the classes above them. And on the basis of that friendship he appeals to them. "Children of the future, whose day has not yet dawned," he calls them, "you, who with all your faults, have neither the aridity of aristocracies, nor the narrow-mindedness of middle classes, you, whose power of simple enthusiasm is your great gift."

And so in a mood at least analogous to that of the Communist Manifesto, he summons them to lead the way into the future. "But you, in your turn, with difficulties of your own, will then be mounting some new step on the arduous ladder whereby man climbs towards his perfection: towards that unattainable but irresistible lodestar, gazed after with earnest longing, and invoked with bitter tears: the longing of thousands of hearts: the tears of many generations."

"Longing" and "tears." Those are the final words of England's

[16] A French Eton, p. 117.
[17] Ibid., pp. 120-121.

inspector of schools in the reign of the good Queen Victoria. As he labored in the schools Arnold discovered that England could not educate her children because she herself was uneducated. Following the lines marked out by John Locke she had created a world-wide empire of industry and commerce and finance. But, by that very achievement, she had brutalized and stupefied her people. Of what use to talk of "methods of teaching" when the nation, as a whole, was destroying the truth and goodness and beauty which her schools were called upon to teach? How shall men teach if they do not understand?

Chapter 5. THE FORCES OF DISINTEGRATION

THE story of the disintegration of Protestant education has thus far been told in personal terms. There were three characters, a hero, a villain, and a victim—Comenius, Locke, and Arnold. All three of these men were pious Christians. They were all alike loyal to the tradition of Christian life and Christian teaching. And yet their roles are radically different. Comenius is a builder. Locke is an underminer. Arnold finds himself living among the ruins of an old order, yearning for the building of a new one.

The import of our story must now be translated from personal to impersonal terms, from the form of direct experience into that of general ideas. Direct experience does not, as such, "transfer." It does not explain or interpret. Only as experiences and situations are generalized by ideas and principles does their meaning become usable in dealing with other situations and experiences. That translation we must now attempt. We have seen the serene, harmonious, unified planning of Comenius replaced by the confusion, the incoherence, the futility by which Arnold was surrounded and depressed. What were the intellectual and social forces which had brought about the change? What was it that Comenius had had which Arnold had lost? If we can answer that question we can interpret the course of Protestant education.

As we turn now from the personal story, kindness, if not justice, would seem to require that one more word be said about Locke. We have described him as villainous, as the destroyer of the faith in which he believed. He was, we have said, double-minded. He had the characteristic duplicity of the ruling class Englishman. Those statements are, I think, true. And yet, they need interpretation. Apparently Locke was not, in personal relations, a malevolent man. He was kindly and gentle. He was not consciously dishonest or selfish. He had a genuine passion for human liberty, together with an eager desire for human understanding. He wanted clarity of mind, freedom from traditional illusions. Why then was he a villain? The answer is, I think, that the civilization for which he spoke was, as judged by its own standards, essentially a self-contradictory one. The Christian culture was, in its Protestant form, destroying itself. And Locke's mind was of the pliable type which responded with great sensitiveness to all the forces which played upon it. In his day the tremendous currents of the new science and the new commercialism were gathering impetus. Locke felt them keenly and deeply. His genius responded to them and put them into words which would make them practical and efficient. But, meanwhile, he held fast to the old faith. It was out of such duplicity of allegiance as this that there emerged Christian Capitalism, the culture which could follow two gospels at once, the gospel of the Bible and the gospel of the ledger, God and Mammon. Locke did not make that culture. He was rather its spokesman, loyal to all its traditions and tendencies, loyal both to church and state. He was a good member of a bad society.

I

If we search through the mind of Locke to find the central tendencies which, by their boring from within were to reduce to ruins the Christian plan of teaching, three different phases of his thinking demand our attention. In the field of ideas, he argues for toleration. In the field of morals, he accepts a Puritan individualism. In the field of politics, he works out a characteristic "social contract" theory of the state. And in each of these cases, his results have direct and decisive bearing upon the theory and practice of education. Always he is destroying the foundation of unity upon which Comenius had built.

So far as beliefs are concerned, and especially with respect to religious beliefs, both Comenius and Locke were ardent advocates of toleration. Both of them had suffered from the conflicts of the sects. Both had been driven into exile by such conflicts. For Locke, that had meant a few years of relative ease and freedom for study and writing in Holland. To Comenius it had brought lifelong wandering, dependence, insecurity, disappointment. Each, in his own way and his own degree, had personal reasons for reflection on the madness of the religious wars. But the forms of their reflections were characteristically different. Comenius was an advocate of the reconciliation of the churches. It was his hope that even Catholics and Protestants might be brought into a single church. He says, "Christ, whom I serve, knows no sect." But Locke, in spite of some earlier hopes for Comprehension, had given up, when he wrote on toleration, all hope of genuine unity such as this. His program was one, not of peace but of armed neutrality. He recognized, as matter of brute fact, an actual multiplicity of religious opinions. He felt driven to accept the differences between those opinions as irreconcilable. The mind of Comenius was fixed on the hope for unity, for mutual understanding. The mind of Locke was concerned with the hard, cold, present fact of multiplicity, of hopeless misunderstanding. And from these two different attitudes the two men drew two theories of toleration which were, in effect, as far apart as are the assertion and the denial of the truth of Christianity.

There are two kinds of toleration. One of them springs from hope. The other springs from despair. The first is a form of intellectual co-operation. The second is a form of mutual noninterference. The toleration which arises from hope regards men as working in a common cause. As they use their minds, individuals or groups are grappling with a common problem. Each of them, working with his own powers and his own materials, makes such contribution as he can to the common task. And when they find their separate intellectual results opposing one another they recognize that each must take account of what the other is doing. Each finds in the work of the other a correction, a supplementing of his own partial achievement. This is the toleration which a group of scientists have for one another. They are workers in a common enterprise. They differ, but even those differences are of value in pointing the way which all alike must travel if the common work is to be done. This is the toleration which men like Comenius advocate as the proper basis for all human relationships in the various fields of opinion and action. It is the toleration of mutual respect and co-operative effort.

But there is another toleration which springs, not from hope but from despair. It accepts differences of belief as final, as irreducible. It regards the minds of men not as working together but as working separately and independently. Each individual, in his own way, is building up his own reaction to his situation, his own interpretation of the world about him. If those views conflict, what shall be done about it? The answer is "Nothing." Each man must accept the brute fact of difference. On that basis they can make a bargain with one another. "I will agree not to interfere with your belief, if you will agree not to interfere with mine. Let it be understood between us that each man's opinion is his own private business." This is the negative toleration of noninterference. It has none of the quality of intellectual co-operation. It is simply a practical man's way of avoiding trouble. I would not disparage too much the avoiding of trouble. Sometimes, though not very often in the work of thinking, that may be necessary. But to confuse the avoiding of trouble with the active creating of intellectual unity in the life of a society, is to lose all proper sense of intellectual values and intellectual possibilities. At this point, the victory of Locke over Comenius means that one of the unities upon which Comenius had counted is gone. For the followers of Locke, there is no human brotherhood of the mind. There are merely many men holding many opinions which sometimes differ and sometimes agree.

The practical, human significance of this difference in the interpretation of toleration is nowhere more clearly revealed than in the field of education. It is one thing to teach young people to think together in a common cause, in search of a common truth. It is a wholly different thing to train them to "tolerate" other minds with whom they have nothing in common except a dread of mutual persecution. The skeptical implications of this second procedure are strong and inescapable. If I must "accept" the opinion of another man, not because it seems to me worth considering, but simply because he and I will do each other external damage if I interfere with him, and if, likewise, his toleration of my view carries with it no recognition that it has even a partial validity for him, then we are not far from the conclusion that all opinions are alike worthless and invalid. At this point, it did not take long for the logical mind of a Scotsman named Hume to make clear the skeptical implications which a typical Englishman had left obscure. If my beliefs cannot be "justified" to my neighbor that means, to anyone who can think objectively, that they cannot be "justified" to me. Locke's toleration, formulated for the Protestant world, is an admission that Protestant beliefs are held without reason, that men have no intellectual right whatever to declare them true. Comenius had planned the teaching of human beings on the basis of the assumption that they were all alike seeking for a common truth. As Matthew Arnold discovered two centuries later, the Lockian education had taught Englishmen to think, each "what he pleases." And that meant that he had taught them not to "think" at all. It was that mental irresponsibility, that destruction of intellectual comradeship, that logical atomism, which had broken down the Protestant culture, had made impossible the education of the English people.

2

The same atomism which dominates Locke's thinking about logic also dominates his thinking about morals, and with the same destructive effect upon the Christian theory and practice of teaching. Locke has all the moral individualism of the Puritan. Here, again, he begins to wear down the presuppositions which Comenius had taken for granted. The teaching plans of the follower of John Huss were based upon the assumption that all humanity, taken together, is one moral brotherhood. That assumption Locke accepts, as a dictum of theology. But, when he speaks of the actual working relations of men to one another, he proceeds to establish an individualistic atomism which breaks the human society into scattered fragments. In the realm of conscience, for the Puritan Locke, each man lives his life alone and independent. In a moral isolation, he faces his own God. In that unique relationship of one man, one God, the whole drama of moral responsibility is played. One ruler; one subject,—that is the basic society so far as conscience is concerned. Morally speaking, there is not one human society. There are as many moral societies, each with its own independent authority, as there are human individuals. And the relations between these atomic societies are not those of fellowship in a common community. They are accidental and external. I am not morally responsible to or for my neighbor, nor is he, to or for me. Each, through his own conscience, deals directly with his own God. And, so far as morality is concerned, he deals with no one else. When men are thus regarded as morally irrelevant and accidental to one another, human society no longer exists. There is no human brotherhood. Mankind is merely a miscellaneous collection of unrelated individuals.

And the same atomism holds true for the Lockians in the field of external interest and action. Here, whatever prudential arrangements and contracts they may make, the ultimate appeal is always to the separate and distinct interests of separate and distinct individuals. Those self-interests may be found, or may be made, to coincide. An "intelligent self-interest" may, therefore, with shrewd and clever eye, search out these coincidences, may even arrange that the interest of another shall agree with one's own. But, in the last analysis, each man is playing to his own hand. Men are not a society. They are an accidental collection of human atoms, each following its own path. Sometimes they go the same way. Sometimes they clash and block each other. Beyond that there is nothing more to be said, except that in such a dangerous world, prudence is a primary virtue.

This moral atomism of the Puritan has also profoundly affected the work of the teacher. He faces, in his classroom, not the potential members of a moral community, but a number of solitary individuals. Each of these is to be separately educated, whether it be in the field of conscience or in that of external conduct. By one set of lessons, the pupil must be prepared to meet, alone and independent, his own fate at the hands of his own God. His own soul must be saved. By another kind of teaching, each pupil must be equipped to manage successfully his own fortunes. He must always follow his own self-interest, however "intelligent" that self-interest may become. It is that atomism which lies at the basis of Locke's two plans for the education of two sets of young Englishmen. In the teaching of his "young gentlemen," tutors are hired, not to create a human society, but to ensure, each for his own pupil, the separate salvation, the separate worldly success of a young man of property and social standing. And, meanwhile, other young men and women, the members of the "abhorred rascality," are given no education at all. They are not dealt with as members of a human society. They are herded together in droves, driven into "parish working schools" which will fix upon their bodies and minds, the habits and endurances and stupidities and subserviences which will make them a good working class to serve their masters. Such a double plan of education is a characteristic product of moral isolationism as expressed in the unholy alliance of Christian piety and practical common sense.

3

But the idea of Locke which cuts most deeply into the basic beliefs of Comenius, which has brought the Protestant theory of education into the most destructive conflict with itself, is to be found in his version of the "social contract" theory of the state. Locke accomplishes here the ideal theology for Anglo-Saxon "practical common sense." He combines assurance that God exists with equal assurance that He will not interfere with the "sensible" management of human business by businessmen.

Locke wrote, as everyone knows, two treatises of civil government. The first of these proved to his own satisfaction that the authority of the state did not come from God. The second proved that the state was made by men, that it was a human arrangement. It is now customary to disparage the importance of the first of these two treatises. And it must be admitted that, as we read it today, the argument is curiously dull and unconvincing. It proceeds, by a detailed and literal examination of the Bible, to demonstrate that nowhere within its pages can one find a delegation of civil authority from God to Adam, nor after him to a supposed line of rulers who might have inherited their kingship in his succession. The argument is, as we now read it, antiquated and silly. And yet it was, I am sure, for Locke and for his contemporaries, the crux of the political controversy in which they were engaged. Their primary question had to do with the authority of the state over the individual. Where did that authority come from? Was it unlimited or limited, absolute or conditional? Are there limits to the obedience which a citizen is required to render to his government? If so, what are those limits? Under what conditions, if any, is a citizen justified in disobeying and even in rebelling?

Now, in Locke's dealing with these questions it is the negative answer of the first treatise which is decisive, more than the positive answer of the second. If God had given authority to the rulers of men then that authority would be unlimited, unconditional. There would be no right of disobedience whatever. And, further, for Locke and his contemporaries, the only possible source of such absolute authority was the mind and will of God. If that could be eliminated, if it could be shown that there is no divine right of succession in virtue of which certain men rule over their fellows, then the threat of absolutism is gone. That threat Locke eliminates by his first treatise. Speaking for a society which wishes to set limits to what a government may do, which insists that, only so long as certain specified conditions are met will its members acknowledge the civil authority of the state, Locke, first of all, proceeded to exclude the state from the only field in which unconditioned authority can be found. Devout believer as he was in his God, he cut off the state from the sphere of the activity of the Divine will. And in so doing he led the way in that process of disintegration by which the structure of Christian citizenship and Christian education was to be broken down.[1]

In the second treatise Locke develops the positive contention which is the necessary complement of the negative argument of the first. Government was not established by God? By whom then, and for what purpose, was it created? The answer is clear and—for a believer in the Christian doctrine—terribly significant. The state is a human arrangement, a human bargain. It springs not from the will of God, but from the prudence of men. Its authority rests not in Divine law, but in human convention. In the hypothetical "state of nature" which, Locke tells us, precedes the creating of established governments, men are not safe. Their "rights," granted to each man separately by his God, are often invaded. Their needs, for the satisfaction of which they seek to have and to hold property, are denied satisfaction. In a word, when human living lacks governmental regulation, men interfere with one another. And in this insecure and disastrous situation they are driven by prudence to make a compact, to set up, by common consent, a controlling, authoritative government. It is agreed among them that a state shall be established and maintained for the protection of the citizens and of their property. That state has such authority, and only such authority, as

---

[1] The dictates of the Divine Will had made mankind a "community." They had not made it, or any part of it a "state."

is stipulated in the bargain. Its sanction is to be found, not in the Divine will, but in human prudence. Its authority is such as human prudence dictates and, from time to time, from situation to situation, maintains and modifies.

Now the destructive element in Locke's thinking, which smashes directly against the Christian unity which Comenius had taken for granted, is found in the sharpness of the separation here made between two realms of human conduct—the realm of conscience, in which men are subject to the laws of God, and the realm of prudence, in which men are subject to the laws of the state. Human conduct thus falls into two sharply separated fields. And these two fields are not only radically separate in sphere, they are also radically different in content. In his relations to God, an individual is subject to moral authority. Here the law reads "you ought; you ought not." This moral law divides the right from the wrong. It is a distinction perceived by a man's conscience. But, in the other field, that of the state, no individual is ever told what he ought or ought not to do. The state has no authority over a man's conscience. It can appeal only to his self-interest, to his prudence. Its imperatives are conditional rather than absolute. It says, "If you do this act which I forbid in the common interest, I will see to it that you have cause to regret your action: I will arrange that you shall lose more than you gain by your act of disobedience." And this means that the only civil reason for observing the law is regard for one's own self-interest. If a man can so arrange that, by breaking the law, he will gain more than he loses, the state, at least, cannot charge him with moral turpitude in doing so. That question he must settle with his own conscience. The laws of the state rest, not upon the eternally valid moral principles of the Divine will and reason, but upon the conditional, prudential arrangements of men who, in specific situations and under specific conditions, have made a bargain for the furthering of their own self-interests. That bargain they will keep so long as it pays them to keep it, and, if they have common sense, they will keep it no

65

longer. The appeal to reason, to love, to conscience, of the moral field is here matched by a distinct appeal to fear, to worldly wisdom, to prudence, in the field of external action.

Here is, I am sure, the chief source of the duplicity which has infected England's spirit as her people have, during the last three centuries, fought their way up to dominance over the industry and culture of the modern world. Locke does not deny God. But he does limit the field of His action. He debars Him from interfering when questions of the "rights of property" are at stake. Those questions are to be settled, not as matters of conscience, but as matters of bargaining between men of shrewd, practical common sense. With moral right and wrong, the church, as God's spokesman, may of course deal. But it had better be silent about wages and working hours, about starvation and sanitation—except as these come within the field of private charity,—even about freedom and equality. As men deal with the affairs of this world they have two distinct and separate questions to answer. They must ask, not only "Is it right?" but also, "Does it pay?" and Anglo-Saxon morality has never been able to decide on the proper relations of these questions. It is that moral ambiguity which, more than any other factor, has enabled Britons and Americans to combine, and yet to keep apart, piety and worldly wisdom, but which has thereby destroyed the spiritual integrity upon which the Christian system of education had been built.

How profound is the social effect of this separation of the moral and the prudential is revealed by its influence upon the work of the teacher. He has now, not one, but two sets of lessons to teach. He must bring his pupil into right relations with God. But he must also establish him in proper relations with his fellow citizens and with the state. And since these two sets of behaviors spring from different sources, depend upon different motivations, they require two different kinds of teaching.

It is this cleavage which gives to Locke's lists of teaching aims their strange sense of inner incongruity. On the one hand, the teacher must inculcate piety and virtue. On the other hand, he must build up physical health, good manners, worldly wisdom, love of reputation, technical skills suitable to his pupil's station. And, as between these two, the function of learning is uncertain and equivocal. On the whole, learning is, for Locke and for his fellows, a servant of prudence rather than of virtue. Great knowledge is not needed to make a man acceptable to God. "Simple piety" will do—in fact it may be preferred. But if one wishes to get on in the world, to advance one's own self-interest, then one must study men and the world to see how they may be used for the realization of one's purposes. Education becomes deeply vocational in intention. Learning is no longer a following after the Divine reason. It is an instrument of worldly success. The "adamantine chain" of Comenius has been broken in two. One does not say, in speaking of a human being, that "it is only by a proper education that he can become a man." One comes nearer to saying that education is a way of becoming a good businessman.

Locke's apostasy has also had a profound effect in starting the drift which has carried the school out of the hands of the church and into the hands of the state. If the division of human conduct into two distinct fields be accepted then it inevitably follows that neither church nor state is fitted to take charge of education as a whole. The church, representing God, may well undertake to teach piety and virtue. The government, if it can teach at all, may instruct young people in the ways of prudence, the customs and habits suitable to the social contract which guards their interests. But neither institution is fitted to give guidance in both realms. An unworldly church cannot teach common sense. Nor can a state, whose motivations go no deeper than self-interested prudence, be expected to impart private virtue, generous sentiment, human aspiration. If Locke's moral dualism is accepted, then, at one stroke, both church and state are found to be unfitted to take charge of education as a whole. As one searches out the motives which have prompted the transferring of the control of the schools from one institution to another, it is that double unfitness which seems to be the most powerful influence. "Neither of them can do it," we have said; "therefore turn it over to the state."—It is little wonder that our Protestant-capitalist education has collapsed. It is little wonder that the civilization which gives and receives that education is now involved in desperate self-destroying strife.

Book II

THE PROBLEM OF RECONSTRUCTION

Chapter 6. JEAN JACQUES ROUSSEAU

THE man who leads the way out of the disintegration of Protestant education into the creation of "modern" teaching is Jean Jacques Rousseau. It is this eighteenth century thinker who really breaks loose from older ideas, who defines the new problem with which later thinkers must struggle, who points the way toward its solution. He is the most stimulating, the most suggestive, the most provocative of all recent students of a society and its teachers. As we try, therefore, to get the "feel" of our contemporary situation, we cannot do better than to take our cue from Rousseau.

Rousseau's mind is, in every respect, at the opposite pole from that of Locke. Both in social and in educational theory, Locke was his chosen enemy. In the Englishman, as we have seen, all incongruities between ideas are blurred. His genius is that of holding together, in a foggy unanimity, points of view which are fundamentally incompatible. Problems, as he deals with them, are not solved: they are dissolved. He muddles through. He has common sense. He is practical. Rousseau, on the other hand, has no common sense. He is absurd. His creative, tumultuous mind rushes to extremes. But its peculiar genius lies in the fact that, when contradictory ideas are being dealt with, he rushes to both extremes. He presses the claims of unity just as clearly and passionately as those of diversity. He fights for individual freedom with an intensity and effectiveness which few men have equaled. But, on the other hand, his doctrine of the social authority of a General Will which is absolute, which is infallible, marks the outer limit of the belief in a "social control" to which human beings must submit themselves. This is the sort of mind which is needed as a disintegrating culture is torn to shreds, and preparation is made for the forming of a new culture to take its place. It is easy to disagree with Rousseau. He is essentially a transitional, a preparatory thinker. Few men of sober mind would be inclined to accept his theories as he frames them. And yet he cannot be ignored. He is absurd. But he is never ridiculous. The problem which Locke blurs and hides, he brings out into the open. He forces upon the attention of the modern world the issues that must be faced, the factors that must be considered as men move forward in the desperate attempt to make a new society and a new education.

The peculiar quality of Rousseau is well depicted by George H. Sabine as he assigns to the writer of the *Social Contract* his place among his contemporaries. He says,

A really satisfactory arrangement of this complex material is probably impossible but on the whole it seems clear that one figure in the French eighteenth century stands apart, Jean Jacques Rousseau. He himself felt it and suffered from it; his acquaintances felt it and detested him for it; all discerning critics have tried to take account of it. Lytton Strachey has said, "He possessed one quality which cut him off from his contemporaries, which set an immense gulf between him and them: he was modern."[1]

It is characteristic of Rousseau that in the same year, 1762, he published two of the world's greatest books—the *Emile*, a study of education, and the *Social Contract*, a study of the theory of the state. His "Republic" was written in two separate treatises. It is equally characteristic that on the surface the two arguments seem to be contradictory. But one does not understand Rousseau, nor does one grasp the essential problem of modern culture, unless one sees that they are really one argument. In the *Emile* Rousseau preaches the gospel of individual freedom in teaching. But a careful reading reveals that freedom is to be found only in conformity to the demands of an authoritative society. In the *Social Contract*, Rousseau discovers the absolute authority of a General Will. But the purpose of that will is, we are clearly told, to make individual men free. Freedom and authority—those are his two dominant motives, and he will not let either of them

[1] *A History of Political Theory*, Henry Holt and Co., 1937, pp. 544-545.

go. That double insistence enables him to state with provocative clarity the political educational problem which men are still trying to solve.

I

The basic conflict of ideas and of motives with which Rousseau is grappling is seen most clearly in his discussion of education. In this field he was, as everyone knows, the prophet of what we now call "progressive" teaching. He hated instruction by the imposition of authority. He rebelled against the requirement of obedience. No one ever had a more lively contempt for verbalisms of every sort. No one ever saw more clearly the necessity that teachers discover and pay regard to the individual differences of their pupils. He was sure that you cannot proceed to make a pupil what he ought to be unless you know accurately and sympathetically what he now is.

Treat your scholar according to his age: put him in his place from the first and keep him in it, so that he no longer tries to leave it. Then before he knows what goodness is, he will be practising its chief lesson. Give him no orders at all, absolutely none. Do not even let him think that you claim any authority over him. Let him only know that he is weak and you are strong, that his condition and yours puts him at your mercy; let this be perceived, learned and felt. Let him early find upon his proud neck, the heavy yoke which nature has imposed upon us, the heavy yoke of necessity, under which every finite being must bow. Let him find this necessity in things, not in the caprices of men; let the curb be force, not authority.[2]

But the same Rousseau who said, when prescribing the methods of teaching: "The very words *obey* and *command* will be excluded from his vocabulary, still more those of *duty* and *obligation*,"[3] said also: "There is only one science for children to

[2] *Emile* or *Education*, J. J. Rousseau, trans. by Barbara Foxley, Everyman's Library, 518, p. 55.
[3] *Ibid.*, p. 53.

learn—the duties of man."[4] And in another place he tells us: "From the first moment of life, man ought to begin learning to deserve to live; and, as at the instant of birth we partake of the rights of citizenship, that instant ought to be the beginning of the exercise of our duty."[5]

It will not do to interpret this man too simply. Here is a mind which can think two different thoughts at once. His thinking does not play the game of "following the leader," as so many of the believers in "individual differences" have followed one of his leads. He is forever grappling with two or more ideas which seem so contradictory that they cannot live together within the unity of a single mind. With respect to the method of teaching, Rousseau is a romantic individualist of the most extreme kind. But with respect to the content and aim of education he is equally extreme in his idealism or humanism or rationalism or rigorism or classicism or whatever be the title which we give to those who, in the name of "duty" and "obligation" have fought the battle for authoritative human values and principles. On this side, he is both the pupil of Plato and the teacher of Kant.

It may, of course, be taken for granted that Rousseau does not solve his problem. He is never a finished, a systematic thinker. But he does state the problem—as few men have done. And this makes him one of the decisive figures in European culture. It is not enough to say of Rousseau that he speaks in paradoxes. He speaks in paradoxes because he grapples with fundamental human dilemmas.

2

The one-sidedness of much current educational theorizing is seen in the fact that, when speaking of Rousseau, his interpreters deal so grudgingly with the "duty" element in his teaching. "Progressive" educators can hear him when he speaks of

[4] *Ibid.*, p. 19.
[5] *The Social Contract and Discourses*, Jean Jacques Rousseau, Everyman's Library, 660, p. 268.

freedom, of individual differences. But they seem strangely deaf
when he advocates the claim of authority and obligation. Joseph
K. Hart, for example, warns us against a strange, unintelligible
element in Rousseau's thinking. And to account for it, he says,
"Rousseau was scarcely a normal person, scarcely a person at all
in most ways; he was a sort of natural phenomenon expressing
himself as the spirit of utter revolt against the institutions and
artificialities of the eighteenth century."[6] But to say this is to
see Rousseau only as a destroyer of the past, not as the creator
of the future.

And John Dewey is, I fear, open to the same criticism. In his
early writings he recognized Rousseau's kinship to Plato and
Kant. But when *Democracy and Education* is written, the *Emile*
is dealt with as if it were purely naturalistic in meaning. The
writer of the *Social Contract* is even chided for lack of proper
regard for the "social" factors in education. His authoritative
General Will is referred to only in a footnote[7] as "a much-
neglected strain in Rousseau tending intellectually in this direction," a direction counter to his dominant naturalism. And,
unfortunately, Dewey's curiously partial interpretation does
little to remedy the neglect of which he speaks. No student of
education has provided more carefully than did Rousseau, in
the *Emile*, for the deliberate guidance of the life of a growing
individual, so that it may conform to the authoritative will of
a society. Throughout Emile's career, his tutor has foreseen
every event, has planned for it, has measured its good and its
evil possibilities, has provided for obtaining the one and avoiding the other. At every moment Rousseau's pupil is under a
guidance which will mold and shape aright his mind and body
and will. And yet Dewey and his colleagues seem to interpret
Rousseau as believing only in the "spontaneous development"
from within of the "native organs and capacities" of the pupil.

But this will not do. Rousseau is a naturalist—in teaching

[6] *Creative Moments in Education*, Joseph K. Hart, Henry Holt & Co.,
1931, p. 252.
[7] *Democracy and Education*. Henry Holt & Co., 1916, p. 109.

method. But he is also a rigorist—in teaching content and intention. He believes both in the freedom of the individual and in the authority of society. He believes that either of these is unintelligible without the other, and from this it follows that to make him merely a naturalist is to lose even the meaning of the naturalism which, as one factor in the situation, he does so strongly stress.

3

Sabine and Strachey have told us that, in the political field, Rousseau was "detested" by his contemporaries. He is still detested.[8] Few men have been so bitterly hated by traditionalists, past and present. He is a dangerous, a revolutionary, thinker. With a strange, unerring, intuitive insight, his ironical mind points out to a dominant culture its denials of its own beliefs. And, more than that, the same insight gets, at least, a glimpse of what are to be the principles of the future.

The central problem with which Rousseau is concerned—with which all Protestant social theory has been concerned—is that of the relations between a human individual and the organized society of which he is a member. This is the problem in dealing with which Locke had given expression to the characteristic Anglo-Saxon moral duplicity. Rousseau abhors that duplicity. All his thinking is a keen and desperate attempt to expose it, to recover human integrity. But to do that requires cultural surgery. Rousseau therefore slashes with brilliant satire at traditional beliefs and customs. That is why he is so bitterly hated. He cuts where it hurts.

Throughout the Protestant era, whether in its days of flourishing or in those of its decay, we Anglo-Saxons have taken it for granted that an individual has "rights." Those rights we Protestants have been ready to defend. We have, therefore, been

[8] As an expression of a Catholic detestation of Rousseau read the characterization of him by Jacques Maritain in *Three Reformers.*

critical of the claims of authority over us. As against all human "authorities" we have insisted upon our private freedom and independence. We have demanded that our rights be recognized and respected and guarded. Every man, we have said, has a right to worship God as he deems best—or to declare that there is no God to worship if that seems to him best. Every man has a right to think his own thoughts and to express them openly and without fear, either by speech or by writing. Every man has a right to assemble with his fellows, to discuss with them matters of private or public policy and to present a statement of grievances whenever a wrong seems to have been done. Every man has a right to "own" property and to have an equal share in the protection which the government has agreed to give to all alike in the acquiring and holding and using of the means of livelihood. These and like matters are specified in the first ten amendments to the Constitution of the United States, our American Bill of Rights. In the Declaration of Independence they are covered by the oft-quoted words—

We hold these truths to be self-evident: that all men are created equal; that they are endowed by their creator with certain inalienable rights; that among these are life, liberty, and the pursuit of happiness. That to secure these rights, governments are instituted among men. . . .

Now it is here, in dealing with "rights" and "authorities," in defining the relation of the individual to his government, that the intellectual chasm opens up to separate the new world from the old. This is where Rousseau and Locke part company. The Englishman speaks for the past. The Frenchman speaks for the future.

If we say that men have "rights" which other men must respect, which their governments are founded to guard and to maintain, the question arises, "What is the source of these rights; where do they get their validity?" If a man says, "Every human being has a right to be free!" sooner or later he must face the question, "What right have men to be free? Who gave them that right? Where does it come from? How do you justify the claim to freedom?"

If one wishes to "face the crisis" in modern society or modern education, no intellectual issue is more significant than this. It lies at the heart of all our discussions of "democracy" and "totalitarianism." It is the basic issue of the World War. It is involved in all our attempts to interpret the meaning and authority of the Constitution of the United States in relation to the "freedom" of the individual citizen. It is decisive in its influence upon our theory of education, as the "state" undertakes to teach our children. What is the source, the basis, the justification of our individual demand for freedom, for equality, for justice, for security? And especially how is that demand related to the authoritative purpose of the political state?

The conflict between Locke and Rousseau at this point is of peculiar interest to Americans because these were the two men whose ideas most powerfully influenced the making of our political institutions. And the curious and disconcerting fact is that, in spite of their contradictions of each other, we, as good Anglo-Saxons, accepted them both. Since their lists of rights were apparently the same, though based upon conflicting sets of reasons, we adopted both sets of reasons. The resulting confusion in our political theory and action would be hard to measure. For the most part—as may be seen in the Declaration of Independence—we use the medieval words of Locke. But, meanwhile, the inexorable logic of Rousseau's modernism drives us on. And for this reason we find continually that one set of our words denies another. We still declare that all men are endowed by their Creator with certain "inalienable" rights. And at the same time, day by day, our courts and legislatures are solemnly determining under what conditions those rights may be alienated.

Here is an issue which is basic to all social and educational theory and practice. In every school and college in America, in every class of adults, pupils should be studying John Locke's *Treatises of Civil Government* and Jean Jacques Rousseau's *Social Contract.* Taken together in their opposition to one another these two men define the "problem" of our democratic institutions. They show us the vital break in our Protestant-capitalist civilization. If we can understand them we shall be able to see why the control of education has gone over from church to state. We shall see also why government, as we have interpreted and fashioned it, is so sadly unsuited to the teaching responsibility which we have laid upon it.

4

Locke and Rousseau are agreed, in general, as to the origin of the state. For both of them, it is made by men. It arises out of a social contract. Both thinkers describe this human achievement by drawing a contrast, which is rhetorical rather than factual, between human life in a "state of nature" and human life in a "civil state." They are not saying, when they use these phrases, that men ever did live in a state of nature. They are merely imagining what human living would be if there were no political institutions. By this rhetorical device they try to single out the influence of the political factor. It is their figurative way of expressing the relation between the state and the rights of the individual.

The difference between Locke and Rousseau at this point can be more clearly seen if we relate them both to Comenius. The Czech bishop had no doubt that both the state and the individual were created by God. That was the medieval point of view. The English public servant takes half the step from this medievalism to modernism. Locke's theory is that the individual was made by God but that the state was made by men. Rousseau takes the full stride into modern thought. Both men and the state are made by men. Civilization, whether in its individual or its social phases, is a human achievement.

79

The essential duplicity of Locke's social theory, which has made him the accredited spokesman of our Protestant-capitalist culture, appears in his account of individual rights. In the biblical, theological account of humanity which the Englishman gives, it appears that when God created men and gave them the earth for their use, He established them in the state of nature. But He did so in accordance with the laws and principles of His own will. "Natural" men were, therefore, subject to a law of nature which, being divine, was also a law of reason. And this law of reason, defining the relations of men to one another, was the basis of their "rights." As members of God's community they were endowed, eternally and inalienably, with the human rights to freedom, equality, property, justice, and the like. But at this point in Locke's theory the action of God ceases. The Divine will does not proceed to establish government among men. That they must do for themselves. And they are driven to do so by sheer necessity. For it appears that, though God has "given" men rights inalienably, they do not always "get" them. Individuals in the state of nature seem little concerned about the rights of their fellows. They interfere with one another. They take what they can get. They plunder and kill. Each, seeking his own self-interest, refuses to recognize the claims of others even though those claims are eternally valid.

It is this situation which drives men to the establishing of government. The political state arises as a secondary social phenomenon. It arises out of human prudence. By mutual consent, as a device of self-interest, men give to government authority over themselves and their possessions. It is the task of the government to "secure" the "rights" whose validity had been assured prior to and in complete independence of the government itself. Those private rights, it is essential to note, are the ultimate social facts. They are morally grounded in the will of God. The state, by contrast, is a nonmoral human contrivance. As to the validity of rights it has nothing whatever to say. Government is not moral. It is merely prudential.

Rousseau's theory of human rights is the exact antithesis of this. In his "state of nature" there are no "rights" whatever. Men living without government, he tells us, can have neither "rights" nor "wrongs." They have neither "laws" nor "reason." They can have no property since the owning of property implies a contract, an agreement, as to the conditions under which it shall be held and used. And such an agreement can be made and enforced only by the will of a political state. Unless such a state exists, men can "have," but they cannot "own." In the state of nature, also, there is no justice, since there are no laws. Neither is there any equality, since all individuals differ in their abilities to grab and to keep what they want. Freedom, too, is wholly lacking. In its place is the complete license, in accordance with which each man proceeds separately to the satisfying of his own desires and interests. When men have no government, they can have no morality, he also tells us. The distinction between good and bad behavior is made and maintained only as men, by means of the conventions of an organized society, agree and enact legislation decreeing certain acts lawful and certain others unlawful. Rousseau even goes so far as to suggest that reason is man-made and conventional. It, too, as well as morality, is a political invention rather than a divine gift, a "natural" possession. He does not think through this last suggestion, not being a student of the theory of logic.[9] But the implications of his position inevitably lead along the road which it indicates. For him, the political state is not a secondary institution. It does not merely "secure" rights which men have received from God, prior to their citizenship. Government is primary. It creates "rights" and "wrongs." They are meaningless and impossible without it. The state is the creator of mankind. It makes civilization, makes culture, makes human beings. To paraphrase Comenius we may say that "only by becoming a citizen does one become a man." Human rights are whatever the changing activities of organized living require

[9] The line of that suggestion is to be found in the moral and political theories of Immanuel Kant and of his followers.

of human reason that they should be. This does not mean that the state exists first, and then, afterward, brings the qualities of social living into existence. It means only that these two sets of facts are complementary, are the individual and social phases of one fact. Human rights are political. To be a member of an organized and governed society is to have rights. And vice versa, to have civil rights is to be a member of an organized, a governed, society. Locke's "natural rights" are nonsense. Man is a political animal.

5

The conflict between Locke and Rousseau as to the origin of individual rights, especially when seen in relation to the faith of Comenius, reveals the significance of Rousseau for the modern world. It also explains why he is "detested."

Rousseau challenges the licentious individualism which Matthew Arnold found a century later, destroying the social and intellectual integrity of England and America. He sees through the duplicity of idea and motive on which that individualism rests. For Comenius, the rights of the individual and the authority of the state had been equal in moral status. Both came directly from God, hence, in case of conflict between them neither could claim moral priority over the other. Neither could appeal to the Divine reason as giving sanction to its demands, while denying like sanction to those of its opponent.

But the Puritanism of Locke destroyed this balance. In his hands the rights of the individual acquired a moral superiority over civil law and order. Rights, he tells us, are established by God. They express His Will. They are eternal, inalienable. Civil laws, on the other hand, are made by men. They are merely human contrivances. The level of their authority does not rise above that of expediency. The conscience of the individual, his dignity, his worth as a person, are absolutely justified. But the action of the state has no such sanction. It has no "moral" standing whatever. And from this it has followed that whenever, in the Protestant-capitalist world, the morality of the individual and the prudence of the government have met in conflict, the individual has brought to the advocacy of his claims a smug and dogmatic moral superiority by which mere "political" considerations have been shamed and driven from the field. "One with God is a majority" we Protestants have said. And since each of us has found "the voice of God" in his own conscience each of us has been that "one." Each of us, with arrogant assurance, has regarded the concerted political judgments of his fellows as something essentially inferior in kind to the dictates of his own will. It is by mental jugglery such as this that a disintegrating religion has tipped the moral balances of an Anglo-Saxon world. It has enabled us to combine righteousness in morals with success in business.

But the drastic surgery of Rousseau cuts through this duplicity of standards. For him, the rights of the individual and the authority of the state spring from the same stock. They have the same moral status. Both are made by men. And if there be conflict between these two, they meet on equal terms. Neither one of them can claim a backing of "reason" which is not available to the other. The human wisdom, out of which they both come, to which they are both responsible, is their final and common court of appeal. In a word, individual rights are principles of action of a politically organized society. They are not "prior" to that society. They are created and sustained by it. They are the forms of human relationship and behavior which it approves and enacts. And they have no other "justification" than this.

It is not hard to see why Rousseau is detested. He has committed two grievous sins. First, in theory, he is accused of degrading man by secularizing his rights. He is, therefore, an enemy of religion. Second, in the field of practice, he has invalidated the claim of the individual to be superior in status to the government of which he is a citizen. He is, therefore, an enemy of private morality and of private enterprise. Those charges have been pressed in manifold forms of misrepresentation. But the motive which underlies them all springs from the fact that Rousseau slashes at the very nerve of Protestant-capitalist self-seeking. The only freedom which can be justified, he is saying, is not freedom "from" the state. It is freedom "in" and "by" the state. The only rights men have are those which citizenship in a political society confers upon them.

6

With one of the favorite misinterpretations of Rousseau we must deal here, because of its special significance for education. Rousseau, we have said, places individual and political standards of conduct on the same level. For the Lockians this would mean that they are both degraded to the lower level of prudence. Since government is made by men, it is merely prudential; it has no moral status. But also, since men are made by the state, they, too, are merely prudential, merely self-seeking. In both cases, morality, when it is secularized, ceases to be moral. But Rousseau has no such meaning as this. For him both the state and the individual are on the upper level. His secular state speaks of duty, of obligation, of moral commitments. As he sees them, both the individual and the state are morally grounded. He has a human substitute for the will of God. It is the General Will of men. That General Will, as he interprets it, has all the authority, all the absoluteness, formerly assigned to the dictates of the Divine Being. The state, he tells us, is a moral institution. More than that, it is—he says in brilliant paradox—"a moral person." Upon the acts and decisions of that "person" the whole structure of human intelligence, human society, human education, rests. His state is fitted to replace the church. That is why the churchmen "detest" him. But that also is why he points the way for the "moderns."

84

7

If Rousseau is right, then one fundamental question concerning contemporary education is on its way toward solution. In our first chapter we asked, "Can a state teach? Can a government do the work which, in the days when religion was dominant, was assigned to the church, but for which the church has now become unfitted?" To that question Rousseau offers an affirmative answer. If morality and intelligence are fundamentally political, then political institutions may be trusted to teach them. The first principle of all teaching is that a person can teach what, and only what, he himself is doing. If it be true that the state is the maker and maintainer of freedom and justice, of equality and intelligence, of industry and ownership, then the state through its agents can teach those lessons to its citizens young and old. In that case, the putting of our schools into the hands of our governments may not have been a "colossal blunder." It may be that we moderns can create a nontheological civilization which can carry on the work of morality and intelligence. It is that possibility which Rousseau has suggested to the contemporary world. It is that clue which we now try to follow.

Chapter 7. THE FIRST OF THE MODERNS

IF WE take our cue from Rousseau we are bound to interpret the school as expressing the wisdom and the will of a community. Every school, we shall find, is established by some social group, large or small. And from this it follows that the purpose of teaching is to be found, not primarily in the will of the pupil, not primarily in the will of the teacher, but rather in the will of the society by which the school is conducted. To that society both teacher and pupil "belong." The teacher is an agent—usually a paid agent—of that community. Since he is a teacher, he must be free in his teaching. And yet the ultimate fact can never be escaped that the purpose to be realized by the school is not, in the first instance, that of the teacher. It is that of the group which puts the teacher to work. And, in the same way, the will of the pupil is likewise secondary. We may, perhaps, find in him the explanation of learning, but not that of teaching. The provision for his education is made, not by him, but by the community which cares for him. We know what a school is doing only in so far as we know what a community is trying to do.

In what has just been said I am not suggesting that the teacher and the pupil should not be free, the one in his teaching, the other in his learning. Like Rousseau, I would fight to the bitter end for unqualified freedom for both teacher and pupil. But I am saying that the justification of classroom freedom is to be found, not in the private rights or demands of the teacher or pupil, but in the public purposes and intentions of the group to which the school belongs. If that group chooses to be democratic, it will make its teachers free because, only by so doing, can it realize its own purpose. And the same holds true of the pupil. Why should he be free in his learning? Why should the school devote all its efforts to the building up of the independence of his mind and will? It is only because the community which establishes the school, which engages the teacher, which entrusts to him the pupil, has a purpose of its own—the making of free people. The justification of academic freedom goes far beyond the private wills of teachers and pupils, or even those of parents. It is to be found in nothing short of the General Will of the group which provides that teaching shall be done, whether that group be home, church, city, state, nation, or any other agency which assumes responsibility for carrying on the work of educating youth.

There is, however, lurking in what I have said, an assumption which many students of society and of education will challenge. It is the assumption that social groups have "General Wills," that communities have purposes, that a society has intentions, which underlie such institutions as the school. Are there, as matter of sober fact, such social wills and intentions? Or are they mere fictions, ideas which exist only as the sounding of words, without usable meanings? I need hardly say that Rousseau's General Will, after which we are here following, has been violently attacked as just such a fiction. All "wills," we are told, are individual. A social will is a myth. To accept Rousseau as one's guide is evidently not to escape from controversy but rather to be plunged into the midst of it. And yet the presupposition of "the will of the community" seems to me so essential to the understanding of teaching that I cannot give it up. We must rather try to find what clear and defensible meaning it can be made to have.

The term which in our own current discussion seems to come nearest to Rousseau's General Will is that of a "culture" or a "pattern of culture." I propose, therefore, that we examine this term and see where it may lead us.

A "pattern of culture," as the term is used in our ordinary speech, is a social consensus of approvals and disapprovals of human behavior. It expresses the attitude of a social group as it works out a mode of life which claims and exercises authority over the conduct of individual members, of constituent groups, and even of itself as a total society. In all three of these relations, the culture approves and disapproves, accepts and rejects, praises and blames, establishes and destroys. Essentially a pattern of culture is an authoritative custom of evaluation.

This notion of evaluation, of approval and disapproval, lies at the heart of any plan of teaching. Except as a school is trying to direct the growth of a pupil along some chosen line, except as it tries to prevent his growing along other lines, education is a meaningless process. But the notion of evaluation is quite as difficult as it is significant. By what mental process does a society pass judgment upon its members and upon itself? Where does it find standards of judgment? What assurance is there that these standards themselves are valid? Throughout the history of European culture no set of questions has been more baffling or more persistent than these which lie at the foundation of any understanding of teaching.

I

What, then, is a general will or a pattern of culture? And how does it evaluate? I would suggest that we seek help by comparison with a musical theme

When we speak of a group of people as having a pattern of culture our idea seems to be closely akin to the experience of music. In any musical composition many different notes are bound together into some coherent design. These notes are heard together and also in succession. But however divergent they may be there is running through them all a relation of congruity, of common significance, of aesthetic interconnection. It may be that a single melody runs through them all. It may be that different themes are brought together, each dominating its own movement and all fusing into one varied, inclusive, masterful whole. But however simple or complicated the pattern, the essential fact is that, within the whole, the different notes do "belong" together.

88

Each has its part to play in the total enterprise. The dominant theme or themes run through them all. And with a peculiar sense of fitness, the composition selects those notes which "belong" to it, rejects those which are not "fitting." In this sense, the whole, as an organized unity, has authority over its members. It has the power of acceptance and rejection, of approval and disapproval. It distinguishes what is right from what is wrong. The general will of all the notes seeks expression, and claims the right to expression, in every one of them.

Now it is much this same relationship which we have in mind when we speak of a social group as having a pattern of culture which claims and exercises authority over its members. In the community, the successive experiences and actions of individuals do not simply accompany and follow one another. They need one another. They imply each other. They are so related as to create and sustain the chosen pattern of the group. Or, on the other hand, they fail in congruity. And they are judged, are approved or disapproved, according as they do or do not "contribute" to the life of the community. As social happenings, all human behaviors are experienced in relation to some "pattern of behavior." To say then that a society has a pattern of culture, a general will, is to say that running through its career there is a dominant theme or set of themes in terms of which human significance and value are measured. And that means that we can understand a society culturally only in so far as we catch its themes, recognize their dominance, and see every event, every action, in terms of its fitness or unfitness for meeting the requirements of the pattern which together those themes create.

2

If we accept this figure of speech as suggesting the character of a society, two features emerge which are significant for a study of education. First, a musical composition endures; it runs through time. It binds a series of notes together. Throughout that series, runs the same theme or group of themes; it is one from beginning to end. And, second, the whole has, in some sense, authority over its members. It has the right of exclusion and inclusion, of approval and disapproval. It lays down the law for the separate notes. It requires that, at any given instant, this note rather than that shall be struck. At any rate, it determines a limited field within which selection must be made. And, in this character, it creates the distinction between what is right and what is wrong. "That will not do." "This is what I want."—these are the judgments of the creative musical mind. Its essence is the judgment of value. To be a master in this field is to have in unusual degree the power of creative selection in both positive and negative ways.

And these same two characters are to be found in any social group which is regarded as having a culture of its own. First, the life of any community is a continuing enterprise. "Rome was not built in a day," we say. So too, the making of the Athens of Pericles, the building of the British Empire, the creating and enriching of a home, the organizing and guiding of a labor union, the conducting of a business, the leading of an orchestra—all these are enterprises which take time. I do not mean that they last forever—tunes are not unending either—but only that they last. In every one of them a dominant congruity runs its course, changing at every moment, varying, it may be, with tremendous range as circumstances vary. And yet, so long as the group exists, the congruity remains. It is the congruity which defines the group, makes "it" exist. And if that sense of unity is lost, as it often is, the group ceases to be, even though some lifeless hulk or some scattered fragments may be left to caricature the living reality that is gone.

And, second, every pattern of culture is, in its very nature, a criticism of behavior. It praises and blames, accepts and rejects. It establishes codes of approval and disapproval. One may not do in Middletown what one does in Paris or Vienna or Moscow. Words which will win applause from the chamber of commerce may be greeted with hootings and groans at the meeting of a labor union. Since you and I belong to social groups, what we may do or say is subject to judgment. It is fitting or right or decent or magnificent or, on the other hand, it is evil, inappropriate, atrocious, unbecoming, according as it carries on or fails to carry on the theme dominant in the group to which we belong. A pattern of culture is, of necessity, a custom of approval or disapproval. It is an assertion of cultural authority.

3

If now we apply to the field of education the idea which our figure of speech suggests we are brought to a first, preliminary definition of the social intention of teaching. It is a dangerous definition to give in the present state of political theory and practice. And yet, fundamentally, it seems to me valid. *The purpose of all teaching is to express the cultural authority of the group by which the teaching is given.* In the words of our figure, a school intends so to mold and inspire a pupil that at every moment of his experience he will, both in thought and in action, strike the right note in the composition which his community is playing. The society wills that the pupil shall be, in terms of its intentions, a good member—rather than a bad one—of its social order. It commissions the teacher to bring that about. It has work to do. It, therefore, wishes the pupil to be fitted to do that work. It has values to interpret and to maintain. It wishes him, therefore, to be sensitive to those values, to devote his life to their service. Every social group, as such, draws its own distinction between "good" and "bad" behavior and builds its system of teaching on that distinction. The terms "good" and "bad" as so used take their meanings from the preferences of the society by which the teaching is set up. They express the authority—the cultural authority—of the group. And, under the sway of that authority, the aim of any plan of teaching is to increase the number of good people in the community, to decrease

EDUCATION BETWEEN TWO WORLDS

the number of the bad, to make good people better and bad people less bad. In a word, education is the agent of a social, cultural intention. It has authority. Without such authority, teaching does not exist at all.

4

As I look back at this statement and at the figure of speech upon which it rests I am painfully conscious how dangerous they are, how absurd they may seem, how easily they may be mis-interpreted. Authority is not, just now, as we watch events in Europe, and Asia, a favorite term among us. And the picture of a young person as waiting, at each moment of his life, for his social cue to tell him just what thought he should think, what action he should perform, is not, for most of us, an alluring one. And yet I am sure that the statement, properly interpreted, is essentially valid, both for life and for education. Especially is it valid as we try to make a democracy. A society which takes the democratic mode of life as its dominant aim is not living without pattern, without general will. It is attempting to create the most difficult, the most complicated, as well as the most sublime, of all social compositions. It can succeed only in so far as the au-thority of that purpose is accepted by every member of the group. Unless the citizens of a democracy are intelligently, sensi-tively eager, in every passing situation, to play their proper parts, to serve the common cause of freedom, the theme simply cannot be developed. It breaks down—as today in America it has at so many points broken down—into a welter of clashing, meaningless acts. Without cultural authority, there is no social order. With-out it, men are not human beings. And to talk of education without it is to use words which have no meaning.

No one who follows social and educational discussion needs to be told that we have now come to a point where controversy rages, where misunderstanding threatens to control the field. That is what one must expect if one follows Rousseau. Taking our cue from him we have said that teaching attempts to bring a pupil into conformity with a pattern. The school asserts social authority. It is the attempt of a society to make its members what it wishes them to be. In a democracy, for example, a state demands that its members be free. Education approves one mode of behavior and condemns another. It is authoritative—in a cultural sense.

But whenever this position is stated, protests arise. "What then of individual freedom?" men ask. Is a human individual simply a thing to be used by the society to which he belongs for purposes of its own? What of his own separate interests and intentions? Does not your social authority destroy his personal freedom? That ancient protest has always been made. But today, as we see national states going mad in their inhuman, irrational assertion of governmental power, it takes on new intensity, gives expression to new terrors and abhorrences. It has found philosophical expression in the pragmatic writing of William James and John Dewey and their colleagues. The antipathy of James was directed chiefly against a "block universe" which he found so rigid and unalterable, so dominating in its control of its parts, that these could have, in their separate fields of action, no alternatives, no freedom whatever. And, along the same line, the antagonism of John Dewey—since his work is primarily that of a logician—has been directed against an Absolute Mind which, by its prior possession of an eternal truth, so knows in advance the nature of things that the finite mind has no independent work to do. It can only "copy," come into line with, the truth which is already there before the human inquiry has even begun.

This is not the place to answer these protests. That they are based on misapprehension seems to me certain. Both James and Dewey are still caught in the false individualism of a disintegrating Protestantism. Authority and freedom are not contradictory notions. And my hope is that, as we examine their meanings in the field of education, their supposed hostility will give way before the perception of their congruity and mutual implications.

That is the cue which Rousseau has given us. As we turn again to follow him, two preliminary explanations may well be made.

First, the musical figure of speech which we have used should be guarded at one point. When we suggest that a society is playing out, experience by experience, a career which has something of the dominating congruity of a musical composition, we do not mean that that composition has been previously created by someone else. The social group is not repeating a tune which others before it have played. It is composing, creating, as it goes. No two groups play the same tune. No group knows in advance how its themes will develop and change.

And, second, I must say one more word for Rousseau before we leave him. In these days of bitter conflict men will call him and his followers Fascists or Nazis. They will declare his insistence upon social authority to be destructive of human freedom. But when these charges are made it is well to remember that he too is on record as a lover of freedom. However loudly any present-day advocate of the liberty of the individual may raise his cry, Rousseau will shout even more loudly in the same interest. However passionate may be our demands for individual initiative in education, for recognition of personal differences of taste and capacity, Rousseau will press them even further. He is hard to beat at the game of going to extremes. Freedom, he is telling us, can be gained and kept only by action of the political state. We do not make men free merely by saying that they are free, nor even by wishing that they were free. Liberty is won only by vigorous co-operative action. The theories of democracy and of laissez-faire are flatly contradictory of each other. We will not make a free society by letting each man separately fight for his own freedom. We will create and sustain freedom only by fighting together, with common purpose, in a collective action which recognizes and is directed by the social authority of that common purpose. Human freedom is not freedom from the state. It is freedom in and by the state. Only as the governmental tyranny and despotism of a Nazi or a Fascist state finds itself faced by the governmental freedom and justice of a democratic state will it be overthrown. Rousseau speaks, therefore, for the strong, free state. He speaks for a form of human government which is authoritative over every one of its citizens because those citizens, as a group, have made up the group-mind that, whatever the cost, its members shall live in relations of freedom and equality with one another. Such a state does not merely "secure" a liberty which individuals already possess. It creates a liberty which, without its action, is both impossible and inconceivable.

Rousseau is—one must admit—paradoxical. But so, too, is freedom. Our American individualism has been far too simple, far too childish a theory of human experience to account for the facts. As we teach a young person it is not enough to teach him to "be himself." We must teach him to "be himself in an organized society." To comprehend the mingling of individual freedom and social authority which that statement intends is the intellectual task of modern education. It is that task to which Rousseau has summoned us.

Chapter 8. CUSTOM AND INTELLIGENCE—TWO AUTHORITIES

As WE now proceed to interpret the authority underlying any scheme of education as expressing the pattern of culture of some social group, several consequences of great importance to our schools are seen to follow.

First, it appears that in any human situation with which we have to deal, there are many distinct social groups, many different patterns of culture. And this means that there are many cultural authorities and hence many different educations. As we try, then, to understand teaching we must examine, not simply one social group with its prevailing mode of life but many such groups, each with its own distinctive codes and customs of behavior. Educational theory is, then, at once plunged into a sea of multiplicity. Wherever, in human experience, we find a group of people who are linked together by a common custom of approvals and disapprovals, there we have the materials out of which a distinct scheme of education may be made. Such groupings are not only political in interest. Any human association may undertake to teach. Within the same civic community of men, radically different cultural groups may be teaching their youth in the light of radically different theories of human behavior, in the direction of radically distinct human intentions. We have to interpret, then, not one education but many educations.

It would be of great advantage in the study of education if we could list with accuracy and comprehensiveness the different cultural themes which are, in actual practice, serving as the bases of plans of teaching. In what forms, in actual human experience, do we find men united by common beliefs and tastes into such groupings that they can carry on, each in its own way, the initiation of its younger members into the ways of life which it approves? If we could do that listing, we should have a cultural survey of the society with which we were dealing. And we should have, therefore, a survey of education. Without such a survey our grasp upon the concrete processes of teaching must be fragmentary and ill-arranged. It is difficult, if not futile, to discuss the nature of education in general unless we know what specific kinds of education have been, and are, and probably will be, going on in an actual society.

Cultural history and social psychology have not yet worked out, so far as I know, such a listing of cultural groupings as our study would need if it were to be thoroughly done. For the present I can only give a few illustrations which may serve to suggest the outlines and general character of the field.

I

As seen by the teacher, the most striking social grouping is, naturally, that of the scholars. In numbers this group is not large. It is however very closely knit. And its range, both in time and space, is wide. Its members are to be found in the past, so far back as records of study can go. And, in the other direction, it is always looking forward to the accession of new members who, it is hoped, will succeed in the solving of problems by which the scholars of the present are still baffled and beaten. All these members, past, present, and future, belong to a fellowship. They have a common purpose. They depend upon each other. Whatever one of them accomplishes is the achievement of them all. They are participants in a common, and a single, undertaking— the creation of knowledge. And from this it follows that the work of each one of them is judged, is appraised, in terms of its contribution to the intellectual undertaking as a whole. "Thales led the way," men say. "Aristotle thought into order what the Greeks had done. Plato suggested one line of interpretation. Democritus suggested another. Newton laid foundations for modern physics. Later students are re-laying them. Darwin was

right. Lamarck was wrong. Freud has let loose a flood of significant suggestions."—and so it goes. All these achievements fall
within the scope of a continuing fellowship, a continuing theme
of purpose. And, on the basis of their membership in the group,
all scholars are directed and co-ordinated; they are criticized and
evaluated; they are inspired and instructed; they are given standards of intellectual behavior which they accept as the principles
of their work.—Here clearly enough, is a pattern of culture out
of which can be made a plan of education. It means something to
teach a person to be a scholar. No other human association is, so
far as I know, so sure of its fellowship, so definite in its purpose,
so confident of the allegiance of its members, so authoritative in
its command over their behavior. It knows weakness and failure
among its members. But, practically speaking, it does not know
refusal to recognize its authority.

A second cultural group, which also has great teaching significance, is that of the men of business. This fellowship is more
numerous and not so closely knit as that of the scholars. But it is,
apparently at least, more effective in its teaching influence. It,
too, has a pattern of culture which it accepts as authoritative.
Its code has to do with ways of creating and distributing human
wealth. And the group has, on the level of custom, of tradition,
of "common sense," strong convictions as to the proper forms of
human conduct in this field. It recognizes a difference between
business vices and business virtues. It can impress upon its initiates the contrast between right and wrong modes of behavior.
Its principles differ from those of the guild of scholarship in that
they are chiefly volitional and emotional rather than intellectual.
But there can be no doubt that the cultural attitude of "business" is enormously effective in determining the beliefs and
tastes of such a country as America. In fact its influence is so
pervasive that its social grouping seems at times to include all of
us. Men and women and children are alike molded by it. We
are a "business" civilization in a sense and to a degree in which
no stretch of the imagination could regard us a "scholarly"

civilization. And this means that, in the education of our youth, the business code is more widely recognized, more readily followed than is the code of scholarly achievement. If someone should say, "Our scholars must find businessmen to do our trading," the words would sound strangely to our ears. But there is nothing strange or shocking in the common notion that our property holders engage teachers to advance knowledge for them and to instruct their youth.

Other cultural groupings which, more or less explicitly, exert teaching influence are all about us. A college football team with its coaches; an orchestra with its conductor and concert master; the American Legion or the Communist Party; a golf club; a single church or an organized sect; the legal or the medical profession; a Parent-Teacher association; a picnic party; an audience with its lecturer, or the spectators at a play. Each one of these groups fuses into some sort of unity which finds expression of its attitude or intention in some code of behavior. And each of them thereby becomes a controlling, teaching influence, a source of authority which must be recognized if the association is to be true to its purpose. Its members must learn to conform to its principles. It is by the multifarious human associations of this kind that, in the large, the teaching of the human race is done. Educations are, beyond question, many.

2

But, second, patterns of culture and the social groups to which they belong are not only many. They are also shifting and transitory. They come into being. They change, sometimes with great rapidity. And they "go to pieces." A football team, a home, an orchestra, a nation—these do not last forever. Nor do they remain static and rigid. Their essential quality—if we may return to our musical figure—is that of the development of a theme. And the theme, however unified it may be, is never the same at any two successive moments. And this means that the teaching which is given by any cultural group is constantly changing. More important even than that, it means that whoever explicitly assumes the task of teaching for any group must himself be constantly changing. He must develop with his group, keep pace with it. No mind which is dead can be an adequate teacher of "a way of life."

Anyone who sees the realities of our present situation, in its social and educational aspects, can see that just now our cultural themes are shifting with great rapidity. Such a story as Marquand's *The Late George Apley* gives a striking example of the fact. It is a favorite theme of other storytellers as they picture the individual caught in the swirling currents of social attitude which play upon us. Twenty-five years ago Thorstein Veblen brought it into the foreground of our discussions of social theory. And this means that the bases of our plans of education are rapidly changing under our feet. The content and the aims of teaching must take ever new forms. We must recognize that the pupils who enter the school today are, in disposition and in interest, quite different from what their parents were. And also the world in which they are to live is, in terms of its cultural significance, radically transformed from that of forty or fifty years ago. It would be idle to elaborate an insight which is today so startlingly upsetting and, at the same time, so generally recognized. But the fact is there and must be faced—our many educations, conducted by shifting and transitory groups, are, of necessity, shifting and transitory things.

3

A third feature of our social controls, which deeply affects the work of the teacher, is the crossing and interweaving of patterns of culture. One person may be a member of many different social groups. Each of these has its own code of behavior. It follows, therefore, that the same person has, not one "way of life," but many "ways of life." He recognizes many different authorities.

He is, then, subject to many different educations. Each of these is leading him, controlling him, molding him into the pattern of its own approved behavior. The scholar, whose life is devoted to the cause of learning, may be also the "head of a family" and may find some strongly compelling claims in that relationship. And it is always possible that these different loyalties may be involved in curious relations of divergence and strain. A man may belong to the Democratic party, to a golf club, a college fraternity, a Rotary Club, a church, a Parent-Teacher association, the American Civil Liberties Union, the management of a fruit-growing industry. Each of these has its own shifting but authoritative code. Each exists for a purpose. And by his membership in the group, each person is bound to allegiance to that purpose. By one such loyalty he is united with one set of people. By the ties of other cultural unities, he participates in, becomes a member of, many other social groups, no two of which are identical in their ideas or in their membership lists. We not only have many shifting educations. We have many different and shifting educations for the *same* person.

4

And finally, from this third feature of our cultural groupings and controls a fourth arises. Authorities come into active conflict with one another. They do not simply exist side by side. Their opposing claims involve them in strife, more or less consciously directed. In the unconscious form, the different groups rub and grind against each other. England and Germany, for example, or Athens and Persia, at an earlier time—each, with its own dominant values, beliefs, and interests—find themselves inevitably thrown into contact and communication with one another. Neither of them can fail to become aware of this other code of behavior which is different from its own. In our own country, at present, Catholics and Protestants live side by side, work in the same offices and factories, share the fortunes of the same city.

Groups of employers, fused together into acceptance of one set of ideas, must deal with groups of workers who continually startle and shock them by the rapid and apparently ruthless development of a different view of industrial relationships. It is here, as everyone knows, that commerce has had its profound cultural effects of confusion and disintegration as well as of stimulation. Whenever, by the growth of travel and trade, different peoples have been brought into touch and acquaintance, there has been forced upon their attention the startling fact that the "way of life" which seems to each of them so valid, so sacred, so authoritative, has no authority whatever over other human beings with whom it seems possible to associate for mutual advantage. There is much truth in the observation that it is in the market places of the world that human beliefs and values are shattered and broken. Unfortunately, we are not quite so clear as to where they are mended. But, in any case, the principle holds true that in such a world as ours, distinct groups, fused each into its own unity and segregated by customary taste and belief, are forced to recognize the existence of other groups and other codes quite alien and, it may be, hostile to their own.

5

Now it is obvious that all this multiplicity and changing and crossing and fighting of cultural codes has a profound effect upon the work of the teacher. How can he settle down to teach one "pattern of culture" when he sees all around him many other modes of life which claim exactly the same kind of authority and with, apparently, exactly the same kind of validity? In a human world whose codes are multifarious and shifting and conflicting, which code shall he teach? To this question it is sometimes answered, by the "mere intellectualist," that the teacher's task is only that of calling to the attention of his pupils the fact that codes are multifarious and shifting and conflicting. But to do that is not teaching. Such information would be a sorry diet on which to feed the minds of young people. It would have all the effectiveness of giving, in place of breakfast, a lecture on the varieties of breakfast foods. In spite of all complexities, the first principle still holds. Teaching must find its roots in some active code of behavior. It must express some authoritative pattern of culture. It must believe something. Some social group must be speaking through it, impressing its way of life. Nothing short of that is education. But the question is, which code shall it be? In the midst of our shifting, uncertain, self-contradictory world, what shall we teach? That is the puzzling baffling problem into which everyone is sooner or later plunged who sees teaching as the activity of a specific social group. It is, I think, the most significant form of the question with which the contemporary theory of education is called upon to deal.

6

At this point of ultimate confusion and conflict, the human being reacts in one of two different ways. The first way, which has already been suggested, is a process of external attrition by which opposing cultures wear each other away. When conflicting habits of behavior come face to face, they begin, on the unreflective level of life, to grind each other down. Thus, for example, the sects of Protestantism, living side by side in our Anglo-Saxon civilization, have, by a process of stubborn, dogmatic, intolerant wearing upon each other, ground into dust the validity and authority of their respective traditions. How can a group of people continue to believe in the truth and indispensability of the doctrine of Infant Baptism when all around them is the evidence that, as between those who go through the rite and those who do not, there is no assignable industrial or aesthetic or moral difference whatever? Such an argument is not ordinarily made verbally explicit. Its reasoning takes place in the "unreasoned" sentiments and attitudes of people who are in touch with one another. But it is nevertheless enormously effective. In this way every complicated civilization finds its convictions ground away. Codes of behavior, of morals, of taste, of belief, of play, of adornment, weaken and rob each other of authority. When many conflicting claims seem equally valid, the blind, inherent reasonableness of human nature is driven to condemn them all. It can feel that the holding of any one of these creeds, as against the others, is quite indefensible. Dogmas become, then, mere personal or tribal peculiarities. What belief one holds is mere matter of chance, of birth or station. "You have been conditioned to think this: I have been conditioned to think that; and there is nothing more to be said." By such mutual grinding, all validity is destroyed. Naive dogmatism gives way to an equally naive skepticism. No belief, no code has any authority. And with the going of authority, education goes too. There is nothing left to teach.

7

But, second, human beings, when faced by cultural conflict, are said, at least, to engage in another form of activity. The work of our "minds," as we call them, is not all done on the unreflective level. Sometimes we "reflect" upon the confusing and contradictory situation. We study it, as we say, in intellectual terms. We analyze it. In a word, we try to "think" about it.

When patterns of behavior confuse us by their multiplicity, when they shift and change beneath our feet, when by their conflicts they break down their own certainties and validities, we are sometimes stirred to this other, noncustomary activity. When all patterns disagree, we are evidently facing a situation with which no one of those patterns can deal successfully. We need, therefore, still another pattern, different from them all, which can deal with them all. We are driven to search for, to create another mode of activity which can mediate between changing and conflicting codes, which will undertake to construct out of their confusion a new basis for life and for teaching.

It is this attempt which we call "thinking" or "reasoning." A human being who finds his accepted views of life challenged by other men, challenged by himself, seems to be more or less capable of framing the question, "Which of these two conflicting views is right?" Apparently we are able to "consider" our codes and customs, to "reflect" upon them, to "criticize" them, to attempt to make out of them all a wider or deeper view which includes them all and gives to each its proper place. Apparently we approve and adopt codes of behavior, not only by blind custom but also, in some measure, by critical intelligence. Now if this is true—or rather, so far as it is true—there is present in human life a second factor which is of the utmost importance for the teacher. Both life and education are bound to recognize at this point another authority which claims the right to direct them. Whenever this happens, human beings have undertaken the task of setting up over against, or supplementary to, or critical of, the authority of habit and custom as seen in accepted codes and patterns, a new form of control—that of reason or intelligence.

I speak of this second activity in tentative terms because around it center all the problems, both of life and of education. The idea of critical intelligence is a problematic one. And yet, if the notion is valid, it has the most vital consequences for all our interpretations of human living. This new pattern of behavior, in whatever form it exists, holds a relation to all the other patterns essentially different from any which they hold to each other. It "thinks" about them. It "examines" them. It claims critical authority to pass judgment upon them.

Perhaps the most startling claim which is made by this new authority is that of its "unity." Customs divide men or, at least, assemble them in separate groups which, among themselves, differ in taste and experience. Intelligence, on the other hand, intends to fuse all reasoning men into one group. There are, as we have said, many customary patterns of belief and behavior. But—and here is the vital issue—there is only one pattern of critical intelligence which is the same for all men. When one tries to "think" one is engaging in an enterprise in which all "minds," no matter how varied their cultures, may, so far as they succeed in "thinking," take part, on the same terms, in the same spirit, for the same end. My reader may, at this point, observe that, if "thinking" be so defined, there is very little of it going on in a contemporary world. And with that statement I should have no quarrel. And yet I am sure that the human attempt at intelligence is made and that, when it is made, it is motivated by the demand for unity of understanding of which I have spoken. To choose not to seek for that unity is to choose not to think.

8

By the use of a striking phrase to express a fruitful insight Walter B. Cannon has indicated, in biological terms, the relation of which we are speaking. There is, Cannon says, a "wisdom of the body." That unconscious wisdom, he tells us, has provided for men the adjustments of living in the physiological sense. Through the practical lessons of countless ages, the human body has learned how to be alive. "The remarkable effectiveness," Cannon says, "of the regulative processes of the department of the interior in preserving fitness is one of the marvels of biology." And again, "Here is an outstanding achievement, the result of evolutionary processes during immeasurable eons of past time. We are warranted in examining this supreme triumph of organization by nature for possible light on present defects of organization by man." The habits of the physiological body of man, it would seem, are intelligent, even when not consciously so. And in a corresponding way, as Cannon goes on to suggest, the unconscious wisdom of the body politic has great achievements to its credit. It has given us language, the family, and society. These general structures of human life have been "unconsciously" built. The "social body" has acquired a wisdom of its own.

But it is equally clear that men have another way of adjusting themselves to their world. Under certain conditions, they become "aware" of what they are doing. They examine their behavior, studying the conditions out of which it arises, the results toward which it leads. By such procedure we human beings have "criticized" language, the family, society. We have envisaged "ends" which might be realized under existing conditions and have directed our activities toward the realizing of those ends which seem best suited to our needs. This is what we call the "wisdom of the mind." It is the way of study, of investigation, of reasoning, of intelligence, of conscious control of human behavior. Now it is the relation between these two kinds of wisdom —the wisdom of the body and the wisdom of the mind—which gives us the basic problem of educational theory. What is "conscious" intelligence? What is its bearing upon those "nonreasoning" activities out of which it grows, by which it is nourished and blocked and supported? This is the problem which any philosophy of human behavior undertakes to answer. It tries to put "reasoning" in its proper place among the activities of mankind.[1]

9

One further point must be noted as of immediate importance to the teacher. If we admit the existence of intelligence in human behavior, it sets up over the teacher a second "authority"

[1] To make this statement complete we should, I presume, list four related factors, rather than two. Human experience contains unwisdom as well as wisdom. And this distinction holds on both levels. The body fails as well as succeeds. It makes bad adjustments as well as good. The mind too reasons both successfully and unsuccessfully. Teaching, therefore, is concerned, on the one hand, with the wisdom and unwisdom of the body and, on the other, with the wisdom and unwisdom of the mind. A complete theory of intelligence would take account of all four of these types of activity. Certainly the teacher has to deal with all four of them.

to which he must give heed. He has now two masters rather than one. The authority of custom, of the accepted "pattern of culture," is confronted with a rival authority—that of reason or critical intelligence. We have seen that social groups set up codes of approval and disapproval for human living, and that these control teaching. But here we are faced with an agency which subjects those codes themselves to approval and disapproval. The judges are judged, the critics, criticized. It is the very function of reasoning to pass judgment upon "ways of life," to accept them or to discard them as they do or do not meet its demands. Here is an authority which claims the right to rule over all our other authorities—of custom and of tradition. The task of the teacher is not, then, so simple as we had thought. He must obey, not only his master, but also the master of his master. It was bad enough when he was forced to recognize that the code of the social group which he serves is simply one of many codes of equal standing, that they all alike shift and change, collide and go to pieces. But now it appears that he must acknowledge still another ruler who is superior to them all. The teacher of a "pattern of culture" must be also the servant of cool, detached, disinterested critical intelligence. If we could understand how one person can perform both those functions we should know what teaching is. We should know what men and their societies are.

Chapter 9. THE TEACHER HAS TWO MASTERS

~~~~~~

WE ARE now face to face with Rousseau's dilemma. It is the crucial problem which confuses and baffles the modern teacher. Perhaps I should say "which confuses and baffles all teachers," since every teacher is, in his own day, modern. It is the problem of the relation of intelligence to custom, of inquiry to belief.

So far as teaching is seen as the expression of an uncriticized code of behavior, it is relatively easy to understand—or, rather, there is no felt need of understanding it. If, in any given community, a cultural authority is accepted in the form of traditional ideas and attitudes, then the work of the school is simple and uncomplicated. The dominant theme, undisturbed by discord, flows on from one generation to another. Pupils learn to live as their elders live and have lived. They have no "reason" for wishing to do otherwise.

But with the entrance of doubt and reconstruction upon the scene, the situation of the teacher is transformed. What shall teaching be in the midst of a society which doubts its own beliefs, which questions its own principles of behavior, which passes judgment upon its own standards of judgment, which, in some sense, recognizes another cultural authority as superior to that of its own code? What, in that situation, shall our young people learn to think and be and do? Shall we lead them to believe or to question, to conform or to rebel, to live in harmony with prevailing social attitudes or to break out in revolt against them? Shall our education express our tradition or our criticism of that tradition, our customs or the intelligence which summons those customs to appraisal and to acceptance or rejection?

Can the teacher serve two masters? There is no doubt that that is just what, in any present-day social order, he is called upon to do. And there is no school or college or university in our scholastically untutored America which does not give tragic illustration of the conflict. This is the point at which questions of "academic freedom" arise. There are, in the field of education, two "authorities" rather than one. Both of them must be obeyed. And they are in conflict with one another.

The sharpness of this conflict is often dulled and the point of the controversy lost by a false statement of the issue. We are told that the struggle is one between authority and intelligence. And the suggestion here given is that, while customs and traditions are authoritative and dominating, the claims of intelligence and criticism are merely personal, express nothing more than the individual choice or preference of the "critic" who is trying to "think." Surely nothing could be further from the truth than this. Men do not leave "duty" and "obligation" behind when they enter the ranks of intellectual inquiry. The mind has its own "pattern of culture" as truly as has any uncriticized code of behavior. The man who studies physics or art or history or philosophy finds himself quite as much under the dominance of rules and standards and principles as does the member of a Rotary Club or a golf club or an evangelical church. Reasoning is not merely the "free association" of ideas, the mere allowing of unregulated notions to run riot through one's mind. It is the strenuous, desperate attempt to get something right that has a powerful drive toward going wrong. Its most characteristic words are "ought" and "ought not," "true" and "false." As one surveys the intellectual history of mankind there can be no doubt that intelligence has a code,—or codes. It approves and disapproves, accepts and rejects, establishes and destroys. Thinking may be a way of escape from one authority—that of routine custom. But the escape is accomplished only by the recognition of another authority as superior to the first. It is the function of intelligence, as we say, to make men free. But that does not mean "free from intelligence." The teacher—may I say it again—has, like all

other "modern" men, two masters. Which of them shall he obey?
He must obey both.

I

Now the difficulty in this problem lies chiefly in the difficulty
of finding the social source, the origin, the basis of the authority
which intelligence claims. It is relatively easy to "place" the
authorities of social customs. Each of them is established and
sustained by some specific social group—a city, a nation, a
church, a political party, a family, a social class, a baseball club,
or a school of art. Each of these is a definite, ascertainable social
unit which follows a way of life and which therefore engages
teachers to instruct pupils in the following of that way of life.
But what club is the sponsor of intelligence? What social group
assumes responsibility for seeing to it that the principles of the
mind are learned and obeyed? If intelligence is a "pattern of
culture," of a peculiar type, what is the society whose behavior
is dominated by that pattern? I hope it will be noted that I am
not here speaking of the sponsorship of scholarship. The intellectual process, in the narrower sense of the pursuit of learning
in laboratory and library, by the use of the abstract symbols
which specialized investigation has devised, that process is, as
we have said, sponsored by a definite and closely knit social
group—the scholars of past, present, and future. They are an
authoritative fellowship. But intelligence is, in scope, far wider
than scholarship. Not all human thinking is done by professors.
Is there then a wider human group to which human inquiry
belongs, by which it is established, from which its authority is
derived? If intelligence is a way of life, *whose* way of life is it?
We moderns are rightly hostile to a supposed Platonism which
represents reason and understanding and thought as other-
worldly influences, descending, as it were, from heaven upon
the human scene, bringing to bear upon men's lives a control
essentially alien and superior to human nature itself. We know

now that whatever reason may be, it is human. It is made by men. It arises out of customary human activity. It has work to do in the rough and tumble of ordinary experience. And yet, to say that does not answer our question. What is the "human" basis of reason? What backing has it? If thinking is authorized by certain men or certain groups as conventions and customs are, we must know who those men or groups are and, especially, why they want thinking done. Whatever else may be true or false about the activities of the human reason, one thing is certain. It has been carried on through the ages at the cost of enormous volitional effort. It expresses struggle and purpose and persistence unsurpassed by any other human activity. What is that underlying purpose—or those underlying purposes—of the use of the mind? Whose purposes are they?—That is a question for which the teacher, who tries to cultivate intelligence, must find an answer. He is working for someone. Who is it? The Christian teacher was working for God. For whom are the moderns doing their study and teaching?

2

The dilemma of which we are here speaking is not limited to the work of the teacher. It affects also every phase of the life of the community within which and for which the teacher is at work. Here, as always, the processes of education reveal with peculiar clarity and urgency, not only the aims of a people but also the difficulties, the perplexities by which the mind of that people is beset. It may be worth while, therefore, to try to see the teaching problem with which we are dealing as one aspect of a wider problem which torments all our contemporary Western culture. We commonly speak of it as the dilemma of liberalism.

The term liberalism, as used in our tradition, indicates a pattern of culture which criticizes itself, which challenges its own validity. Such a culture has a double pattern. It has customs and standards of behavior. But it also has the habit, the attitude, of free and active questioning of its own dominant beliefs and standards. And this means that in a liberal social order both customs and intelligence hold sway. It has a "way of life" which is authoritative. But it has also activities of criticism by which that way is tested. Neither of these can replace the other. It is by a combination of the two that liberalism is created and sustained.

It need hardly be said that the "liberal" state of mind, as thus defined, is an uneasy one. It is easy merely to believe—if you do not doubt. It is easy to doubt—if you find no basis for belief. But the liberal is not content with either of these "easinesses." He will both believe and doubt. He doubts what he believes and believes what he doubts. To give up either of these is to abandon the way of intelligence, to cease to be a liberal. If a man or a society stops doubting its convictions, it is dogmatic and despotic. If a man or a society stops believing, it has nothing to live for, nothing to do, nothing to teach. That is the way of futility and loss of nerve. But the mind and the will of the liberal are made of sterner stuff than either of these. He is determined to establish and maintain an active, forward-moving, but self-criticizing culture. It is an amazing combination of the demands of the authority of custom and the authority of intelligence. The liberal responds to the claims of customary authority but—apparently on the basis of some other "higher" authority—he questions and even opposes the action of the society to which he gives his allegiance. He is a critic of his own way of life. He makes the criticism of customs one of his established customs.

It is one of the absurdities of current social discussion that men speak of liberalism as if it were organically connected with the cotton mills of Lancashire. Apparently they regard it as an invention of the English Liberal party. They deal with it as if it were an offshoot of the individualism of the laissez-faire theory of economics. They talk as if Socrates had been born in Manchester. And from this point of view they lament the disaster which has recently come upon the liberal tradition. We are told that since laissez-faire is doomed and individualism obviously unsound, liberalism too must go. Men speak of the dilemma of liberalism as if it were a recent mishap or disease, due to changing external circumstances which were not present when the doctrine was in its prime. They even suggest that, in its own day, liberalism was a simple, straightforward, uncomplicated, well-adjusted state of mind. But to say this is to miss completely the essence of the doctrine.

Such a picture sets up an individualistic caricature of the liberal mind in place of that mind itself. It sees Mr. Roebuck as a liberal. But a genuine liberal attitude is as old as human self-criticism—and as permanent also. Throughout human rational experience it has been true that to be liberal is to suffer dilemma, to be complicated. If an individual or a group will hold fast both to custom and to intelligence, then its experience will be inevitably paradoxical and divided against itself. The being who seeks intelligence is a divided personality. He leads a double life. And the explanation which tells how double-mindedness was brought down upon him by changing industrial circumstances has the quality of explaining how water has recently become wet. The adventures of the liberal tradition in capitalist England are not the outline of its career. They are merely passing incidents in a deep-running intellectual drive which, long before the industries of England had been dreamed of, brought dignity to the human mind and which, we trust, will continue to exalt that dignity long after those industries have had their day and ceased to be.

3

What, then, is the crucial task which faces the "liberal" teacher, which faces a social group at whose behest liberal teaching is carried on? It is, I am sure, to discover what intelligence is and does. We must make clear to ourselves what it means to criticize and so to modify our own habits and customs. As an illustration of the forms which that task may take I would like to offer that desperate international situation which is at present puzzling the minds of all of us.

In the *New Republic*, sometime ago, Willard Price told of the tradition of Japan. He spoke of it as "Japan's divine mission."

Every child of the Empire, grows up believing with every fibre of his being that:

> Japan is the only divine land;
> Japan's emperor is the only divine emperor;
> Japan's people is the only divine people;
> Therefore, Japan must be the light of the world.

Here, Price seems to say, is a code of belief and behavior which, for a long time, has had dominance over the national life of a people. And as Japan, in the rush of her rapidly changing economic and social situation, proceeds to express her beliefs in action, her armies march into China. She makes demands upon the Chinese government and the Chinese people. But these demands are in direct conflict with the beliefs and customs of the invaded nation. China does not agree that Japan is divine. She does not acknowledge "the divine mission." She has a mission of her own. And so she fights back. Men and property are destroyed. It is true that under the rapidly changing international codes, war is not declared. And yet brutality is established as the way of settling the dispute. This is what happens when two social groups, with two hostile social codes, clash without "criticism," grind each other down without the saving grace which comes from a common appeal to intelligence.

But what on the other hand is the appeal to intelligence? What is the method of peace? What happens in a human mind which tries to "understand" such a human situation? How does it differ from what happens when no such effort is made? As one hears that question, familiar words of which we have already spoken quickly come into the foreground of one's attention. We would say that a man who thoughtfully judges between China and Japan should be cool, fair, detached, trustworthy, judicial, impartial, objective, disinterested. Now all these terms indicate a mental attitude more easily assumed by an outsider than by a partisan to the dispute in question. In general we would say that the Chinese and the Japanese are both biased, both prejudiced. But the "intelligent" mind, we assume, would rise above these limitations. It would be "disinterested." What does that word mean? It suggests a human quality which lies at the very heart of all organized society, of all genuine education. Every teacher would wish his pupil to become not only "interested" but also "disinterested" in his judgments of human affairs. We shall not understand either society or education except as we are able to give exact and dependable meaning by which to control the use of that term.

4

What, then, does it mean to be "disinterested"? One interpretation can be immediately discarded—though it is all too frequently used. It certainly does not mean that a man who judges fairly has no interests, that his thinking is indifferent to human values. For example, a proper umpire between China and Japan would have an active regard for the interests of both of them. If that were not true, how could he assess their values, how decide between them? That suggestion will not do. To be "disinterested" does not mean to be "lacking in human interest."

Our impartial judge is, then, concerned about the welfare of both China and Japan. But he has other interests too. What are they? Whose are they? Are they "his own"? May he use his position as umpire for the furthering of his own private ends? Unanimously we would reject that suggestion. A man who regards certain interests as more important than others because they belong to him is wholly unfit to "judge." That would be partial rather than impartial, self-interested rather than disinterested. Week by week, month by month, in the early years of the struggle between China and Japan we shuddered with fear and horror as the press brought to us the possibility that England or France or Germany or Italy might be called in to arbitrate the Far-Eastern dispute. We did not trust them. We knew their international records too well to think of them as impartial. They would have used their judgeship for the furthering of the wrong interests—those of the judge.

What group, then, does an impartial mind serve? Whose interests dominate him and determine his decision? He must have some ends to further. Otherwise there would be no use in making a judgment. What are those ends? To whom do they belong? This is the question which, some years ago, the American people were discussing when President Roosevelt made suggestions as to ways of choosing the personnel of the Supreme Court. And the waging of that dispute gave far too convincing evidence that the terms "judicial" and "objective" and "disinterested" have not for us, as a people, any clear or dependable meaning. Our national institutions, we all know, make their final appeal for direction to the decisions of the courts. At this crucial point we assume "disinterested intelligence." That is the form of judgment of any society which is governed by laws. And yet we do not know what the assumption means. We even doubt at times whether it has any meaning whatever. We doubt, therefore, whether we have any intelligence to teach.

Here, finally, is the problem which our modern, nontheological development has forced upon us. We cannot longer say to the man who is to judge between China and Japan, between labor and capital, between isolationism and internationalism, between Germany and England, "Follow after the mind of God: come as near as you can to the decision which He would make." We must have a man-made meaning of objectivity, of disinterestedness. Without that meaning our plans for social practice, for the conducting of our schools, are vague and fluctuating and lifeless. Unless we know what a man's mind should be we do not know either what a human society or what a school should be. What is a mind for? What does it do when it is working properly?

5

The statement of this problem brings our study of education to the point at which John Dewey and his pragmatic colleagues come upon the scene. And here I must pay tribute to the man who, more than any other, has dominated, during the last fifty years, the theory and practice of American education. Dewey has done that. And he has done it chiefly by focusing attention upon the problem which we have been trying to state. His chief preoccupation, both in the social field and in that of education, has been to discover the role and the nature of human intelligence. Throughout his career he has found human beings doing their living with greater or less understanding of what they were doing, with greater or less intelligent criticism of their procedure. And that has always seemed to him the human distinction with which education is chiefly concerned. Individual and social action, he has said, must be made more and more "aware" of what it is doing. To bring that about is the purpose of all teaching. Dewey has seen, and has tried to make others see, that if we wish to understand society or education, to understand them together, we must know what human intelligence is and does, as it arises out of customary human experience.

Our next task is, then, to study the educational theorizing of the pragmatic school. And both because of his leadership and because of his especial interest in education, I choose Dewey as the representative of that school. He and his colleagues came into the field at the time when the ideas and appreciations for which Matthew Arnold had spoken were losing their force. As against the older culture of "sweetness and light," of "right reason," the pragmatists have pressed the claims of the "modern," the "scientific" interpretation of what intelligence is and does. We must now try to see what they have accomplished. What has Dewey done with the problem with which Comenius, Locke and Arnold were grappling? What, especially, has he answered to the queries and dilemmas of Rousseau? If we can answer those questions we shall, I think, know where contemporary educational theory stands. We shall be face to face with the task of teaching as it now presents itself to a distracted and bewildered world. What, then, is the pragmatic theory of intelligence as the "critic" of human behavior?

Chapter 10. GENERAL FEATURES OF PRAGMATISM

DISCUSSIONS between pragmatists and non-pragmatists are seldom satisfactory. On the whole they seem to produce more heat than light, more misunderstanding than agreement. And the reason for this difficulty should be clearly evident to anyone who sets out to follow such a discussion. The pragmatist, it must always be remembered, claims to have devised a modern, a new, account of what reasoning is and does. But, presumably, his opponent does not accept the new theory. Each maintains therefore his own different interpretation of what they are doing together. It is little wonder that they fail to understand each other. Their relations are those of war rather than those of peace. Each tends to say of the arguments of his opponent, not that they are false, but that they are irrelevant or meaningless. Their minds seem not to meet.

In this situation I choose to follow, as well as I can, the example of Socrates. The Athens of his day faced an intellectual crisis closely akin to our own. And in dealing with it, Socrates adopted, if he did not invent, a unique mode of discussion. He declared his willingness to limit the argument to the evidence presented by his opponent. He himself would present no case. He would accept, provisionally, both the evidence and the method of his adversary. He would ask only, "What do you mean?" And, in the attempt to answer that question, the two together would follow wherever the evidence and the method might lead them.

The next few chapters will, then, attempt a Socratic examination of pragmatic thinking in its bearing upon education. Dewey and his colleagues have undertaken to do something. I propose that we try to understand that attempt in its own terms.

We can then ask whether, as judged by its own standards, it has succeeded. Does Dewey's theory "work" as a way of dealing with the problems which he is trying to solve?

I

There can be no doubt that Dewey has, for fifty years, directed the attention of American reflection toward its most significant problem. He has tried to discover what intelligence is and does. And he has done so in "secular," in "scientific" terms. At this point his likeness to and difference from Comenius are striking. In teaching attitude and disposition the two men are alike. They are both "progressive." But the difference between their theories of human nature is the difference between the medieval and the modern worlds. Just as Comenius is theological, so Dewey is biological. Just as Comenius finds his wisdom in the Bible, so Dewey finds it in the *Origin of Species* and the *Descent of Man.* Just as Comenius regards human understanding as an imitation of the Divine mind, so Dewey regards it as a unique and novel human invention, devised by "intelligent" animals to meet their organic needs.

Pragmatism, we are saying, attacks the problem which Rousseau had indicated. But it does so with new hope of success. There is now available the Darwinian advance in biological theory. Dewey follows Darwin. Pragmatism is Darwinism applied to human intelligence. It is scientific naturalism, as opposed to a theological supernaturalism.

I am tempted at this point to note that the Darwinian discoveries are as acceptable to Dewey's philosophical opponents as they are to himself. This is as true of the realists and idealists whom he attacks as of the pragmatists whom he leads. Naturalism, in this biological sense, is not the private possession of any one school of contemporary reflection. It is the working hypothesis of all schools which are in active touch with scientific study. The question which divides philosophical theories is not, "Is

Darwinism true?" but "What does Darwinism mean?" But, in pressing this point, I am perhaps falling away from the example of Socrates. Our present business is not to confront pragmatism with an opposing theory. It is to ask, "What is the pragmatic account of human intelligence and what are its implications for human society and human education?"

2

Dewey's argument centers upon the relation between what we have called the wisdom of the mind and the wisdom of the body. His main purpose is to interpret that relation in Darwinian terms. As already noted, the most striking feature of the Darwinian theory is that it discards theology. It undertakes to account for the origin and the functioning of human nature, not in terms of a kinship with, and difference from, God, but in terms of a kinship with, and difference from, our fellow animals. Thinking therefore is seen as a biological process. It is one of the many closely interrelated activities of a complicated animal. Its origin is not supernatural but natural. The human individual comes into being, lives his life, reproduces his kind, and dies, just as does any other organism. All the activities of the mind, such as discovering, experimenting, theorizing, doubting, verifying, valuing, are, like those of the contracting of the muscles or the circulating of the blood, merely organic responses to specific stimulations. Their function is to contribute to the life of the organism within which they occur. Like any other animal activity, thinking has a part to play in the total complex of activities to which it belongs. And the playing of that part is all it has to do. Its business, as so defined, is not to copy an eternal truth but to create whatever ideas the organism needs for the carrying on of its living function.

Against this general background, the outline of Dewey's view of the thinking process is not hard to grasp. It is essentially dramatic in statement, and has easily seized upon the imagination of a wide body of readers and nonreaders. Here we find the well-known doctrine that men think, or may think, when they are in trouble. It tells us that, in the ordinary course of its "unconscious" living, the human organism goes about its business in ways which are established as customary, habitual responses to familiar situations. It acts as a smoothly running body. When, however, those responses do not work successfully, when they block each other, when they fail to accomplish our ends, when they do not fit new situations, we are thrown into a condition of strain, of inner conflict, of confusion, of frustration. It is out of this condition that thinking arises. Under the stress of strain, the human being becomes "conscious." He "recognizes" the factors in the situation. He "reflects" upon them, "investigates" them, sees their relations to one another. He assesses each in its bearing upon the ends which it serves. He assesses those ends in terms of the possibilities which the factors in the situation suggest and permit. This awareness, this assessment, this reflection, this critical reconstruction of ends and means, is the work of thinking. And, according to the doctrine, that work goes on until the strain is relieved, until the contradictory situation is resolved, until unity is restored. At that point, thinking ceases. Life goes on again in its new, modified, customary, unconscious ways. The body has been educated.

3

With the main intent of this doctrine I do not see how anyone can quarrel. Conscious thinking is an episode in the life of an organism whose behavior is, for the most part, unconscious. Human living is largely unaware of what it is doing. And again, critical study is a response to difficulties. Its function is to solve problems. And, that being true, it follows that when a problem has been solved, there is, in that case, nothing left for conscious thinking to do. The only use of that intelligence which results from knowledge is to give guidance to behavior, when and where such guidance is needed. In a word, a mind is an educated body. Theory is the servant of practice.

All these statements are true. And they go directly to the heart of the teaching problem. The purpose of our schools, in so far as they are intellectualized, is to use knowledge for the advancement of intelligence. The teacher takes under his charge the unconscious behavior of the pupil. He introduces into that behavior the methods and results of deliberate and conscious study. And he does this with the conviction that knowledge will improve human adjustment, that a person who knows and understands will live more successfully than a person whose mind has not been awakened.

This general statement of the relation between knowledge and intelligence is, I say, true. It is also enormously significant. And yet one hears it, or reads it, with an uneasy sense of ambiguity. It is true that theory serves practice. But it seems equally true that theory intends to guide practice, to control it, to direct it, to be its master. Intelligence is án "instrument" of human behavior. Its only justification is its usefulness to mankind. And yet, it seems equally true that intelligence is itself the highest and most valuable form of behavior. Intelligence, we commonly say, is freedom. As such, it is the goal of all human endeavor, conscious or unconscious. It is an end as well as an instrument.

Now it is this ambiguity which chiefly concerns the reader of the pragmatic theory of education. No teacher doubts that knowledge can be, and should be, used for the improving of intelligence. And yet, that statement leaves essential questions unanswered. There are, as all men know, "learned fools." There are also, as is equally well known, wise, gentle, sensitive men and women who know little of books. The having of knowledge may be useful for intelligence, but it is not identical with it. And the relation between these two is the primary question of educational procedure. It is that question with which Dewey's thinking is chiefly concerned. Our primary task, as we read him, is to find, if we can, his answer to it.

4

Now the charge which, as a follower of Socrates, I bring against Dewey's account of intelligence, is that it is disastrously ambiguous. It is obscure at the point which is most important for education, namely, that of the relation of an individual to the larger group of which he is a member. In two different social moods Dewey gives two different accounts of the activities of problem solving. One of those accounts is predominantly individualistic. The other is equally socialistic. And Dewey's argument goes from one to the other with no clear marking of the transition. It is the confusion and conflict between those two interpretations of intelligence which makes him so hard to understand. At a time when we are trying to think our way out of a broken-down individualism into some kind of co-operative action, that confusion is peculiarly harmful.

If we say that thinking takes place as the result of "strain" in human experience, the most popular and widely accepted pragmatic interpretation of that statement is subjective and individualistic. It finds both strains and the easing of those strains located in the experiences of separate individuals. This view regards a problem as solved, for an individual, when, in the experience of that individual, the feeling of strain out of which the problem came, dies away. The individual in question is no longer disturbed. His problem is solved. That Dewey gives basis for this popular interpretation is beyond question.

But he has also another account of problem solving which is far more difficult to construe and which has won no such wide acceptance. The strain of a problem, he often tells us, is not in any individual alone. It is "in the situation." It is objective. It is social. And this means that a problem may remain utterly unsolved even though any given individual may have been freed from the strain of it. Such a person may have tired of the difficulty and gone to sleep. He may have been diverted to something else. He may have drifted into some conventional or traditional makeshift of opinion which brings ease of mind by its popular resolution of human dilemmas. There are many non-thinking ways of securing release from intellectual strain. But these escapes of individuals do not mean that the "objective problem" has been solved. The disturbance is still there, "in the situation." It is true that only those who are intellectually awake will be tormented by it. But, until solved, it is a defeat for all of us, even though in the minds of the dull, the lazy, the dishonest, it is evaded and ignored.

Dewey, I am sure, holds to both these interpretations, without reconciling them. But there is a further difficulty. As the two conflicting statements stand side by side, they are not kept in even balance. One of them is clear and convincing. The other is unclear and hesitating. Dewey's statement of the claims of individualistic multiplicity is sharp and forceful and persuasive. But his corresponding statement of the purposes and methods of objective criticism and unification is vague and constantly shifting. He easily translates the relativity of Protagoras into Darwinian terms. But he cannot give the same modern translation to the words of Plato. And from this it follows that his popular influence is always heavily weighted on the side of its subjective, its individualistic meaning.

5

It is important to note the peculiar effect which the acceptance of Dewey's individualistic account of problem solving has had upon the planning of education. If we say that thinking occurs only when a strain is felt in the experience of some isolated individual, and if those strains arise separately, each out of its unconscious background, the activity of inquiry becomes a broken series of disconnected episodes rather than a permanent and continuing enterprise. The mind, as so regarded, becomes merely a trouble shooter. It has no general supervision over the business of living. On the contrary it comes into action only as, now and then, it is summoned to deal with a specific situation.

And if we ask why this trouble shooter is summoned it appears that thinking is concerned, not with the positive, continuous carrying on of human activity, but only with the removing of temporary obstructions in its course. It deals, not with the creative organization of the drives and tendencies of the human being, but only with their mutual frustrations and contradictions. It acts only as "situations," arising in the "unconscious" behavior of men call it forth. Its separate responses are not, so far as thinking is aware, bound together by any common intention. They occur as, one by one, strains arise. And, one by one, the conscious activities of inquiry and reflection resolve these strains, dispose of them, and then, having done their work, they sink back into the darkness out of which they were called. Human thinkings have, then, no continuing quality, no unity of aim. They deal with a "plurality of problematic situations" which occur on separate occasions. They deal with them one by one as incidents in the continuing life of an organism may require. The activities of the organism are continuous. But the activities of thinking are discontinuous. And from this it has followed that pragmatic plans of teaching, especially with respect to content, have had no unity or coherence of purpose. They do not express one intelligence. They express a multiplicity of disconnected intelligences.

6

The reader of Dewey encounters a second ambiguity which is, however, rhetorical rather than logical. Its influence has been felt chiefly among the nontechnical readers. As already noted, Dewey's chief concern is that thinking shall be practical. His theories are called upon to work in everyday experience. In words which have been often quoted, he tells us that "Philosophy recovers itself when it ceases to be a device for dealing

with the problems of philosophers and becomes a method, cultivated by philosophers, for dealing with the problems of men."
That statement is valid in so far as it is intended to rebuke
scholars who live in ivory towers, who deal with problems which
have no bearing upon actual living. The only knowledge worth
getting is the knowledge which tells us how we should live.
And yet Dewey bases upon this insight a rhetorical procedure
which is confusing. He speaks to two different audiences at
once. Since the "philosopher" and the "plain man" are ultimately
interested in the same problems he addresses them both in the
same terms. But such double speaking as this is doomed to misunderstanding. Whatever their fundamental identity of interest,
these two groups do not use words with the same meanings nor
in the same way. Plain men are concerned primarily with "action," with getting things done. Theirs is the wisdom of the
body. Scholars, by contrast, are concerned with theories, with
principles and methods by which to understand what is, and
should be, done. And, however, true it may be that ultimately
these two interests are one, the immediate fact is that the mental
processes of the two kinds of activity are radically different.

The distinction which we are here making is suggested by
Dewey in his book, *The Public and its Problems*. Speaking
there of such practical causes as universal suffrage, majority
rule, and the like, and of the ideas underlying them, he says:

Looking back, with the aid which ex post facto experience can
give, it would be hard for the wisest to devise schemes which, under
the circumstances, would have met the needs better. In this retro-
spective glance, it is possible, however, to see how the doctrinal
formulations which accompanied them were inadequate, one-sided,
and positively erroneous. In fact they were hardly more than political war-cries adopted to help in carrying on some immediate agita-
tion or in justifying some particular practical polity struggling for
recognition, even though they were asserted to be absolute truths of
human nature or of morals. The doctrines served a particular local
pragmatic need. But often their very adaptation to immediate cir-

cumstances unfitted them, pragmatically, to meet more enduring and more extensive needs. They lived to cumber the political ground, obstructing progress, all the more so because they were uttered and held not as hypotheses with which to direct social experimentation but as final truths, dogmas. No wonder they call urgently for revision and displacement.[1]

Now the distinction which Dewey here draws between social movements and the ideas which accompany them has direct application to his own writings. Pragmatism has advanced both war cries and theories. It has been both a social movement and a philosophy. If we wish to see it clearly, these two phases of its work must be separated.

As a program of reform pragmatism came into being about fifty years ago. It happened chiefly in America. It was called forth as a response to the intellectual and social conditions of that time and that country. And, more specifically, it was a negative reaction. It was an attack upon a set of human arrangements then existing. It was, as we say, a revolt. It demanded reform of society and of education. It fought for the displacement of institutions which had been found, in actual human experience, harmful and destructive. In this capacity we can understand the drive of pragmatism only as we see it launching its attack upon the social and educational structure which, fifty years ago, was established in the English-speaking world and, especially, in America. In this concrete phase, pragmatism is not a theory. It is a social movement of reform. And its enemy is Victorianism.

But pragmatism as a philosophy cannot be defined in such concrete, specific terms as these. The instrumentalist theory, on the side of its theoretical meaning and intention, goes to the limit of abstractness. Its primary interest lies in the field of "method." And to say that is just another way of saying that it deals with "universals," with the nature of activities "as such." It studies, not contemporary America, but human nature and conduct in general. Certainly no more abstract or far-reaching

[1] *The Public and Its Problems*, pp. 145-146.

principle of human behavior was ever formulated than that of the "experimental way of knowing." In terms of a single idea, it deals with the nature of experience as such, the nature of thinking as such, the nature of morality, the nature of habit and custom, the nature of beauty, the nature of freedom and of slavery, the meaning of democracy, of liberalism, of aristocracy. Each of these taken separately and all of them taken together, fall within the wide, inclusive sweep of a single generalization about human behavior and the human world. On the side of its abstract meaning pragmatism is a theory which intends to be true of and for all men, at all times, in all situations.

A familiar illustration of the distinction which we are making can be found in the double functioning of the doctrine of natural rights. That doctrine was a theory. But it was also a weapon to be used in social conflict. In this latter role, its service was magnificent. As an instrument of attack upon entrenched power, entrenched caste, entrenched wealth, it was admirably suited to its purpose. But in its capacity as a general idea, as a theory of the nature of man and of society, the belief in the inalienable rights of man was, and is, intellectually untenable. No critical account of human society can assign validity to those rights as they were interpreted by many of the men who prepared the way for the writing of our own Declaration of Independence. The theory was useful for fighting purposes. It was even valid in a relative sense. Certainly it was much closer to the facts than were the claims of the divine right of kings, the sacred sanctions of property, the feudal privileges of an upper class, against which its assault was directed. In the field of concrete action, it deserved to win.

But in the other field, that of general theory, it is clearly one of those doctrines which, as Dewey says, "call urgently for revision and displacement." We cannot possibly allow it the kind of intellectual validity which, for example, the "theory" of pragmatism claims for itself as a theory of human experience. It was useful in its day. It is still useful in America as men fight for their "rights" against other men who, with seventeenth century minds, are determined to keep the right to invade them. But there is little hope for genuine progress toward mutual understanding among us except as we see that neither set of rights, as construed by these fighting factions, has any clear or defensible meaning. Abstract thinking is not well done with war cries. It must use ideas. It must test and verify those ideas by the methods of cool, scholarly, objective intelligence. In its practical bearings it must have regard for "more enduring and more extensive needs" than those of any immediate, local situation. In this sense, thinking is always theoretical rather than practical.

7

Now if this be true, it follows that our study of pragmatism must be carried on in two different fields. First, we will examine and try to assess the pragmatic attack upon Victorianism, as an established but disintegrating "pattern of culture." Second, we will consider a philosophical theory, which, as against other like theories, has attempted a new interpretation of human nature and, especially, of human intelligence.

In its first capacity there can be no doubt that pragmatism, by means of its war cries, has had enormous influence for good. It has stirred men to social conflict. It has been a fighting faith. On the popular level, it has been a sharp and powerful force wherever men have differed as to the forms which society and education should take. As Matthew Arnold had told us, there was, in Anglo-Saxon culture fifty years ago, "a particular, local, pragmatic need." The time had come when the ruins of the Victorian manner of life should be swept away. The complications and absurdities of that culture and of its education had become intolerable. And on the positive side, there was the still more urgent need that a new social order, a new plan of teaching, be invented and established among men. It was not only pragmatists who saw and felt that necessity. Thomas Carlyle,

Thomas Hill Green, William Morris, Karl Marx, Ralph Waldo Emerson, and many other non-pragmatists were stirred by it to raise their voices in urgent demand for action. And yet it cannot be denied that, especially on the negative side of this revolution, Dewey and his colleagues have played a leading part. On the social level they have enlisted men and women in an ardent crusade against ancient evils, against time-honored injustices and absurdities. One may question their positive success in devising a new social order or even in suggesting its principles. But no one can deny that they have furnished slogans for a revolt—a revolt against that "pattern of culture" which we call Victorianism.

But meanwhile Dewey has been writing—and the philosophically minded among his followers have been reading—*Essays in Empirical Logic, Studies in Logical Theory, Outlines of Ethics, Human Nature and Conduct, The Quest for Certainty, Experience and Nature, Art as Experience, Logic, The Theory of Inquiry,* and so on. In the arguments of those books he has been grappling with Plato and Aristotle, Spinoza and Locke, Kant and Hegel, Bradley and Bosanquet, Royce and Creighton, McGilvary and Cohen. As against all these, he has brought fundamental criticism to bear upon traditional philosophical methods and results. He has also pointed the way toward what he regards as a new and revolutionary method of philosophy. Speaking of the significance of this intellectual achievement in which he has played a part, he says, "It is not too much to say, therefore, that for the first time there is made possible an empirical theory of ideas free from the burdens imposed alike by sensationalism and rationalism. This accomplishment is, I make bold to say, one of the three or four outstanding feats of intellectual history."

8

Here, then, is the outline of our study of pragmatic thinking. Dewey is both social reformer and philosophical thinker. He has devised both slogans and ideas. That these two operations are, in fundamental purpose, identical, I fully agree. And yet, intellectually they represent different levels in the attempt to realize that purpose. Leading men by means of slogans is not the same as leading them into the use of ideas. As we try to understand Dewey and his influence we must keep this separation clearly in mind. We shall therefore, as we assess the contribution of pragmatism to educational theory and practice, deal with it, first as a set of war cries, and, second, as a philosophical theory of human experience.

The next step in our argument will be an attempt to deal with the "movement" which, under the general slogan "Be Scientific," has waged war upon the Victorian education of "Culture."

Chapter 11. THE WAR CRIES OF PRAGMATISM

IT HAS been one of the disastrous features of education in America during the pragmatic era that our teachers have been taught to know Dewey, not in terms of his theories but in terms of his war cries. They have been led, in some measure, to participate in his emotional and volitional drive against a Victorian social order. They have not been led to think through the philosophical problems with which Dewey himself has been grappling.

This condition is disastrous chiefly because it indicates that our scheme of national education is built upon the supposition that the teachers cannot be expected, in any genuine theoretical sense, to understand what they are doing. They themselves are "led" rather than "taught." Dewey, their leader, finds it necessary, as we have said, to grapple with Plato and Aristotle, with Spinoza and Locke, with Kant and Hegel, with Bradley and Bosanquet, with Royce and Creighton, with McGilvary and Cohen. His understanding of essential human problems has taken form from his agreements and disagreements with these other scholars. The teachers in our schools, on the other hand, are not asked to follow these discussions. Practically all they hear about them is that the pragmatic logic has refuted, once for all, some strange and old-fashioned ideas. Plato, they are told, was an aristocrat. He may therefore be ignored. Kant believed in *a priori* categories. That is enough to know about him. We moderns discard as meaningless and useless such outmoded, un-American ideas. With characteristic frontier independence, we start from scratch to make out of our own experience a new and unique view of society and of education. But the trouble here is that the teachers are doing the exact opposite of what Dewey himself has done. His thought has grown out of a critical examination of non-pragmatic theories which he himself at one time accepted. His followers, on the other hand, are expected to grow the same thoughts out of ground which lacks that cultivation. And that means, in effect, that they are blindly following their leader, accepting his ideas with no proper understanding of their meaning. They are "unconscious" pragmatists. The current training of our teachers is thus affected by a peculiarly vicious type of intellectual aristocracy. We take it for granted that they "cannot understand." Our schools have undertaken to teach intellectual independence and initiative by means of teachers who are trained to intellectual dependence and subservience. That is the weakness of education by war cries.

I

In the writing which has come out of the pragmatic school, whether political or educational, three slogans have been most clearly heard, most widely influential. They are first, "Down with dogmas and fixed beliefs and absolutes!" second, "Have done with useless knowledge!" and, third, "Away with aristocracy!"

Now the chief defect of these war cries is that they are negative, as war cries tend to be. They have summoned teachers, as well as other social workers, to attack an old order. They have not led them to the building of a new one. The animus of pragmatic education has been directed against Victorianism. With greater force and with sharper weapons it has fought essentially the same fight as that in which Matthew Arnold was engaged. Its weapons of destruction have been far more efficient and powerful than his. But on the positive side, it stands practically where he stood. Like him it has been unable to take the next step, from breaking down to building up. And this means that, in the crisis of our social disintegration our education has provided no positive intention or direction. We must examine the war cries of pragmatism to see whether or not that charge can be sustained.

First, then, the attack on dogmas! Is that merely negative? This attack is not, as we all know, a modern invention. It has been pressed in every period of European "Enlightenment." Whenever a settled scheme of life has lost its grip, whenever customary beliefs and values have lost vitality, the demand that changing conditions be recognized by changing ideas has gathered force. And that demand has commonly been stated in terms of a universal principle, a fighting faith. Old theories, men have said, are not adequate for new situations. In a world in which everything changes, beliefs too must change. To let customs of thought or of behavior harden into uncriticized traditions which demand, in the name of loyalty, unquestioning adherence, is intellectual and social suicide. Our fathers made their own creeds. If we are loyal to our heritage, we too will make ours. Beliefs are not eternally valid, are not sacrosanct, are not fixed absolutely in the nature of things. They are our inventions. And we must forever try to remake them to suit our changing needs.

This attack upon an established order, we have said, has been over and over again pressed at the turning points in Western culture. But the coming of Darwinism gave it new power and effectiveness. To the earlier notion that the world, about which men think, changes, there is now added the perception that the thinking man himself, being a part of the world, is essentially a changing thing. If—as the new account of human behavior tells us—human intelligence is simply one of the characteristic responses of a living organism to its changing situation then it follows inevitably that intelligence itself is an activity of transitory adjustment. Each new mental happening is a new step in the growth of a living being. Its function is to serve the needs out of which it springs. It must then vary as its needs vary. The traffic rules of a motor-car society differ from those of the horse and buggy days.

That observation of the relativity of ideas and values has been taken by our social and anthropological sciences into every corner of human experience, into every type of human society. And everywhere they have found it, so far as they have gone, valid. Human behavior, including the behavior of the mind, is a growing, changing, adjusting thing. We find among men, not one fixed and final code of morals, not one eternally valid system of beliefs, not one absolutely established set of social institutions, but rather a constantly shifting multiplicity of human behaviors. Victorianism is, then, not the last word in human wisdom. It is merely the word current in English and American society in the latter half of the nineteenth century. Its history is that of a passing episode, different from those before and from those which will come after. A new time requires new manners of thought and behavior. Down with the dogmas of the past! Up with the non-dogmas of the immediate future!

As a negative war cry this principle of the "cultural lag" has had, in pragmatic hands, enormous effectiveness. Before the onslaughts which it has incited, Victorian beliefs and customs have gone tumbling into ruins. Matthew Arnold would tell us that the foundations of those beliefs and customs were already in ruins before the attack was launched. He would, I think, describe the warlike achievement of the pragmatists as one of "mopping up" after the battle is finished rather than one of active conquest over a fighting enemy. And yet the fact remains that during these last fifty years the Victorian scheme of life has crumbled and fallen. And in the field of popular education, of popular social practice, the battle cry, "Down with ancient dogmas" as used by the pragmatists, has undoubtedly played an important part.

But on the other, the positive side, the principle of the cultural lag has no such achievement to its credit. As old ideas and customs are cleared away, the human mind—so far as it has influence—faces a second task. Practical living cannot be well guided by an absence of ideas and customs. It is not enough to know that old dogmas are false. Unless a new pattern of culture is ready to replace the old, human experience is thrown into just that chaos, that futility by which our own is at present obsessed. What help, for example, does the principle "Down with dogmas" provide in the present conflict between democracy and dictatorship? We Americans have, in the past, assumed that democracy would gradually spread over the face of the earth as other nations grew in intelligence. But the social conditions of the nineteenth and twentieth centuries have brought rapid and disconcerting change. The triumphant march of democracy has been widely checked. In Germany, in Italy, in Spain—perhaps in Russia—dictatorship has emerged. It has arisen out of changing conditions. It is a response to new and complicated and desperate situations. But one of its most striking features is its challenge to democracy. Government by consent of the governed seems to the advocates of the new polity old-fashioned, out-of-date. So strongly are they convinced that parliamentary institutions are inefficient and evil, as compared with their own, that they are ready to engage in crusading wars to spread the new gospel. Are they right? That is the crucial question of our era. Time, it would seem, is on the side of the dictators. They are more "up to date" than we are. Democracy is comparatively ancient. It arose under human conditions quite different from those which now prevail. But how shall we or Germany or Russia decide which is for us now the better form of government? Obviously our problem is created by the fact that there are now, under present conditions, at least two conflicting theories facing us, each of which claims to be the more suitable to our needs. And we must choose between them. At this point of positive choice it is of no use to say "Down with dogmas!" Since both beliefs are open to our question as we try to assess their merits, neither of them is, by us, regarded as a dogma. We cannot say that an idea is false because it was believed a hundred or a thousand years ago. We cannot say that an idea is true because it has just now, for the first time, popped into the mind of some specific individual or nation. Every human situation produces conflicting ideas which claim to serve as its interpreters. Errors are quite as much "up to date" as are insights. And the attempt to correlate validity with dating is a vast and disastrous illusion. The principle of the cultural lag is, on the popular level, a powerful weapon of attack upon ideas which are already, on other grounds, discredited. But as an instrument of positive planning, of creative thinking, it is irrelevant and meaningless. It supplies little more than epithets. The burning political question of our time is "What form of government shall the world have?" And for the answering of that positive question, the pragmatic condemnation of dogma has no contribution whatever to make. In an era of reconstruction the complaint that old ideas are static has become one of the most static of our ideas.

2

The second pragmatic attack upon Victorianism is one which we have found used both by Comenius and by Locke against the schools of their own day. It accuses the teachers of an established order of giving to their pupils knowledge which is useless. It therefore declares the work of the school to be useless.

Here again, the bringing in of the Darwinian analysis has given to an old argument new vigor and effectiveness. In its earlier form this battle cry summoned social reformers to an attack upon leisure-class education. It found the social order of England and America divided into two levels, the upper and the lower. It found also that it is a characteristic of the life of the upper-class man that he has leisure. This means that he does not need to work. His "work" is done by someone else. It is not necessary, so far as he has leisure, that he do anything for himself. He can therefore afford to waste his time. Perhaps better, since we are speaking of education, he can afford to waste his mind. Since his servants will attend to all practical matters he can devote his mind to nonpractical matters. He can let his spirit of intellectual curiosity wander freely through the universe wherever it pleases, with no sense of responsibility, individual or social, to hinder or restrain it. His thinking is done for the sheer fun of the game. Its aim is "knowledge for its own sake."

Meanwhile, in the other division of the social order, are men and women who must work in order that they may eat. For them eating might be classed as a leisure activity were it not for the fact that their eating is justified by its contribution to their working efficiency. They must, men say, have a "living wage," which seems to mean that they must be kept alive so that they may do the tasks assigned them. In this curious circle, their leisure is invaded by their work, is perhaps negated altogether. They are the working class.

As a battle cry to stir men and women to fight against the cruel injustice of an established social order the argument, as thus stated, has had immense effectiveness. The contrast between the pampered children of the rich and noble, educated to a life of unearned enjoyment, and the children of the poor and lowly, who are condemned and trained to labor in the production of goods in the enjoyment of which they will have no proper share —that contrast, when really seen, will arouse any normal human being to fury and rebellion. Out of it there can be made a stirring battle cry.

But the Darwinian modification of the argument has given to it even greater force. To moral indignation it has added scientific knowledge. In his *Human Nature and Conduct* Dewey has riddled and ridiculed the Victorian view of the human individual. The mind, he shows us, is not related to the body as is the "master of the house" to the "tenement of clay" which he inhabits. Mind and body are not separate things, one of which uses the other as its servant. On the contrary, there is only one human being—the living organism. And within the life of that being it is the function of all activities, including thinking, to be useful. Mental effort occurs when it is needed. Men learn to think when the necessities of their experience confront them with difficulties which can be successfully dealt with only by the way of inquiry. The mind is not a useless appendage of life, not an idle spectator, sitting on some grandstand to watch the spectacle of life go by. It has work to do. Its success or failure is judged by its doing or failing to do that work. Ideas emerge from living. They refer to living. They return to living and are tested by it. A human being is not an animal whose anatomy has been taken over as a dwelling place by some superior thinking angel. He is an animal who, as the needs of his living require, learns to make theories and to use them. He is homo sapiens—a complicated biped in whom there has occurred some slight development of that peculiar form of practical activity, that "aptness of the body," which we call "intelligence."

Here is an argument which is valid as well as effective. It is a war cry which springs out of reason. As it is used, naturalism drives out supernaturalism. Science replaces theology. The new view of man plunges him, his mind, his will, his spirit, his body, into the midst of nature. In spite of his essential differences from other living things, he is shown to be of the same stuff, involved in the same process, sharing the same precarious and transitory fate. And in that setting, the leisure-class theory of thinking is seen in its true colors, as a kind of intellectual perversion. The unnaturalness of the leisure-class interpretation of human thinking is so depicted as to make men who waste their minds in useless knowledge, ashamed of themselves.

And yet, at one significant point, the "uselessness" argument, as negatively formulated by the pragmatists, misses fire, or rather turns its fire upon friends instead of enemies. It is a colossal blunder to interpret upper-class education as giving only useless knowledge. The major vice of that education has been, not its lack of efficiency, but its dreadful effectiveness. The young people of the upper class are taught by it, not only how to enjoy special privileges, but also how to get and to keep and to enlarge them. The aristocrat, whether Victorian or not, is not merely an enjoyer of life. He is also the master, the manipulator, the controller of human society. From the Greek and Roman civilizations which, as Dewey says, the upper-class man has so eagerly studied, he has learned that knowledge is power. He knows that he too, if he and his dependents are to enjoy life, must work, not at a trade but at the controlling of tradesmen. When he is most dangerous he knows that he can dominate and use his fellows only so long as he understands them better than they understand themselves. And his opponent who pictures "the exploiters of the people" as idly reclining on cushions of ease, as idly contemplating and appreciating the world which passes by, is making the worst of tactical blunders. He is underestimating his adversary. As against a Victorian foe who has known the necessity of keeping the agencies of learning and of teaching under his control the pragmatic war cry against useless knowledge is a gallant but largely futile gesture. It attacks an enemy at a point where he is willing to be driven back. And meanwhile the main positive issue, "What is useful knowledge?" is lost from sight. On that issue, "scientific" pragmatism has had relatively little to say.

3

The third war cry is a wider and deeper version of the second. It incites men against aristocracy. And here, I think, the ruling passion of the pragmatic movement finds its best expression. Dewey's great book about teaching is *Democracy and Education*. And that book thrills with hatred, not simply of uselessness in the schools, but of special privilege of every sort. Its fundamental demand is that all young people shall have an equal chance at the experiences of living. It is with Comenius. It is against Locke.

This war cry, as Dewey uses it, is attacking not only a conventional system of education but also, in the same words, a conventional social order. The principles of teaching are, for him, the principles of society. A community teaches, not so much by what it says as by what it is and does. This insight, formulated for our culture by Plato and again by Rousseau, is basic to the pragmatic argument. Aristocracy in schools is merely one phase of aristocracy in society. Victorians, like other aristocrats, have

offered instruction on two different levels because they believed
there were, because they intended there should be, two different
kinds or classes of people in their community.

Our study of Comenius, Locke, and Arnold has shown, I
think, that, in direct contradiction of the religious principles
which it acknowledged, Victorian culture was and is, in this
sense, aristocratic. This is true for America, not only in the
South, with its traditional segregation of one race from another,
as essentially lower in quality. It is just as true in Rhode Island
when a mill-owning and managing class has imported "aliens"
to be its workers, and is forever shuddering lest, under the spell
of democratic institutions, these outsiders should claim and
should secure equality with themselves. And it is, in the same
way, true in California as the owners of the land bring in still
other "aliens," whether of foreign or of native birth, to cultivate
and harvest their crops. Anglo-Saxon civilization is, in the nature
of its industrial organization, a two-class society.

And it is equally clear that for these different types of human
beings different kinds of education have been devised and established. That difference may be obscured by such a glittering
phrase as that of "equal opportunity for all." But the looseness of
the phrase unfits it for any active, efficient meaning under the
actual conditions of social life in the South, or in Rhode Island,
or in California. There are in those communities two classes of
pupils, each with its own distinctive lessons to learn. Pupils of
the upper class must be trained to keep and to enjoy their su-
premacy. It is theirs to control, to direct, to manage, the affairs
of the community. It is theirs also to have more, to enjoy more,
to appreciate more, to be more cultivated and sensitive. And,
on the other hand, the workers too must be educated for their
station. They must, first of all, take on the vocational characters
of the worker—technical skill, physical endurance, obedience,
etc. But they must also learn contentment with their lot, pride
in their inferior station, enjoyment of the place which God has
assigned them. Two classes of people—two educations! What-

ever its protestations as to equality of opportunity, that is, in the large, the social arrangement of Anglo-Saxon civilization.

Now there can be no doubt that, as against this prevailing aristocracy, pragmatism has raised, or has joined in raising, the battle cry of democracy. We Americans are determined that there shall not be in our society two kinds of people. We will not have two kinds of schools—one for gentlemen and ladies, the other for workers and servants. We believe that every man and woman should be a "worker." We believe that every man and woman should be "cultivated." We believe that all men and women should govern. We believe that all men and women should be governed. All the members of our society must have both liberal and vocational education. There shall be one set, and only one set, of schools for all people, whatever their age, whatever their race, whatever their sex, whatever their personal quality, whatever their economic conditions. The first postulate of a democracy is equality of education. The gospel of Comenius is still true.

As one surveys the lifelong fight which Dewey has led in this battle between democracy and aristocracy it would be idle and absurd to say that his personal attitude has been a negative one. Everyone who knows him, knows that he has wanted for America not only the destruction of Victorianism but also the creation of a new social order in which men and women and children shall have far more of freedom and equality and justice than are now available. And yet even here, his influence is a curiously divided one. While his emotional and volitional drive is clear and unequivocal, his thinking about the nature of society and the nature of human intelligence seems always to block that drive, to thwart it by negations. In the last resort he is far more successful in telling us what human society is not than what it is, what human intelligence does not do than what it is and should be doing. And so it has come about that his influence upon the presuppositions of education in America, upon the determining of its direction and goal has been largely negative. This is true not only in social practice but also in social theory and in logic. Our next task is to see whether, in these theoretical fields, where the intellectual bases of education are to be found, the same charge of negativism can be justified. And this inquiry will, of course, take us out of the field of war cries into the field of philosophical discussion. We shall be asking what Dewey has said about human nature, about society, about democracy, and hence, about education. But, most important of all, we must discover what he thinks concerning intelligence. What is, for him, the nature, the function, of objective, disinterested criticism?

4

As we leave behind the discussion of pragmatic war cries, one summarizing remark is needed. Pragmatism has not, in popular terms, given us a positive alternative for the Victorianism which it has attacked. And in the present critical world situation, that failure of American thinking may prove to be of tragic importance. The Victorian scheme of life is gone, so far as human effectiveness is concerned. But in its death struggle it has called forth an opposing spirit which threatens all mankind. Dictatorship is ready to take the place of what it regards as a dying democracy. It too hates Victorianism. But it has also a positive program—a program of brutal despotic domination. It will destroy the virtues as well as the vices of Victorianism. To meet that attack the forces of democracy must have an equally positive program, though not an equally dogmatic one. And the chief defect of our pragmatic culture as a popular attitude, is that it has no such affirmative or directive meaning. For that reason the day of pragmatism is done. The movement which, for fifty years, has so gaily consigned older theories to oblivion because they were outmoded, were out-of-date, is now itself open to the same treatment. It, too, grows ancient. If I may again use Dewey's words with regard to other popular movements, I should say that, as a war cry, pragmatism has "served a particular, local, pragmatic need." But with the passing of fifty years, it also has "lived to cumber the political ground, obstructing progress, all the more so because it has been uttered and held not as hypothesis with which to direct social experimentation but as final truth, dogma. No wonder it calls urgently for revision and displacement." Whatever we may find to hold true with regard to Dewey's theories, that characterization of the war cries of pragmatism is, I think, valid. Democracy desperately needs the formulation of a positive program of action, both national and international. And pragmatism, in the face of that emergency, does not work. It is irrelevant.

Chapter 12. KNOWLEDGE AND INTELLIGENCE

WE TURN now from the war cries of pragmatism to its problems and theories. As we do so it is important to note how closely connected is Dewey's study of education with his study of philosophy. In his great book, *Democracy and Education,* Dewey says, "Philosophy is the theory of education as a deliberately conducted enterprise."[1] Again, "Philosophy may even be defined as the general theory of education."[2] And still again, "The most penetrating definition of philosophy which can be given, then, is that it is the theory of education in its more general phases."[3] And, finally, "Education is the laboratory in which philosophic distinctions become concrete and are tested."[4] It is clear that we shall not know Dewey's theory of education unless we know what his philosophy is.

Now the central problem of Dewey's philosophy is the central problem of every student of teaching. It has to do with the relation between theory and practice, between facts and values, between knowledge and intelligence. Every school which relies upon words and symbols is trying to use knowing in such a way as to make behavior more intelligent. These two are not identical. A man may "know" without "being wise." He may be wise without having much formalized knowledge. A chemist, for example, may be learned about the behavior of gases, and may yet be foolish about the use of gases in warfare. Intellectual skill is not identical with practical efficiency. And yet knowledge can be useful. It can contribute to intelligence. To make it do so is the primary business of the school. To understand how it does so is the primary business of educational theory.

[1] *Ibid.,* p. 387.
[2] *Ibid.,* p. 388.
[3] *Ibid.,* p. 386.
[4] *Ibid.,* p. 384.

The problem which arises as we relate theory to practice is familiar but elusive. If, for example, we are studying the housing conditions of a great city the search for knowledge will reveal, in detail, the fact of social inequality. Some families are lavishly supplied with rooms and equipment. Other families are living in conditions which are, as we say, "unfit for human habitation." Our procedures of investigation will make that information exact, complete, and orderly. But, then, another question arises. It is a question, not of facts, but of values. Is it wrong or undesirable that there should be such inequality of living standards? Should action be taken to change the situation? Our knowledge of the facts alone does not answer that question. It merely provides usable information. But the question itself arises from our conviction of the relative merits of equality and inequality. If I believe that such inequality is evil, then that belief becomes a ground for action. If I have no such judgments of value then action would be meaningless. In a word, intelligence needs not only knowledge of facts but also principles of judgment. And the question as to the relation between theory and practice is "Where do these value principles come from? On what basis are they founded?" That question is primary for any theory of society or any theory of education.

I

Now Dewey's clearest statement of the relation between facts and values, between theory and practice, between knowledge and intelligence is given when he draws the distinction between the sciences and philosophy. The sciences are, for him, the culmination of the human striving for knowledge. Philosophy, on the other hand, is our most deliberate and systematic attempt at wisdom. "Inquiry" seeks to discover what the world is and does. "Reflection" tries to assess the values of life, to determine what men should be and do. These two intellectual enterprises represent the attempt to "know" and the attempt to "be wise" at their most highly conscious levels. If we can see how they differ, how they are related, how they work together in the lives of men, we shall have Dewey's account of what is, for the teacher, the most significant aspect of human behavior. We shall have at once his "philosophy" and his "general theory of education."

2

The most striking defect in Dewey's "general theory of education" is its disparagement of intelligence. He does not deny the importance of "wisdom" which is "based in knowledge." On the contrary no one has insisted more eagerly, more vigorously than he, that knowledge shall be intelligently used in the guidance of human behavior. But he does cast doubt upon the "objective validity" of that procedure. In what may be called his "subjective" mood he draws the sharpest of contrasts between the scientific and the practical activities of mankind. The findings of the sciences are tested and verified. They are warranted by evidence. But the judgments of wisdom, the choices of value, have no such warrant in evidence. They are untested, unverified, unwarranted. And, that being true, the whole structure of education which rests upon them, is likewise lacking in support. It is equally true, however, that Dewey has another, an objective mood, in which judgments of value are said to be criticized, tested and evaluated. Both these moods are present throughout his thinking. In fact his intellectual career is largely one of conflict between them. But that conflict is never resolved. As we attempt to follow his thinking about society and education, the course of that struggle is, of necessity, the dominant motive of our discussion.

3

In *Democracy and Education* Dewey formulates the problem of which we are speaking. And he deals with it chiefly in his subjective mood. All knowledge, he tells us, comes from the sciences. "Knowledge, grounded knowledge, is science; it represents objects which have been settled, ordered, disposed of rationally."[5] All knowing, it would seem, is obtained by the sciences. In so far as they have finished their work there is no more "knowing" to be done. What then does philosophy do? If the philosopher does not add to the stock of human knowledge about men and the world, what is his business?

In the twenty-fourth chapter of *Democracy and Education*, which deals with the philosophy of education, Dewey's answer to this question is explicit, if not altogether clear. "It is for the sciences," he tells us, "to say what generalisations are tenable about the world and what they specifically are. But when we ask what sort of permanent disposition of action toward the world the scientific disclosures exact of us we are raising a philosophic question."[6] Philosophy, he seems to say, does not tell what men are nor what the world is. It tells what men should do with their world. It seeks for principles of behavior. Those principles, it appears, are not "known." How then are they acquired? On what basis are they held or discarded? How are they justified or repudiated? What does "exact of us" mean as describing the procedure by which philosophic action goes beyond scientific knowledge?

The answer to that question is given, in the chapter on the philosophy of education, where Dewey reviews his argument as a whole. He has advanced, he tells us by three steps. First, there is an account of "the general features of education as the process by which social groups maintain their continuous existence."[7] This general study takes "no specific account" of "the *kind* of society aiming at its own perpetuation through education."[8] The second step describes democracy and aristocracy as opposing "kinds" of society. It also adopts democracy as its program, rejects

[5] *Democracy and Education*, Macmillan, 1922, p. 380.
[6] *Ibid.*, p. 379.
[7] *Ibid.*, p. 375.
[8] *Ibid.*, p. 375.

aristocracy, and analyzes teaching on that basis. The third step considers the "present limitations" of the "actual realisation" of the enterprise.

Now, in the progress of this threefold argument, it is the second step which is taken by philosophy. When democracy and aristocracy have been set face to face as opposing social programs either of which education might serve, a choice is made between them. That choice is not made by any science nor by any combination of sciences. It is made by philosophy. Dewey, as a philosopher, has adopted "a permanent disposition of action toward the world." He is a democrat.

But how is the choice made? Is it justified by evidence? Is it "grounded" like the conclusions of science? We could answer that question if we could understand the phrase "exact of us," in the passage already quoted. That phrase suggests that the values come out of the facts, are "exacted" by them. But the suggestion is not there clarified. Dewey does, however, tell us, in another statement how principles of values are chosen. They are "taken for granted." In describing the second, philosophic, step in his argument he says, "The sort of education appropriate to the development of a democratic community was then explicitly taken as the criterion of the further, more detailed analysis of education."[9] And again, "Save for incidental criticisms designed to illustrate principles by force of contrast, this (philosophic) phase of the discussion *took for granted* the democratic criterion and its application in present social life."[10]

Here then, so far as the argument of *Democracy and Education* goes, is Dewey's separation of science and philosophy, of knowledge and intelligence. The sciences have to do with knowledge of objects. Philosophy has to do with the direction of action. And these two mental operations are radically different in kind. The conclusions of the sciences are "grounded" in evidence. The conclusions of philosophy are ungrounded, are "taken for

[9] *Ibid.*, p. 376.
[10] *Loc. cit.*

granted." What then does it mean to say that they are "based on knowledge"?

4

In 1918, two years after the first edition of *Democracy and Education*, Dewey gave a lecture at the University of California, on the topic "Philosophy and Democracy." The problem of that lecture was the one which we are now raising. What is the philosophic basis for that American choice of the democratic way of life which two years earlier Dewey had himself made? And the lecture is an explicit assertion of the arbitrariness, the ungroundedness, of the choice of democracy. The conclusions of philosophic criticism are, as such, made without reasonable justification.

As he seeks for evidence to support this sharp separation between the methods of science and those of philosophy Dewey finds the most striking feature of philosophies to be their multifariousness. While, in effect, there is only one science, there are many philosophies. They are ancient, medieval, and modern. They are English, French, or German. Some day, he tells us, when women have begun to do creative work in the field, we may even have a feminine philosophy as against the customary masculine ones.—We might add here the suggestion that women philosophers too may have their emotional differences, and so still further increase the number of philosophic systems.—And these differences of philosophy, Dewey tells us, express "not diversities of intellectual emphasis so much as incompatibilities of temperament and expectation."[11] They started "not from science, not from ascertained knowledge, but from moral convictions, and then resorted to the best knowledge and the best intellectual methods available in their day to give the form of demonstration to what was essentially an attitude of will, or a moral resolution to prize one mode of life more highly than

[11] *Characters and Events*, Henry Holt & Co., 1929, Vol. II, p. 843.

another and the wish to persuade other men that this was the wise way of living."[12] Philosophy, Dewey says, comes into human living when men advance beyond the work of "knowing" into another kind of work. So long as we are engaged in the sciences, we are truth-seeking. We are looking for that which may be "recognized to be established truth." But the theory of education is not striving for truth. It is attempting to direct action. It arises, Dewey tells us, when men meet the "need for projecting even the completest knowledge upon a realm of another dimension, namely, the dimension of action."[13] And the driving, justifying force of that action is not knowledge but will. "All philosophy bears an intellectual impress because it is an effort to convince some one, perhaps the writer himself, of the reasonableness of some course of life which has been adopted from custom or instinct."[14] It may take the "garb" but not the "form" of knowledge. And in this case, "scientific form is a vehicle for conveying a non-scientific conviction, but the carriage is necessary, for philosophy is not mere passion but a passion that would exhibit itself as a reasonable persuasion."[15]

A "passion that would exhibit itself as a reasonable persuasion"—that is Dewey's characterization of the "general theory of education." That is the theoretical basis which he has provided for American teaching. Philosophies differ, we are told, because they arise in different individuals and groups, from different moral convictions, different attitudes of will. Those differences are not rational. Each philosophy has, as its origin and final justification, a unique and distinct moral conviction, a peculiar set of habits, customs, instincts. And from this it follows that philosophic principles are not intellectually justified or rejected. They are subjectively preferred. They are cultural dogmas. The advocates of these dogmas do not reason with one another. The thinking of the philosopher is not reasoning. It is rhetoric. It is

[12] *Ibid.*, p. 844.
[13] *Ibid.*, p. 848.
[14] *Ibid.*, p. 846.
[15] *Ibid.*, p. 847.

an attempt to give scientific form to that which is not scientific. It is to exhibit as a "reasonable persuasion" a "passion" which is not reasonable. It is an attempt to convince—not to know. It would "convince some one, perhaps the writer himself, of the reasonableness" of customs and habits and instincts which, in their very nature as such, have none of the quality of reasonableness. In a word, education has, as its theoretical basis, unreason, ungrounded and arbitrary choice.

5

Dewey's contention that "the general theory of education" is adopted without justification reaches its sharpest statement in the *Reconstruction in Philosophy*, published in 1920. In that controversial piece of arguing he opposes, "with malice prepense," science and philosophy, with constant disparagement of the latter. The attack upon philosophy, which runs through the book differs curiously in form, though not in intention from that of the paper on "Philosophy and Democracy." Philosophy is here regarded, not as the guide of action but rather as the maker of "general theories." The dominant motive of the book comes to focus in the last chapter, which deals with social philosophy. And the conclusion reached is explicit. It is unwise, Dewey tells us, to philosophize, to have and to use "general theories" of society. This statement presumably applies also to having "general theories" of education. "What is needed," Dewey says, "is specific inquiries into a multitude of specific structures and interactions. Not only does the solemn reiteration of categories of individual and organic or social whole not further these definite and detailed inquiries but it checks them. It detains thought within pompous and sonorous generalities wherein controversy is as inevitable as it is incapable of solution."[16] Such theorizing as this tends to substitute mere abstract ideas for concrete, specific investigations. Science, then, must take charge of action. "We

[16] *Reconstruction in Philosophy*, Henry Holt & Co., 1920, pp. 198-199.

need guidance in dealing with particular perplexities in domestic life and we are met by dissertations on the Family or by assertions of the Sacredness of Individual Personality."[17] The Dewey who writes those words would seem to have little confidence in a "general theory of education." In his hands, philosophy, as the search for wisdom, has fallen upon evil days.

It is, however, obvious that what Dewey says in the *Reconstruction* about the nature of philosophizing is not, and could not be, his total judgment about the business to which his own life has been devoted. What he is condemning here is not "philosophy" but "bad philosophy." After all, Dewey is not a scientist. He is not an investigator. He is a philosopher, a generalizer, a spinner of theories. As already noted, the range of his abstractions takes in at one sweep the whole field of human experience. And the attack of the *Reconstruction*, soberly considered, without "malice prepense," is directed, not at the use of generalizations, but at the abuse of them. Dewey finds that social theorizing, when not based in solid fact, has evil effects. It tends to irrelevance and to dogmatism. It furnishes a way of escape from actual problems. It also sanctifies the *status quo*. And in these observations he is undoubtedly right. These are the fruits of bad theorizing, pragmatic or non-pragmatic. Generalizations are dangerous instruments. But what follows? Shall we cease from using them? In the *Reconstruction* Dewey seems to be very near to that generalization. Certainly his words suggest it. His discussion of social philosophy forbids any general theory of society. His whole argument is a defense of that negative attitude. And that means, for our argument, that he is also denying the possibility of a "general theory of education."

6

The destructive effect of Dewey's subjective account of the process by which knowledge is used for the guidance of action

[17] *Ibid.*, p. 189.

has been, both for studies of society and for studies of education, enormous. Wherever that interpretation has been accepted, social attitudes, and educational policies, have been acknowledged to be founded in unreason. Reasoning, in all its practical phases, has been regarded as "rationalizing." When two "patterns of culture," such as democracy and aristocracy, face each other as rival claimants for the directing of a plan of education, as they do in the text of *Democracy and Education*, Dewey gives us no rational way of choosing between them by a fair, objective impartial, disinterested measuring of their relative advantages. That choice is made, not by reasoning but by moral conviction, by custom, by habit, by instinct. When a society is divided into two social groups, the aristocrats and democrats, these parties are not, in any intellectual sense, in communication with one another. Each of them has "taken for granted" as its basic postulate a "general attitude" which, with equal lack of reason, is rejected by the opposing group. In that situation, there can be no objective attempt by co-operative intelligence to weigh the merits, under actual conditions, of the two basic assumptions. Neither group is criticizing its own postulates. Neither group is trying to understand the other. Each is busy in giving to its own dogma, and the practical consequences of that dogma, the form of demonstration which will make them plausible. This is the procedure which F. H. Bradley so cleverly characterizes when he defines metaphysics as "the finding of bad reasons for what we believe upon instinct," and adds, "but to find those reasons is no less an instinct."[18]

And, at this point, we must, in large measure, hold a subjective Dewey guilty of the charge of giving articulate expression, in the fields of social science and of education, to the belief that, in the last resort, all social thinking, as contrasted with the work of the "sciences," is irrational and dogmatic. It is a serious charge to make because I suppose no other doctrine has done so much to

[18] *Appearance and Reality*, F. H. Bradley, Swan, Sonnenschein & Co., 1893, Preface, xiv.

destroy the foundations of sober inquiry into social conditions and social programs as has the conviction that, in this field, men are not really inquiring but are only "assuming the garb" of doing so. They are not really co-operating in a common intellectual study. They are merely trying to "put something over" on another. As I read parts of *Democracy and Education* and all of *Philosophy and Democracy* and *Reconstruction in Philosophy*, Dewey is clearly on that ground. And the unfortunate feature of his American influence is that it is chiefly the Dewey of this mood who has been accepted as guide in the fields of education and of social science. From one end of America to the other we come upon men working in those two fields who use the notion of "rationalization" as a kind of patter, with apparently no realization of its implications as an account of what they themselves are doing. It is the members of this group who tell us that all teaching is, and must be, propaganda. In the process of developing the minds of their pupils, our teachers have available, they say, only the warring dogmas of conflicting sects, conflicting nations or cultures, each of which is fundamentally unintelligible to the others and to itself. This being true, all that any teacher can do is to pick his own dogma, or obediently accept that of some social group to which he belongs, and proceed to find the most plausible ways of making that dogma acceptable to his pupils. And the irony of that situation is that the men who thus make "rationalizing" the fundamental term in teaching and in social theorizing almost invariably turn to Dewey as their master, regard him as the fountainhead of their wisdom.[19]

[19] The extent to which this point of view has penetrated the field of social study and has destroyed the standards of moral judgment is suggested by the following words of Robert M. MacIver. Speaking of ethical principles he says, "But we discover soon enough that there is no body of accepted doctrine in respect of that problem, and that in the nature of the case there can be none. For if I say that happiness is the supreme end of life and another gainsays me, what way can be found of deciding between our claims? If I meant that men as a rule do seek happiness before everything else, my statement may admit of verification or refutation, but if I mean that what men *ought* to seek is happiness, how can that statement be controverted except by an equally dogmatic statement

In so far as Dewey's writing has had that effect upon the social and educational activities of America it must be said that the pragmatic philosophy has failed to do what it undertook to do. Fifty years ago, the theological answer to the question, "What is objective, critical intelligence?" had lost its meaning. The new naturalism offered to provide, out of the findings of biology, a new answer to replace the old one. But the answer which the *Reconstruction in Philosophy* gives is "There is no objective, critical intelligence." Intelligence is, as such, subjective and uncritical. The outcome of Dewey's search for "a general theory of education" is that general theories are not worth having. As we shall see later, this conclusion is hostile to many of Dewey's deepest convictions. And yet he never abandons it. And what is worse, it is this side of his thinking which has been popularly known and widely accepted. So far as his general influence is concerned, the outcome of his attempt to make human behavior critically and objectively intelligent is the belief that the activity which we call intelligence is neither critical nor objective nor intelligent. A philosophy of life is "a passion that would exhibit itself as a reasonable persuasion."—It is a strange conclusion to be reached by a man whose dominant motive has been to raise the studies of human behavior to a level co-ordinate with that of the physical sciences.

---

that they *ought not* to seek it? Now the distinctive character of ethics is that it is concerned with the question of *ought*, the question of right and wrong, good and bad. It is concerned, that is, with a question lying beyond the bounds of scientific procedure, beyond verification, beyond induction, beyond actuality. Therefore, we can have a history of ethics but no science of it. Instead of a science we must be content with a philosophy—or rather a series of philosophies, varying according to the insight and character of each philosopher, a series whose ethical contradictions and antagonisms can never be dissolved by any scientific procedure. All ethical claims are claims of worthfulness, and we can neither confirm nor refute them save by our own estimate of their worth. In so far as they may mistake the true relation of means to ends, in so far as they may maintain that a system or mode of action contributes to some end to which in fact it does not contribute, we may convict them of scientific error, but in so far as they maintain that an end is good *in itself*, how shall we refute them if we disbelieve—save by denial? *Community*, R. M. MacIver, Macmillan, 1920, pp. 55-56.

7

We have thus far followed Dewey's discussion of the relation between knowledge and intelligence in what may be called his subjective mood. But as already noted, Dewey has also another mood, an objective one. His values are not only "valued." They are also "evaluated," that is, critically estimated.[20] The ideas of philosophy, though based on passion, are yet also based on knowledge. And for this second mood, such choices as that of democracy are not merely arbitrary. They are subjected to critical examination. They are established, modified, repudiated, as they meet, or fail to meet, the tests of criticism. Dewey intends to have an objective criterion by the use of which such choices can be tested.

From the pages of *The Quest for Certainty, Experience and Nature, Art as Experience, Logic, the Theory of Inquiry,* we could select dozens of passages in which this work of critical intelligence is assigned to the philosophic mind. Dewey still separates the fields of knowledge and of action. But philosophy is no longer confined to the latter and excluded from the former. It now deals with the relations between the two. And, that being true, it acquires a status which is independent both of knowledge and of action. It becomes a third party, a referee or judge, who can criticize and evaluate both what men know and what they do. It has authority to bring the knowledge of science and the values of action into right relations to one another.

In the *Quest for Certainty,* for example, Dewey says, "Man has beliefs which scientific inquiry vouchsafes, beliefs about the actual structure and processes of things; and he has also beliefs[21] about the values which should regulate his conduct. The question of how these two ways of believing may most

[20] See *Logic, The Theory of Inquiry,* Henry Holt & Co., 1938, p. 173.
[21] Note that Dewey here apeaks not of "values" but of "beliefs about values." The immediate product of philosophy is not "action" but a "theory of action."

effectively and fruitfully interact with one another is the most general and significant problem which life presents to us. Some reasoned discipline, one obviously other than any science, should deal with this issue."[22]—It is a far cry from the "passion that would exhibit itself as a reasonable persuasion," to that statement which makes the pursuit of philosophic intelligence, a "reasoned discipline" which is "other than any science" and which yet deals with "the most general and significant problem which life presents to us." This does not sound like "taking things for granted."

And again we read,[23] "The problem of restoring integration and co-operation between man's beliefs about the world in which he lives and his beliefs about the values and purposes that should direct his conduct is the deepest problem of modern life." And still again, in *Experience and Nature*,[24] Dewey gives to philosophic thinking a description which marks it off both from active behavior and from the inquiries of the special sciences. "These remarks are preparatory to presenting a conception of philosophy: namely, that philosophy is inherently criticism, having its distinctive position among various modes of criticism in its generality: a criticism of criticisms, as it were." And later we read, "And this effort to make our. desires, our striving and our ideals (which are as natural to man as his aches and his clothes) articulate, to define them (not in themselves which is impossible) in terms of inquiry into conditions and consequences is what I have called criticism and, when carried on in the grand manner, philosophy."[25]

8

In later chapters we must examine how Dewey uses this second method of criticism. That method, too, we must see in

[22] *The Quest for Certainty*, pp. 18-19.
[23] P. 255.
[24] P. 398.
[25] P. 418.

action. For the moment, however, our concern is with the fact that there are two methods, that Dewey has given us two different accounts of the search for intelligence. And, as they are stated, those accounts are radically opposed to one another. For the first, intelligence is "based in passion." For the second, it is the product of criticism. In the paper on "Philosophy and Democracy," the task of philosophy is to "exhibit as reasonable" convictions which are adopted from "custom and instinct." Such beliefs start "not from science, not from ascertained knowledge, but from moral convictions." But in the *Quest for Certainty* and *Experience and Nature*, philosophy has become "a reasoned discipline" whose business is "criticism." In the first case, the attempt of intelligence is to "convince," to "persuade." In the other, it is an activity of "inquiry." In the argument of *Democracy and Education*, a social program is "taken for granted." When Dewey is in his objective mood, all social programs are to be "justified" and "criticized" by an "inquiry into conditions and consequences." Philosophy which, at first, had only the "garb" of reason has now taken on its "form." The phrase "exact of us" has acquired meaning.

I am not saying that these two points of view are wholly irreconcilable. It is obvious that when Dewey makes these different statements, he is, in different moods, looking at different aspects of the human situation. But the difficulty is that those differences are not clearly recognized. And the resulting total impression is one of confusion and incoherence.

9

The depth of the ambiguity of which we are speaking was revealed in a recent interchange of criticism and reply between Dewey and Joseph Ratner. The latter tells us that he has found "a fundamental fault (geologically speaking) which lies deep in the instrumentalism in *Studies in Logical Theory* (1903)." Quoting from *The Need for a Recovery of Philosophy* (1925)

Dewey's statement that "the pragmatic notion of reality is precisely that no theory of Reality in general, überhaupt, is possible or needed," Ratner says, "Here more explicitly than in our earlier examples we find Dewey going from the proposition that there is no 'Reality in general' (which is true) to the conclusion that no general theory of reality is possible (which is false). The passage cited," he continues, "may rightfully be claimed as itself a nuclear or germinal statement of a general theory of reality. But it is quite unnecessary to argue the point. Just as Dewey in *The Public and Its Problems* thoroughly corrected the idea that a general theory of the state and society is not necessary by developing one, so in *Experience and Nature*, which appeared some eight years after the citation above was written, he explicitly developed a general 'theory of nature, of the world, of the universe.' "[26]

Now Ratner's criticism at this point seems to me warranted. Dewey does contradict himself on the question of general theories. He both denies their validity and uses them as valid. And yet Ratner's dealing with the "fault" is not fully satisfactory. He tells us that Dewey has "thoroughly corrected" an error by urging its opposite. The assertion that we cannot have general theories is disposed of by the producing of two such general theories. But surely that "correction" is not very "thorough." Dewey, we are told, has continued to make two contradictory assertions. In adopting the second, which Ratner approves, he has not abandoned the first, which Ratner condemns, even though the second is a denial of the first. If the second is true, then the line of reasoning by which the first was established must have been faulty at some essential point. And correction would be the discovery and elimination of that fault. But that, so far as Ratner tells us, so far as any reader of Dewey can tell us, has not been done. The two contradictory assertions are left face to face, irreconcilable and yet both accepted. And as a result the whole

[26] *The Philosophy of John Dewey*, The Library of Living Philosophers, Vol. I, 1938, p. 66.

discussion of "general ideas" remains involved in confusion and uncertainty. Dewey both condemns their use and uses them.

But Dewey's reply to Ratner gives even more striking evidence of the ambiguity in which his study of knowledge and intelligence is involved. In self-defense, Dewey says, "I did not hit upon my position as a ready made and finished doctrine. It developed in and through a series of reactions to a number of philosophic problems. Under these conditions," he continues, "it is natural that inconsistencies and shifts have taken place: the most I can claim is that I have moved fairly steadily in one direction." And then, in characterizing that direction, Dewey makes one of the most startling suggestions ever made by a writer on philosophy. He suggests that in the course of his life-long discussion "knowledge" and "intelligence" may have been confused, may, at times, have changed places. "Dr. Ratner," he says, "is quite right in indicating that the word *intelligence* represents what is essential in my view much better than does the word *knowledge*, while it avoids the confusion of knowing—inquiry—and attained knowledge which has led some of my critics astray in their accounts of my position. At present, after reading criticisms of the kind of *instrumentalism* that is attributed to me, it is clear that I should, from the start, have systematically distinguished between knowledge as the outcome of special inquiries (undertaken because of the presence of problems) and *intelligence* as the product and expression of cumulative funding of the meanings[27] reached in these special cases."[28]

[27] The phrase "the cumulative funding of meanings" covers a nest of technical difficulties with which this argument cannot deal. It suggests that, in some way or other, after a scientific inquiry is finished, it leaves behind it "meanings" which are "funded." Apparently those meanings are stored away, are kept available for further use by the sciences or philosophy. It would be hard to imagine a more tantalizingly elusive notion than this. Do meanings exist when not in active use? If that is true, its implications for education are very important and strongly counter to the general drift of Dewey's influence.—But the issue is too technical for discussion here. To any reader who wishes to pursue it I would recommend as a starting point, the brilliant study of Dewey's "Epistemology and Metaphysics" by A. E. Murphy in the *Philosophy of*

The effect of that "explanation" upon one who has for many years been trying to understand Dewey's "general theory of education," who has seen that the whole structure of his thought has to do with the relation between "knowledge" and "intelligence," is simply devastating. It is as if Kant should have said, looking back upon his *Critiques*, "Dr. X. is quite right in saying that *a priori* represents what is essential in my view much better than does *a posteriori*. I should from the start have distinguished between them. It was, of course, the latter which I meant when I spoke of the former." For the fact is that Dewey has always distinguished between knowledge and intelligence. From the beginning, his structure of ideas rests on that distinction. It is the crux of all he has to say about the philosophy of society and, hence, of the theory of education. If, as he now tells us, there has been confusion at this point, if one of these terms may be substituted for the other, that confusion goes so deep that no mere abstract redefining or interchanging of the two terms will correct it. There must be radical rethinking of the total set of ideas in which those terms are involved. That rethinking has not been done. And the resulting confusion in this interpretation of the work of our schools and colleges has been disastrous. Every teacher knows, as Dewey assures us, that knowledge must be used for the creating of intelligence. No one denies that. But the question for which we need an answer is "By what process of thinking is knowledge transformed into wisdom?" What is that activity of philosophy or criticism or intelligence which the teacher must attempt to set up in the mind of his pupil? Dewey gives us two conflicting views of that activity. And the difference between those views is decisive for any theory of education. Is intelligence a procedure for rationalizing our passions? Or is it a procedure by which practical beliefs are tested by objective intellectual criticism? Dewey says

---

John Dewey, and Dewey's reply to the question there raised. Murphy doubts whether "inquiry" as Dewey describes it, leaves behind it any cognitive meanings which might be funded or used.

[28] *Ibid.*, 520-521.

both of these. And the result of that ambiguity is that, in the social sciences, in the schools and colleges, which have been influenced by Dewey's leadership, the notion of intelligence is a vague and ineffectual one. No one, in his generation, has pressed more strongly than Dewey the claims of critical thinking. But it is equally true that no one has done more to involve those claims in uncertainty and confusion.

Chapter 13. THE THEORY OF THE STATE

mmmmmmmmmmmmmmmmmmmmmmmmmmmmmmmmmmmmmmmmmmmmmmmmm

FOR a proper understanding of Dewey's account of "criticism," we need a book which he has not yet written. All through his career he has urged that studies of human behavior be raised to an intellectual level corresponding to that of the sciences of non-human action. Social planning, he tells us, should be objective, impersonal, critical—above all, scientific. But that being true, the one book which was needed from his hands was a study of social problems, in which the desired method might be seen at work. The study of aesthetic criticism which was so brilliantly given in *Art as Experience*, needed to be matched by a study of social criticism. What is, in actual operation, the method of objective investigation in accordance with which good social intelligence may be won?

Among the books which Dewey has written the most useful for our purpose is *The Public and Its Problems*, published in 1927. Unfortunately it is not a systematic treatise. But it does give a glimpse of Dewey's mind at work on the theory of the state and the theory of democracy. And since these are the two problems about society which especially concern teaching we shall find in Dewey's discussion of them exemplification of what he means when he speaks of criticism as the activity which is fundamental to all right social thinking, to all sound education. In this chapter we examine Dewey's theory of the state.

I

The argument of *The Public and Its Problems* opens with a sharp, decisive repudiation of the negative attitude of the *Reconstruction in Philosophy*. Dewey still attacks traditional social theorizing. He does not, however, condemn and discard all theorizing as such. "One way out of the impasse," he says, "is to consign the whole matter of meaning and interpretation to political philosophy as distinguished from political science. Then it can be pointed out that futile speculation is a companion of all philosophy. The moral is to drop all doctrines of this kind overboard, and stick to facts verifiably ascertained." But that program which the *Reconstruction* had explicitly advocated, Dewey now rejects. "The remedy urged is simple and attractive. But it is not possible to employ it." As men discuss the conflicting theories which "mark political philosophy," Dewey says:

It is mere pretense, then, to suppose that we can stick by the *de facto*, and not raise at some point the *de jure*; the question by what right, the question of legitimacy. And such a question has a way of growing until it has become a question of the nature of the state itself. The alternatives before us are not factually limited science on the one hand and uncontrolled speculation on the other. The choice is between blind, unreasoned attack and defense on the one hand, and discriminating criticism employing intelligent method and a conscious criterion on the other.[1]

In these words the Dewey of 1927 takes a position radically opposed to that of the Dewey of 1920. He is no longer content to regard intelligence as involved in "the blind, unreasoned attack and defense" which are inevitable when attitudes are "taken for granted." He is now disposed to judge attitudes by the use of "discriminating criticism" of "intelligent method," of "a conscious criticism." Philosophic beliefs are now to be "grounded." They are to be justified. The "many patterns of culture" are to be studied by the "one pattern of intelligence." If Dewey can succeed in that attempt he will have done the work which pragmatism undertook to do. He will have given us a basis for a general theory of society and, hence, for a general

[1] *The Public and Its Problems*, p. 6.

THE THEORY OF THE STATE

theory of education. If he does not succeed, then pragmatism
has failed in its main endeavor.

2

There can be no doubt that the argument of *The Public and
Its Problems* intends to use that method of objective criticism
which Dewey calls philosophy. We shall not understand society, he tells us, by the mere "study of concepts." Nor can we
explain it by "acts of will." What is needed is the "observation
of the consequences of action." Social criticism is "the recognition of consequences as consequences."[2] "There is only one
method by which alteration of political forms might be directed: namely, the use of intelligence to judge consequences."[3]
"Human associations may be ever so organic and firm in operation, but they develop into societies in a human sense only as
their consequences, being known, are esteemed and sought for."[4]

Now the method of observing consequences as used for the
understanding of "the state" might take either of two forms.
We might explain political institutions as "being" consequences
or as "having" consequences. In the first case we should understand the state if we discovered the conditions out of which it
arises. In the second case, we should understand it if we know
the effects which it produces. Our explanation by "conditions
and consequences" might thus take either a "backward" or a
"forward" look in time. It may, of course, also take both.

As one follows Dewey's discussion of the state it is evident
that he is in this case taking the backward look. His question is
"How is a public generated?" Out of what conditions does
political organization emerge? We shall know what the state is
if we know its origin.

The argument, as it stands, rests essentially upon two assertions. First, we are told, the state as contrasted with such "pri-

[2] *The Public and Its Problems*, p. 12.
[3] *Ibid.*, p. 45.
[4] *Ibid.*, p. 152.

mary" associations as those of friendship, art, science, education, sport, industry, and the like, is a secondary institution. Second, the state arises from the interplay of the primary associations. It is unique in being derivative, restricted and accidental in character.

It is, I think, evident that if these two assertions can be established, the groundwork has been laid for such a negative "policeman" view of the state as Dewey adopts. But are they established? On what grounds of evidence, by what method of criticism does Dewey show them to be valid? It is in the answer to that question that we may hope to find a clearer view of what is meant by the "observation of consequences."

3

The primary groups, Dewey tells us, are easily recognizable as primary. Each of them "has its own peculiar quality and value and no person in his senses confuses the one with the other."[5] But the governing state has no such self-sufficient status. It comes into being, as it were, accidentally. Primary groups are drawn together intentionally. They have such common interests as those of sport, art, business, friendship, education. But it is only when the activities of these first associations have unintended, indirect consequences, that "a public is generated." Other individuals and groups who are affected, for weal or for woe, by the behavior of the devotees of sport, art, business, teaching or industry, develop a new "shared" or "common" interest of their own. They are drawn together by the common purpose of seeing to it that these activities which affect them are "taken care of, looked out for." Such activities must be "supervised" and "regulated." As it performs that function the new "public" becomes a "state." Such a state must, in the nature of the case, have "officials." "The lasting extensive and serious consequences of associated activity bring into existence a public.

[5] *Ibid.*, p. 27.

In itself it is unorganized and formless. By means of officials and their special powers it becomes a state. A public articulated and operating through representative officers is the state: there is no state without a government, but also there is none without the public."[6]

Now the whole weight of that argument rests upon one assertion. It is the assertion that the motives which lead individuals to form a political association are radically different in kind from those which lead them to associate in sport, in art, in friendship, in industry, or in teaching. The assessment of the argument must answer two questions—first, what does the assertion mean and, second, by what method of criticism is the assertion formulated and supported?

As to the meaning of the assertion it is, I think, the clear intent of Dewey to make the state what Locke made it. Government is an institution of secondary value. It arises from self-interest rather than from a public interest. Its functions are, therefore, merely regulative, merely negative. The primary associations bind men together by devotion to a common purpose. They express an identity of interest. They are positive and creative in character. But government has no positive purposes of its own. It initiates no activities. It only limits and regulates the activities which other institutions are carrying on. The state, Dewey tells us, does not issue commands. "Rules of law are active forces only as are banks which confine the flow of a stream, and are commands only in the sense in which banks command a current."[7] That is the characteristic political gospel of a Protestant-capitalist society. The state is a "policeman." It does not do anything. It only prevents things from being done. For Locke it is private "rights" which are the prior facts. For Dewey it is private "interests." But the two are agreed in sharply separating private and public activities, and in making the second radically subordinate to and different from the first.

[6] *Ibid.*, p. 229.
[7] *Ibid.*, p. 52.

People do not join together for the forming of a government because they will to do so. They enter the social compact because they are driven to do so.

The motivation underlying the state, as Dewey conceives it, is clearly revealed when he quotes from W. H. Hudson a description of a village community in Wiltshire, into whose life the conscious controls of political organization have not yet entered. To this description Dewey appends a comment which speaks more loudly than could many abstract analyses.

The description reads as follows.—"Consider the village in Wiltshire so beautifully described by Hudson":

Each house has its center of human life with life of bird and beast, and the centers were in touch with one another, connected like a row of children linked together by their hands; all together forming one organism, instinct with one life, moved by one mind, like a many-colored serpent lying at rest, extended at full length upon the ground. I imagined the case of a cottager at one end of the village occupied in chopping up a piece of wood or stump and accidentally letting fall his heavy sharp axe on to his foot, inflicting a grievous wound. The tidings of the accident would fly from mouth to mouth to the other extremity of the village, a mile distant; not only would each villager quickly know of it, but have at the same time a vivid mental image of his fellow villager at the moment of his misadventure, the sharp glittering axe falling on to his foot, the red blood flowing from the wound; and he would at the same time feel the wound in his own foot and the shock to his system. In like manner all thoughts and feelings would pass freely from one to another, though not necessarily communicated by speech; and all would be participants in virtue of that sympathy and solidarity uniting the members of a small isolated community. No one would be capable of a thought or emotion which would seem strange to the others. The temper, the mood, the outlook of the individual and the village, would be the same.

To this idyllic picture, Dewey adds the comment, "With such a condition of intimacy, the state is an impertinence."[8]

[8] *Ibid.*, pp. 40-41.

The crucial point in this picture, as Dewey uses it, and in the comment which he makes upon it, is that the origin of the state is discovered by him not in the "sympathy and solidarity" by which the members of the village are held together, but in the separate, independent, private interests, by which they are held apart. Government, he contends, springs from individual self-interest. As the many villagers go about their separate enterprises they encounter interferences with those enterprises. And when a number of individuals encounter the same interference they become through that "accident," a "public." That is what Dewey means when he says that the state is secondary and derivative. In the face of the organic sympathy and solidarity which binds together the village as a whole, government is something alien, hostile. It is an impertinence.

4

This charge of impertinence may be clarified if we imagine a state arising in our Wiltshire village as a result of such an incident as Hudson describes. Let us suppose that the "strain" set up by the injury to one of its members arouses the community to "awareness," and, hence, to conscious, political action. There are, I think, two different lines along which "public" action might go.

First, along the line of Dewey's suggestion, a number of different "publics" may be generated. In several different ways people will find their private interests affected by the unintended consequences of the cutting of the foot. Some of the villagers may find that their supply of firewood is stopped. They would therefore be driven to take common action to keep themselves warm. Another set of individuals might find themselves called upon to do extra work to replace that of the injured man. Still others might find it prudent to care for him, to nurse him back to health. Each of these groups would thus become a "public," eager "to look out for, to take care of" its own interests. And, somewhere, among them, Dewey would find the origin of the state.

But, in such a community as Hudson describes, another type of "public" reaction may also be expected. These villagers care for their fellows as well as for themselves. They are disinterested as well as self-interested. When, therefore, they see one of their comrades injured, they may ask, "How can this sort of thing be prevented; how, if it happens, can it be alleviated?" And, in this vein, they may proceed to set aside a building, properly equipped to care for Tom or Jim in case he is injured. Would such a beginning of a public hospital be an impertinence? Obviously it would express, not the private interests of separate groups, but the sympathy and solidarity of the whole community. And as the village then proceeded to levy taxes, to establish principles of administration, to select and to pay officials, it would be creating a state, not out of the multifarious self-interests of its members, but out of the common purpose, the common will of "an organism, instinct with one life, moved by one mind."

Dewey, I am saying, chooses one of two alternative explanations of the origin of the state, in terms of its motivation. Political action, as he sees it, is not disinterested. It is selfish. The conscious political institutions of men do not continue that drive toward social integration which marks the unconscious life of an instinctive fellowship. On the contrary, it arises from the accidental coincidence of separate desires. The members of any one of Dewey's "publics" have no primary interest in each other. For the moment they find their separate needs and desires running in the same direction. So long as this is true, they plan and work together. But they are equally ready to separate into hostile factions whenever their interests divide and clash. They have no identity of interest, no interest in each other. Their marriage is one "of convenience." Each is looking out for himself. Each is using the others to that end so long as he finds them useful.

THE THEORY OF THE STATE

5

We have said that Dewey chooses to explain political institutions in terms of selfishness rather than of sympathy. But that suggests the second question which we must ask concerning his argument. It is the question with which the argument of this chapter began. On what basis of evidence, in terms of what "conscious criterion" is it asserted that political action is self-interested? We would expect that "the observation of conditions and consequences" would here be relied upon to justify the assertion. But so far as I can discover in the text of *The Public and Its Problems,* that method is wholly lacking. The assertion that sport and education are primary while the government is secondary is made without any supporting warrant of fact. "Any man in his senses," we are told, can see that other associations are primary. But this means that Dewey is not "observing consequences." He is studying concepts. His theory of the state is as deductive as is that of Hegel. The conviction that the "conscious" action of government is secondary and derivative is deduced from his general theory of "conscious" action. He applies to politics a universal principle which he has derived from a study of human awareness as such.

And, further, it is unfortunately Dewey's subjective and individualistic analysis of the conscious process to which he resorts as giving basis for his political convictions. In Chapter 2 we found that when thinking is regarded as an individual affair, its function tends to become that of a "trouble shooter" rather than that of a permanent and responsible participant in the organic process. Its business is to relieve episodic and disconnected "strains" rather than to carry on a continuous and self-directing enterprise. Now it is that kind of thinking which Dewey assigns to the state and to its officials. His government is a "policeman" and nothing else. As the "officer" travels his beat he finds all about him individuals and groups engaged in activities in relation to which his own are secondary and restricted and regulative and negative. Such governing as he does has no positive purposes of its own. It comes into action only as "problematic situations" summon it into consciousness. It deals, not with values and aims, but only with the conflicts between them. If there are no conflicts then the state, as expressing mind and intelligence, has nothing to do. In that case, any action it might take would be an impertinence. And this means that the agencies of government are not, in any continuing or comprehensive sense, aware of the general ends and values toward which the life and education of a society should be directed. The policeman does not know what the fighting is about. All that he knows is that he is called in to stop it. He is not a judge nor a legislator nor an administrator nor an educator. He is a policeman.

6

Our argument turned toward Dewey in the hope that he would give us in Darwinian terms, an intellectual basis for such public action as that of teaching. And there can be no doubt that his own social attitude is driving in the same direction. Such a book as *Liberalism and Social Action* makes it clear that Dewey does not wish to stand with Locke. He strongly demands public co-operation for the common good. But *The Public and Its Problems* is significant because it shows that Dewey's thinking does not express his own attitude. The pragmatic account of intelligence, as here given, robs it of all objectivity, all disinterestedness. What it offers us is not a state. It is a shifting, whirling collocation of pressure groups, of factions, of parties, in the baser sense of that term. Government becomes, not a unified attempt at freedom and justice, but a miscellaneous collection of "interested" activities, each of which is directed toward the welfare of some individual or private group. In spite of all of his brave attempts to establish and use an objective criterion, Dewey, when put to the test of a concrete situation, drifts back into his subjective mood. The thinking which men do as they carry on the work of governing may put on the "garb" of reason. But, at the bottom, it is nothing else than rationalizing. The motives of government are not such "disinterested" emotions as the love of justice, of equality, of freedom. They are merely individual passions, each of which, as it strives to prevail over others, "would exhibit itself as a reasonable persuasion."

7

It is one of the most tragic features of our contemporary life that this "pressure-group" attitude which Dewey formulates has won so deadly a grip upon our social and political thinking. One of its most familiar forms is the identification of "the consumer" and "the public" which is so common in current economic planning. As we try to deal with the many conflicts between workers and employers we are told that "public" interests need to be guarded against the consequences of those conflicts. When, however, provision is to be made for that guarding it appears that what is needed is the protection, not of the body politic as a whole, but of a third party, namely, the "consumer." It is therefore urged that when plans are to be made for the "regulation" and "supervision" of business procedure the "consumers" should be recognized as "having an interest" which is co-ordinate with that of the "employers" and the "workers." The consumers are, in Dewey's terms, "a public." And from this it follows that whenever owners and workers are planning or fighting about their respective rights, privileges, profits, wages, etc., the "consumer" should participate in the planning or the fighting. He should be a third party in all negotiations. His interest should be "taken care of, looked out for," *by himself.*—It would be hard to express the intellectual and practical destructiveness of that point of view and of the suggestions which follow from it. It is the deepest and most characteristic fallacy of our competitive Protestant-capitalist civilization.

In the first place, consumer interest, as so defined, is quite as "private" as is that of the owner or of the worker. There is nothing "public" about it. The consumer is, in exactly the same sense as either of his competitors, "unreasonable," "self-interested," "subjective." When he enters the scene all that he does is to substitute a three-sided selfishness for a two-sided one. But, equally serious is the fact that consumer "common interests" are not one but many. Men consume shoes, and so become a "shoe" public. They consume clothes, houses, automobiles, books, wide ranges of food, of entertainment, of travel, and so on indefinitely. And for each of these goods there is a different "consumer public." "The" consumer, in any unitary sense, is a myth. The many, multifarious consumer interests are related to each other with all the unreasonableness, all the privateness, of uncorrelated and unregulated desires. And just the same is true of Dewey's "the public." His descriptive phrases, throughout his argument, are those of unity. He regards his thought as leading toward the one Great Community. He speaks, over and over again, as if there were only one "the public," one "shared interest," one "common interest," one "weal and woe of the community," one "good shared by all." But the logic of his argument is driving irresistibly in the opposite direction. It is that pluralistic logic which has tended to make of our American scheme of government nothing more than the competitive clash of "pressure groups," each fighting for its own hand. Each such group, as it is affected by the consequences of the actions of other groups, rushes to its own defense. The body politic becomes, therefore, not an organic unity of sympathy and solidarity, as Rousseau would make it, not an agency for taking counsel together, for establishing disinterested and objective judgment. It is a bedlam of privately warring factions. The method of inquiry into consequences, as Dewey uses it, or fails to use it, does not, and cannot, give an adequate theory of political life. In a world gone mad with self-interest, it provides no sanity. It does not unite men in the common search for justice, for objectivity, for disinterestedness. It splits them asunder into groups, between which such terms as "discriminating criticism," "intelligent method," or "a conscious criterion" can have no meaning whatever. In such a world there is nothing "objective" to teach.

Chapter 14. THE THEORY
OF DEMOCRACY

wwwwwwwwwwwwwwwwwwwwwwwwwwwwwwwwwwwwwwwwwwwwwwwwwwwwwwwwwwwwwwwwwwwwwwwwwww

IN HIS keen and sympathetic study, *John Dewey, An Intellectual Portrait,* Sidney Hook asks, "What is Dewey religious about? What is his God?" And he answers, "It is not hard to guess. If there are any absolutes in his outlook, they are intelligence and democracy, or the ideal of a scientific, democratic, community." In view of our difficulties with the relation between knowledge and intelligence, the ease of Hook's transition from "intelligence" to "scientific" is somewhat bewildering. But with respect to Dewey's devotion to democracy, to his determination that knowledge shall be cultivated and used in the service of the democratic way of life, there can be no doubt that Hook is right. Here again, Dewey is the typical American.

Even more clearly, then, than in the discussion of the state, Dewey's explanation of democracy may serve to bring his pragmatic philosophy to its pragmatic test. Can his ideas account for his own deepest conviction? Does his theory fit his practice, his knowledge support his intelligence? Here, if anywhere, a reader may find basis for judgment upon the final significance of the pragmatic achievement.

I

Dewey's discussions of democracy fall into four different moods or stages. The first of these is pre-pragmatic, pre-Deweyan, as it were. The second, third, and fourth express the pragmatic movement in varying forms.

In the 1890's Dewey wrote his first study of society. It was a paper on the "Ethics of Democracy."[1] The argument was "ideal-

---

[1] University of Michigan Publications in Philosophy.

istic." It advocated the extreme "organic" theory of social relations. Its thesis was essentially that of Plato and Rousseau. Society, Dewey said, is not an aggregate of atomic individuals. It
is an organism. "Human society presents a more perfect organism" than an individual mind. It has a common will, in which
all its members share. In the exercise of that will, the social
group finds a genuine unity which is spiritual. It is that unitary
will which establishes and justifies democracy. "And this is the
theory," Dewey tells us, "often crudely expressed, that every
citizen is a sovereign, the American theory, a doctrine which in
grandeur has but one equal, and that its fellow, that every man
is a priest of God."

But this organic theory of the pre-pragmatic days was quickly
abandoned. Dewey became more "realistic." He lost faith in
"unities" and "entities." It was a first principle of the pragmatic
revolt that such Victorian idealism was untenable. And ever
since that time, Dewey's mood has been one of reaction against
it. In a deep and persistent way he has been a social disorganist.

2

We have already considered the first of Dewey's three pragmatic accounts of democracy. In that discussion democracy was
"taken for granted." Its only justification was an emotional appeal, a moral conviction, which was accepted without question.
In case that appeal were opposed by another, such as that which
now dominates the dictatorship nations, there was, in Dewey's
account of the thinking process, no provision for an objective,
critical judgment upon the dispute. All that human intelligence
could do was to provide that each party to the conflict should
"rationalize" its own conviction, should make it convincing and
plausible to others and to itself. Intelligence was not a judge. It
was an advocate. It was one of the agencies through which conflicting individuals and groups "fight it out."

But we have seen also that Dewey is not satisfied with this

subjectivism, this individualistic irrationalism. In the *Public and its Problems* he intends to apply to all questions of social theory and practice the methods of objective thinking, of disinterested intelligence. What, then, in these terms, are his second and third pragmatic arguments with respect to democracy?

3

The study of democracy in *The Public and Its Problems* takes both the "backward" and the "forward" look. Dewey sees free institutions as arising out of previous determining conditions. He sees them also as producing their own consequences, in terms of which they may be recognized and evaluated. And his thought follows both these lines of interpretation.

The attempt to explain democracy as itself a consequence of social conditions has always been an alluring one for Dewey. It plays a considerable part in *Democracy and Education*. And it runs through all the later writing. Such "causal explanation" has the "garb" of science. It has, therefore, been readily accepted in a so-called "scientific" era. The general thesis has been that, as the social forces which found expression in the organization of a feudal society have given way, other forces working toward democratic institutions have supplanted them. And especially, the inventions of technology have had a profound, transforming effect in that direction. Under the impact of tools, machines, factories, corporations, banks, etc., the old aristocratic regime has been shattered and has crumbled away. And, on the positive side, the same forces have thrust into the foreground of interest, the human individual. The rights of the individual, his claims to the exercise and development of his powers—all these are forced upon human awareness by the achievements of technology. And the idea, the principle, of democracy is simply the growing "awareness," the "consciousness" of these "consequences," of this new social condition. The "idea" does not cause the change. It simply records it, represents it, recognizes it as a consequence. Democracy is in this way explained as an outgrowth of the technological period. We understand it, when we see it, not primarily as a human decision as to how life should happen, but as a human recognition of what is happening.

In support of this way of explaining the democratic form of contemporary society, Dewey quotes Carlyle as saying, "Invent the printing press and democracy is inevitable." And to this Dewey adds, "Invent the railway, the telegraph, mass manufacture, and concentration of population in urban centers, and some form of democratic government is, humanly speaking, inevitable."[2] The current of events, Dewey tells us, "has set steadily in one direction: toward democratic forms."[3] Belief in political democracy "marks a well-attested conclusion from historic facts. We have every reason to think that whatever changes may take place in existing democratic machinery, they will be of a sort to make the interest of the public a more supreme guide and criterion of governmental activity, and to enable the public to form and manifest its purposes still more authoritatively."[4]

Dewey wrote those words in 1927. They were easy to write and easy to believe in the America of 1927. But the course of events between that time and the present has dealt harshly with them. In the flush of the victory of "the three great democracies" over imperial Germany it was easy to draw "the well-attested conclusion from historic facts" that our democratic principles were the principles of the natural order itself. America had always been God's own country. It was now technology's own country. Technology had destroyed feudalism. It had undermined Victorianism. It would now, as an unintended, "indirect" consequence of its triumphal march, create and sustain the democratic way of life. With every passing year, modern society is becoming more widely and more deeply technological.

[2] *The Public and Its Problems,* p. 110.
[3] *Ibid.,* p. 146.
[4] *Loc. cit.*

We may, therefore, take it for granted that, with every passing year, the same society will become more widely and more deeply democratic. Belief in democracy is "a well-attested conclusion from historic facts." American luck still holds good. Fate, in the forms of mechanical invention, has given to us the best government in the world.

Those words, I have said, were easy to write in 1927. They were also easy to believe. But in 1942 men can read them only with bitter laughter. In the last decade and a half technology has begotten other children. It has spawned other broods. Machine industry has revolutionized the life of Japan—but not in the direction of democracy. Italy has been likewise transformed—but not toward democracy. So, too, Russia, plunging with high democratic purpose into the revolution of 1917, has not yet found democracy to be the inevitable output of her factories and farms. And, most significant of all, Germany, gifted with an exceptional talent and taste for technological efficiency, has not used that efficiency for the creating and sustaining of government by the consent of the governed. Democracy, it appears, is not "inevitable" in a technological world. In such a world, despotism sprouts quite as lavishly as does freedom. The dogma of 1927 has been replaced by the problem of 1942. Freedom cannot be taken for granted as a gift of fate. Men can be free only if they choose to be free, only if they are resolute to bend circumstances to suit their wills. Free men must know "why" they should be free. And that reason is not that "freedom is inevitable."

4

From what has been said it is, I think, obvious how inadequate is Dewey's "backward" use of the "method of consequences" for such a crisis as the world now faces. The modern world is called upon to choose between dictatorship and democracy. Can that choice be made intelligently? Is there any "cri-

186

terion" by which the merits of the two systems can be assessed? Have we a method of "discriminating criticism" which is suitable to such a situation? As the human mind faces alternative social programs, to say that "our" program is the inevitable outcome of preceding conditions is so irrelevant as to be meaningless. It is an argument which both sides can use, and do use, with equal lack of validity. In a technological world it has the same relevance, the same logical power, as had the older theological demonstrations which, in every great human controversy, have found God's inevitable decrees pointing toward both sides of the issue. For the plain fact is that Dewey's backward-looking method of social "criticism" does not furnish a way of judging as between alternative social programs. There is no "criticism" in it. It is sheer dogmatism. For the making of a decision it substitutes the observing of a "fact."

But Dewey, it must be said, himself rejects his own favorite and much-used form of argument. Characteristically, he does not discard it. But he does call upon another to correct and supplement it. The technological explanation of democracy, Dewey tells us, may be misleading. "We have in our prior account," he says, "sufficiently emphasized the role of technological and industrial factors in creating the Great Society. What was said may even have seemed to imply acceptance of the deterministic version of an economic interpretation of history and institutions."[5] That determinism is, we infer, invalid. It "ignores," Dewey says, "the transformation which meanings may effect; it passes over the new medium which communication may interpose between industry and its eventual consequences."[6] "It thinks in terms of antecedents, not of the eventual, of origins, not fruits."[7]

Now, here, apparently, our inquiry reaches its goal. Dewey tells us what is the method of social criticism which pragmatism

[5] *The Public and Its Problems,* pp. 55-56.
[6] *Ibid.,* p. 156.
[7] *Loc. cit.,* p. 156.

finally adopts. As between the backward-looking and the forward-looking types of "observing consequences" he prefers the latter. Here is his "criterion" for the study of human behavior. The actions of men, their institutions, on the conscious level, are not satisfactorily explained when we have discovered their origins. They are better known "by their fruits." It is not a wholly new idea. In the fifth century B.C. it was formulated and used by a Socrates who spoke of virtue or wisdom as "the measuring art." And ever since that time it has held a primary place in philosophic attempts at human understanding. And yet, it has not been found, as a method, free from difficulty. For twenty-four centuries men have puzzled over "methods" of measuring values. By what principles do we judge "the fruits of action"? It is, presumably, that question to which Dewey has proposed an answer. All men recognize that values must be measured. But the vital question is: How can it be done? How can we rise out of mere subjective, unreasoned desires and prejudices up to the level of reasoned, disinterested choice and intelligence? It is that question which a biological pragmatism has undertaken to answer. And, more specifically, in the situation now before us, it has assumed the responsibility of showing why we should prefer—or reject—the program of democracy. What, then, is the pragmatic theory of democratic institutions as judged by their fruits?

But at this crucial point in his argument all the subjective negativism of Dewey's attitude comes rushing into the foreground. He has much to tell us about what "judging by fruits" cannot do. He has little, if anything, to say about what it can do. With respect to such a choice as that between democracy and dictatorship, he says,

there is no a priori rule which can be laid down and by which when it is followed a good state will be brought into existence. In no two ages or places is there the same public. Conditions make the consequences of associated action and the knowledge of them different. In addition the means by which a public can determine the government to serve its interests vary. Only formally can we say what the best state would be. In concrete fact, in actual and concrete organization and structure, there is no form of state which can be said to be the best: not at least till history is ended, and one can survey all its varied forms. The formation of states must be an experimental process. The trial process may go on with diverse degrees of blindness and accident, and at the cost of unregulated procedures of cut and try, of fumbling and groping, without insight into what men are after or clear knowledge of a good state even when it is achieved. Or it may proceed more intelligently, because guided by knowledge of the conditions which must be fulfilled. But it is still experimental. And since conditions of action and of inquiry and knowledge are always changing, the experiment must always be re-tried: the State must always be recovered. Except, once more, in formal statement of conditions to be met, *we have no idea* what history may still bring forth. It is not the business of political philosophy and science to determine what the state in general should or must be. What they may do is to aid in creation of methods such that experimentation may go on less blindly, less at the mercy of accident, more intelligently, so that men may learn from their errors and profit by their successes. The belief in political fixity, of the sanctity of some form of state consecrated by the efforts of our fathers and hallowed by tradition is one of the stumbling-blocks in the way of orderly and directed change; it is an invitation to revolt and revolution.[8]

That statement, so characteristic of Dewey and his colleagues, is filled with wisdom. But it is negative wisdom. It lays down principles of limitation which every sober social thinker, pragmatic or non-pragmatic, must, and does, accept. But the difficulty is that these principles do not give us a positive "conscious criterion." They do not help us to choose between democracy and dictatorship.

Who can doubt the following statements—

1. There is no one form of social organization which is best for all social situations.

2. Any "general idea" by which we might guide our social

[8] *The Public and Its Problems*, pp. 33-34.

action will find different expressions as conditions of human living vary.

3. Human planning never reaches its goal in the sense that no further planning is needed as life moves on.

4. All social thinking is, therefore, experimental in the sense that its results must be held tentatively, open to modification as more thinking is done, as further evidence is made available, as conditions change.

5. To regard conclusions reached by our ancestors or by ourselves as holy or sacred, in the sense that they are established for all time as irrevocably valid, is, intellectually, stupid and disastrous.

All these limiting, negative statements are, I am sure, true. I do not see how anyone, however "absolutist," could reject them. But the trouble is that they are all negative. They do not answer the question which Dewey is facing. If we were trying to decide irrevocably the fate of all mankind for all time they would give us timely warning. If, on the contrary, in the present desperate agony of international strife, we are trying to use our heads, to weigh the conflicting claims of democracy and dictatorship, to think as well as to fight, they are useless. It is for the making of such positive, immediate, tentative decisions as this that Dewey has promised us a "method," a "positive criterion." And he does not give it. We wish to know how to make the actual working decisions which, day by day, are presented to us. What, in our changing world of 1942, is the "justification" of democracy? On what grounds of cool, impartial, critical, disinterested judgment can we assess the merits and the defects of dictatorship? Shall we simply "take for granted" our way of life and fight for it with guns and tanks and planes? Shall we say that "history will decide," the implication being that we are freed from that duty, since someone who will be alive after all men are dead will know what decision should have been made? Does the adoption of the "experimental method" mean that we shall try both democracy and dictatorship tentatively and let them fight their way through to some "unconscious" victory for the one or the other? To those questions the argument of *The Public and Its Problems* gives no answer. So far as the merits and defects of democracy are concerned the method of "observing conditions and consequences" remains an abstract and meaningless formula. It gives no "intelligent method," no "conscious criterion," which men may use as they face the trivial or the tragic problems of everyday experience. It is true that we cannot make absolute decisions. Our experience of human errors and human differences has reconciled us to that limitation. But how do we make relative decisions? Is there any "criterion" for that activity? We are told to look at consequences We are not told "for what" to look. The pragmatic method, so far as it is indicated in Dewey's discussion of democracy, does not do its work. Our American political institutions are neither justified nor condemned. We are given neither a working theory of society nor a working theory of education.

5

The statement just made is so severe and sweeping that it must be carefully guarded from misinterpretation. To say that Dewey's thinking does not justify democracy is not to say that he is undemocratic. That statement would be nonsensical. Both his written words and his public leadership would refute it. What we are challenging is not Dewey's democracy but the pragmatic method by which he thinks about democracy in *The Public and Its Problems*.

It is important, therefore, to note that the text of the book suggests several other lines of argument in addition to the main line which we have followed. First, in the sentence preceding the quotation just considered, Dewey says, "Nevertheless, our conception gives a criterion for determining how good a particular state is: namely the degree of organization of the public

191

which is attained, and the degree in which its officers are so constituted as to perform their function of caring for public interests."[9]—That method is, I fear, useless. As we plan for the organization of a society, our "criterion" is to be the degree of organization which is attained in that society. We are to assess the contribution of our officials to the public interest by judging their success in furthering the public interest. Those statements are irrefutable because they have no meaning. The question is, "By what standard do we measure" the degree of organization; the "caring for public interests"? For example, has England or Germany at present a "higher degree of organization"? That question can be answered only if we know "for what" the organization is devised. Is it for peace or for war, for justice or for slavery? And Dewey gives no "common goal," prescribing a "common criterion," on the basis of which the choice of our civilization between two conflicting codes of political organization should be made. He has no "working" criterion which we can now use.

Second, Dewey speaks, in the passage quoted, of "a formal statement of conditions to be met." Such a statement, even though "formal"—or perhaps better, "because" it is "formal"—might be expected to have some usefulness in an "inquiry into conditions and consequences." But for Dewey, the word "formal" tends to be an epithet of reproach. His "forms" are kept far removed from his "contents." And, hence, the formula never comes into active operation. It does nothing in the argument which we have followed.

And, finally, Dewey's lack of a criterion makes him resort again to the method which he most strongly condemns. He "justifies" free institutions by "the study of concepts." He deduces the "idea" of a democracy from the "idea" of a community. A community, he tells us, is, as such, democratic. In the realm of ideas, it cannot be anything else. "Regarded as an idea, democracy is not an alternative to other principles of associated

[9] *Ibid.*, p. 33.

THE THEORY OF DEMOCRACY

life. It is the idea of community life itself."[10] I would not too much disparage "the study of concepts." So long as concepts are kept in living touch with the specific situations to which they refer, that method has far more value than Dewey, in his controversial mood, allows it. But, as used in this case, Dewey's separation of the "ideal" and the "actual" robs the argument of any possible significance.

What does the statement mean for a world in which England and Germany are at war, in which the fate of all other nations, as well as their own, rests on the issue of the conflict? In the realm of ideas, we are told, there is no possible conflict between democracy and dictatorship, as principles of community life. For "thought" the problem is unreal. But we Americans are now living in an actual world in which the problem is real. We are on the edge, and—since these words were first written—over the edge, of the battle. In that situation it does not give us the intellectual help we need to tell us that, in the realm of ideas, a community cannot be a dictatorship. We need to know why, in an actual, present world, dictatorship is detestable and why, as a social alternative, democracy must be maintained. And to those questions Dewey gives no answer. He has a passion for democracy, but no theory of it. The philosophic choice of the values of freedom remains unreasoned, ungrounded.

6

As we look back upon the pragmatic discussion of the "general theory" of education and of society, the conclusion is forced upon us that the ideas of pragmatism are fully as negative as are its war cries. Its fundamental motive is to disprove rather than to prove, to disparage rather than to plan. Running through all Dewey's philosophizing and that of his colleagues is the demand that an old theological absolutism shall be destroyed. That demand is valid. But it is also partial and negative. What struc-

[10] *Ibid.*, p. 148.

ture of belief and planning is to take the place of the old order
in the guidance of human action? To that question pragmatism
has given no answer. It records, with exultant reiteration, the
fact that an old world is dead. But the new world which is to
emerge out of the findings of the sciences is still "powerless to
be born."

This negativism of Dewey's theorizing with respect to the
foundation of education we have found at three points—

First, he gives no clear statement of the way in which "knowledge" may be used to serve the purposes of "intelligence." To
bring that about is the purpose of all intellectualized teaching.
To explain how it may be done is the function of all educational
theorizing. But for many of Dewey's followers this basic problem does not seem to exist. They simply identify "being scientific" with "being wise." They use the words "knowledge" and
"intelligence" interchangeably. And that means that they have
lost sight of the characteristic task of the teacher. They have so
"intellectualized" his problem that it no longer exists.

Second, to a contemporary world which is entrusting its
schools to the control of government, Dewey gives an essentially
invalid theory of political institutions. His state is a medley of
pressure groups with no common, guiding principles of belief
or action, no common devotion to a common welfare. Such a
state cannot possibly teach wisdom. At this point Dewey is
still committed to the chaotic individualism of a disintegrating
Protestant-capitalist culture.

And, third, at a time when we need to understand the "democratic way of life" not only that we may defend it against its
enemies abroad, but also that we may create and sustain it
among ourselves, the pragmatic philosophy would make us as
blind, as dogmatic, as uncritical, as are, in our opinion, the foes
of democracy. It can give no meaning to the words "fair" or
"disinterested" or "objective" or "impartial." Its supposed method
of discriminating criticism does not work.

The basic problem of teaching was stated when we spoke of

a method of thinking which would be able to "criticize" our "unconscious" traditions, habits, customs. Such thinking would distinguish objectively between ignorance and knowledge, between stupidity and intelligence, between prejudice and reasonableness, between a bad social order and a good one, between foolish teaching and wise. But that distinction the pragmatic school is unable to make. We who have lost our theological bearings have not found others to replace them. We who love democracy have not found any "reason" for doing so. Our culture is therefore plunged into confusion and disaster. We shall not find our way up out of the pit into which we have fallen unless our thinking can go farther than pragmatism has gone in defining that "way of intelligence" by following which men may hope to live reasonably and successfully, even though the enterprise must be a precarious and desperate one.

Book IV

THE SOCIAL CONTRACT AS BASIS
OF EDUCATION

Chapter 15. THE DOCTRINE OF BROTHERHOOD

OUR argument comes now to its last step. We have seen a civilization whose beliefs and values had been supported by theology losing those beliefs and values as the strength of theology has dwindled away. Especially in the field of education, we have found that the nature of "critical intelligence," of "objective, disinterested judgment" has lost its grip. And the effect of this disintegration has been to reduce our teaching plans to chaos. Having nothing to teach, we have discussed chiefly methods of teaching it. We have developed an interest theory of education in the sense that, apparently, any "interest" may be taken as the basis of a plan of teaching. Each pupil studies "what he likes." Interests are not criticized because the method of criticism is no longer available.

Now the "vital" question of a modern scientific, nontheological world is this—can we recover the method of criticism; can we give a valid and intelligible and useful meaning to the idea of "intelligence"? To do that would be to construct a "general theory of education." It would, at the same time, give us a general theory of the human society by which education is carried on. It is along that line that our argument must now attempt to make its way.

I

Theological ideas had made intelligence cosmic in origin and importance. For men who believed in God, the universe was an expression of thoughts and purposes because of which the world had been made, for the sake of which it was carried on. But the Darwinian nontheological theory gives to intelligence no such cosmic status. Thinking is, so far as we know, man-made. No other thing, living or nonliving, shares in the conscious attempt to know, to appreciate, to control. The cosmos as a whole, out of which human life emerges, gives no evidence of being, or wishing to be, intelligent. The human spirit is alone in an otherwise nonhuman, nonspiritual universe. Whatever it has, or may ever have, of sensitiveness, of wisdom, of generosity, of freedom, of justice, it has made, it will make, for itself.

Now the transformation of education which is marked by its passing over from the hands of the church into those of the state is a recognition of this revolution. Modern education must teach its pupils to participate, not in an intelligence which makes and controls the universe but in an intelligence which men are inventing as they seek to create meaning and value in an otherwise meaningless world. In that attempt mankind has no backing outside its own ranks. If individuals or groups are to find support, consolation, co-operation, they can find them only by standing together, by uniting with one another. The state, which takes charge of education, can have value and efficacy only as an agency of that attempt at human unity.

If we assume, then, that the assertions, and even the hopes, of theology are gone, that their claim to validity is now negligible, the basic problem of our "modern" society is thrust upon us. Our civilization, our culture in all its variations, our ways of life, all these have been propped up by theological belief. In law, in medicine, in art, in literature, in politics, in science, in morals, in social theory, in education, men have assumed the existence and validity of cosmic principles on the basis of which their work could be, and would be, judged. Though men have striven for human ends, they have done so as servants of God. And now that presupposition is being abandoned. We know no "cosmic" principles of intelligence. We know no "divine" standards or ends. And that fundamental change in belief confronts us with the desperate issue which, at every significant point in our experience, staggers the modern mind. If we can no longer believe in God can we maintain, can we carry on, the civilization which was founded on that belief? Is not civilization itself a veneer, a pretense? The despair which underlies that query has been cutting deep into the foundations of all our institutions. And it still remains to be seen whether that despair can be dispelled, whether confidence can be put in its place, whether, within its own experience, mankind can find a solid basis on which to continue, to enlarge, to enrich its culture.—It is that question which we must answer if we are to have a theory of modern education.

2

The loss of religious faith is, as many of us know, a shattering experience. Individuals have felt in their own lives its bitterness, its disillusionment. And the last three centuries of Protestantism in Europe and America give all too obvious evidence of its destructive, disintegrating consequences for the social order. If one has really believed that the principles of freedom, of justice, of generosity, of sensitiveness, of intelligence are established by God, the loss of the belief that there is a God seems, at first sight, to smash the whole structure of human insight and aspiration.

And, yet, even in the midst of the agony and confusion of the first shock of that experience, one can find evidence that all is not lost. There is, I am sure, a human basis for a new building, for a reconstruction of the old building. Civilization can go on.

In the first place, it requires courage and honesty and love of truth to enable a man to discard a belief upon which his whole pattern of life, as well as that of his community, has been established. To say, "I will not believe beyond the warrant of the evidence which bears upon the question at issue" is to have a principle to whose authority one submits one's thinking. And that principle evidently holds good whether God exists or not.

It is by the authority of that principle that one questions the existence of God. It may be, then, that underlying all our standards of conduct and opinion we can find, in human nature itself, a warrant quite as adequate, more adequate than that which the belief in God had given. There may be human "reasons" for truth and freedom, justice and generosity, which can well replace the divine "reasons" which have previously been given.

And, second, if God does not exist, if the assertions about Him are myths, then the very presence of those myths is a fact of supreme importance for our knowledge of mankind. The Bible, for example, depicts the spiritual life of man as seeking conformity to principles which God has "required of us." But, if God does not exist, who formulated those principles? Who wrote the Bible? It seems clear that God did not do so. Nor did He even "inspire" men to do it. But that implies that the insights, the aspirations of the Bible were created by men, created by their own unaided efforts. The truth is, then, that human prophets have perceived in human nature itself the beauty of holiness, the strength of humility, the magnificence of wisdom. And these qualities seemed to them so great, so significant in their authority over the beliefs and the conduct of men that, without knowing what they were doing, they created the myth of divine origins and divine sanctions. That myth is now fading away. But the human truth to which it gave untenable expression still remains. Courage, beauty, truth, freedom, justice, honesty are still the original facts. The myth was a secondary thing. Its going need not affect the primary values which it was intended to serve. As the sanctions of religion fail us, one consolation is still available. If human values had not been, in and of themselves, good, no sanction by a God could have made them so. Among all the beings whom our imagination might have created no one of them would have been regarded by us as divine unless He had had "reasons" for what He did, what He approved. And when He goes, the "reasons" remain.—Our modern task is to find them, to interpret them, to use them, in their new setting.

3

But the myth which we discard leaves behind it more than consolation. It gives also guidance for study. In the form of religious belief men have thrown upon a cosmic screen their most profound convictions, their deepest insights about themselves. And this means that in the lineaments of the God whom he has imagined, man can discover his own features. If we can know what that God, in the words of theology, has "required of us" then we can know, in modern words, what we require of ourselves. If we can discover why, in our story about Him, He made those requirements, then we can be sure why we should make them, why we have made them.—It will be necessary, as our argument advances, to note the fact that the theological form of statement has distorted and falsified the picture of human nature and human destiny. One cannot use myths as if they were facts without suffering serious consequences of error and illusion. And yet, as the myth is put aside, we can find beneath it the truth from which the myth drew its meaning, its power. What, then, as we look back upon the religious beliefs of our Protestant faith, are the basic ideas and values upon which the structure of our civilization rests? And, especially, what part does intelligence play in that human enterprise which men have described to themselves in mythical terms?

4

In answer to this question I venture two assertions. First, the basic belief of our culture—a belief which our religion has both maintained and concealed—is that men are brothers. Human beings have kinship with one another. And, second, all those activities which we sum up under the term "intelligence" are expressions of that kinship, rest upon it as a final fact.—In the meaning of those two statements is to be found, I believe, all that we have available for the making of a general theory of education.

When we say that men are brothers we are saying that, both morally and intellectually, they are engaged in a common enterprise. That enterprise determines what are, and what should be, their relations to one another. It prescribes both their modes of conduct and their modes of thought. When we have said, in the past, that God created men in His own image, that He cared for them, and that they, therefore, should care for one another, what we were really saying was that human insight has disclosed life to be such that it cannot be lived rightly or intelligently unless men deal with one another as if they were brothers. We were, in that imaginative picture, laying down the fundamental principles of an organized society. Those principles were, of course, only vaguely and inaccurately seen. By differing creeds and sects they were conceived in multitudes of varying ways. And yet, running through all these aberrations we can find a constant clue to guide us in our study. The dogma of the fatherhood of God, which we ourselves created, which, for many centuries, we have maintained, to which, in words at least, we still appeal when basic issues are at stake—that dogma tells us that the men and women of our culture have found the fundamental moral and intellectual fact of human living to be the brotherhood of man. It suggests that, for human aspiration and purpose, and intelligence, if not yet for human achievement, mankind is a fellowship.

5

Is the brotherhood of man a fact? Can we justify its assertion by objective, impartial, secular evidence? The answer to that question is decisive for all educational theory. What we shall teach depends upon our view of the relations of men to one another. And especially are the relations between intelligence and brotherhood significant for any study of education. What kind of intelligence do we wish to inculcate? Is it the friendly wisdom of persons who are co-operating in a common cause? Or is it the cleverness and calculating self-interest of individuals, each of whom is, in the last resort, seeking his own advantage? As we proceed now to face this fundamental question of teaching theory, three preliminary observations must be made.

First, the intimations which are taken over from the "unconscious wisdom of the race" must not be blindly accepted as valid. The notion that humanity is, or should be, a brotherhood must not be allowed to become an uncriticized dogma. It must be dealt with as an hypothesis. As such it may be used to direct investigation with respect to its own validity. It may serve as a focus of relevance around which we can gather information. But the use made of that information must be a testing of the hypothesis itself and, in case it prove unsatisfactory, a finding of another and better one to take its place. The idea that the relations of men to each other and to their surrounding world are such that mankind can be accurately and fruitfully interpreted as a fellowship, is open to sober and detailed verification or refutation by our studies of society. Such studies are too important to be made carelessly. Their findings are basic for the planning of education. We dare not use them unless they are solid and substantial. We must not treat men as brothers unless we "know" that they are brothers.

Second, the idea of a human fellowship, as it passes over from divine to human status, is, of necessity, changed in meaning. At one essential point, this change is very important for education. The religious belief which thought of the human community as established by God, regarded it as already existing, as having existed from the foundation of the world. It was, of course, recognized that men had, in many respects, failed in their responsibility for the fulfilling of the Divine purpose. As in Locke's State of Nature, though men had "rights," they did not always get them. And yet the cosmic fact could still be asserted. God had made men brothers. He had created the human community. Men might ignore the fact, but they could not deny it. It was there, in the nature of things, setting up eternal standards by which the conduct of men would be judged. But the community which human beings themselves are making has no such "prior" existence as this. It exists only in so far as men bring it into being. Men are brothers only as they become so by their own moral and intellectual achievements. The life of fellowship is an ideal, a goal, toward which men may strive. It is an end which, through human wisdom and virtue, may be attained but which also, through human ignorance or wickedness, may, in greater or lesser degree, be lost. And, in the same way, the intelligence of men, when seen as participating in this enterprise, is not the perfect wisdom of God. It is the growing, and not-growing, insight which, by countless ages of searching and striving, men have won for the enriching of their lives, the guiding of their actions.

But, third, it is essential that we note with what intensity of emphasis the religious mind has asserted the authority of the idea of brotherhood. Men have found, in their long experience, a distinction between what they "ought" to do and what they "wish" to do. They have found the claims of justice, freedom, beauty, significance, at war with the demands of immediate desire, immediate impulse for individual satisfaction. And the authority of the ideal, the superindividual, claims has seemed to them so ultimate, so essential that they have projected it upon the very nature of the cosmos itself. As contrasted with "inclination" they have made "obligation" nonhuman, superhuman, divine.

Now, in that form, the distinction can no longer be maintained. All authority over human conduct or belief is human authority. There is no court of judgment beyond ourselves to which appeal can be made for the controlling of our lives. And yet, the traditional imputation of that judgment to the universe as such may suggest to us how deeply significant our unconscious wisdom has felt it to be. Man has found within himself something so sublime, so authoritative in its sublimity, that he has described it as other than, higher than, himself. To follow, from afar, that higher wisdom and virtue has been the supreme law of life. To turn aside from it, to follow one's own individual way, has been the essential human failure. The soul which has thus failed in its love of God has been doomed to eternal damnation. The term "atheist" has, in general, carried with it the stigma of being alien to humanity, of being cut off from the springs of spiritual insight and power. The brotherhood of man, as expressed by the acknowledgment of a common sonship to God, has thus been accepted as the basic presupposition of all our human striving for beauty and goodness and truth. It is that basic presupposition which remains, for our assessment, even when the earlier form of its expression has vanished away.

6

Here, then, is the problem which a departing religion leaves behind it for a Darwinian study of men. Is mankind a fellowship? Are all men brothers? Are we all members of a single family, tied together by the bonds of common purpose, of mutual understanding?

The obtrusive facts of a contemporary world would seem to make that suggestion ridiculous. Men hate. They fight. They misunderstand. They take what they can get. They are alien and unknown to one another. They live in groups which have no effective contacts of sympathy or understanding. How, then, can they be regarded as members of "a single family"?

The facts here cited are obvious enough. But the inference which is suggested does not follow. We are dealing here with conscious human purposes, not with unconscious, nonhuman, happenings. And in the realm of purposes both facts and the principles by which we interpret them take on a peculiar character. The conscious choices by which men control their desires are facts, but they are not mere facts, in the sense of meaningless events. They are facts of value. A choice does not merely happen. It should, or should not, have happened. It is wise or unwise, right or wrong, worthy of approval or of disapproval. And it is this "right or wrong" aspect of human behavior which is before our minds when we speak of men as forming, or failing to form, a fellowship. It is not possible to prove that men are not brothers by showing that they hate each other. They may be bad brothers. What is implied by their fraternal relationship is not that they "do" care for each other but that they "should" care for each other. Their hatred is a human failure. The principles which, from this point of view, explain human choice do not tell us what men always choose. They give or try to give standards of judgment by which we may determine whether any specific choice is right or wrong in the situation in which it occurs. And from this it follows that we can think of men as belonging to the same brotherhood, even though they hate each other, provided we can also say that their hatred is wrong, that they are not dealing with one another as members of the same community should deal with one another. In a word, the essential feature of the life of fellowship is the presence of principles in accordance with which judgments of approval and disapproval can be made. Ignorance of one's fellows does not disprove the fellowship relation, if that ignorance can be judged to be a misfortune. War does not constitute a denial of human brotherhood if we can say that war is a crime. It is taken for granted when the principles of community life are formulated that specific human actions will both conform and fail to conform to their authority. But the basic "fellowship" fact is the presence of that authority. Men cannot fail, unless there is a goal which they fail to reach. They cannot violate principles unless there are principles to violate. And it is those value principles which constitute community life. To belong to a brotherhood is to have one's conduct open to censure and approval.

What has been said in this chapter can be justified only if we

sharply separate the "laws of society" from the "laws of nature."
A law of nature is intended to be a generalized statement of fact.
It says, "Under these conditions, this happens." And the statement, so far as it is true, has no exceptions. It means "always."
But the laws of society, though equally universal, take for
granted their own infractions. When we say, "Men should not
lie," we do not mean that they never "do" lie. We mean that
they never "should" lie. As matter of fact the prohibition
assumes the existence of the offense. It tells us to stop doing
what we are doing. And, as we all know, such prohibitions are
only partially effective. So long as men are men the law will be
needed because, presumably, so long as men are men, lying will
go on. But, nevertheless, the law, if valid, does reveal a fact. It
tells us, at one point, about the society in which the law holds
good. It is a society which prescribes that the truth shall be told.

Now it is prescriptions such as this which furnish the principles underlying education. If we can say, "Men should not do
this: they ought to be that," then the guiding goals of teaching
can be seen. The society for which we teach, in some sense approves actions which it does not fully practice. It both makes
laws and breaks them. And to say that is to say that it has
measures, standards, by which it appraises its own behavior and
that of its members. Those measures and standards are the bases
of educational theory and practice. When they are fully understood they take the form of that "conscious criterion" for which
our argument is seeking. And the suggestion which this chapter
has found in the religious beliefs and attitudes of our civilization
is that our working criterion, both in the moral and the intellectual field, is involved in the notion of human brotherhood. It
is that notion which ultimately tells us both what and how to
teach. It defines the work of intelligence. If we find that notion
to be "justified," then we can assert that our schools and colleges have a goal toward which their activities may be directed,
in relation to which their teaching may be criticized. It will tell
us what "criticism" is.

Chapter 16. THE CUE FROM ROUSSEAU

EARLY in this book it was decided that, when we should try to suggest a positive theory of education, we would take our cue from Rousseau. It is now time to put that decision into effect. We must follow the path which he began to blaze through the tangle of Protestant-capitalist individualism.

The peculiar significance of Rousseau for our Western culture lies in the fact that he leads the way in the substitution of the state for the church as the primary institution of human brotherhood. The belief in fellowship which had formerly been expressed in religious terms he now expresses in terms of politics. As the church loses its grip on the essential principles of human society and human education, Rousseau so describes the state as to qualify it for taking the empty place. The state is, for him, the agency of fellowship. It is, therefore, the source of all morality. And, for the same reason, it is the source of intelligence. Political institutions, as he sees them, are the deliberate attempt of human beings to live together in that friendship which only mutual understanding can give.

If Rousseau is right, we can answer with a strong affirmative the question with which our argument started—can a state teach? Schools and colleges can be, and should be, conducted by governments. But is he right? To minds steeped in Anglo-American competitive individualism, he seems not only wrong but also absurd. And yet I am sure that he is right. If we wish to see clearly those principles of morality and intelligence upon which all theories of education must rest, there is, I am sure, no better line of approach than that which appears if one follows with careful and sympathetic study the attempt of Rousseau to understand that human institution which we call "the state."

I

There are two conflicting types of political theory. On the
one hand is the "organic" theory which Rousseau represents.
Opposing it are "disorganic" theories, such as those of Locke
and Dewey. Organic theories explain social action in terms of a
striving for order and coherence. This does not mean that they
find San Francisco or Peru or Cook County to be a well-
organized and unitary enterprise. It means only that, in the
midst of a vast multiplicity of interests and influences, these
human groups have the task of creating unity of idea and purpose. In so far as they are reasonable that is what they accomplish. Disorganic theories, on the other hand, explain societies
in terms of multiplicity. They find them to be external colloca-
tions of individuals and groups. Each of these has its own purpose or purposes. But the collocation, as a whole, has no purpose.
The relations within it are mechanical rather than organic. They
are relations of power or of force. This is the "pressure-group"
theory of society. Its abstractions ignore the morality and the
intelligence which Rousseau sees as the primary characteristics
of a political society.

The pressure-group explanation is applied by contemporary
thinking both to societies and to individuals. In the social field
it takes the form of what may be called "the sociologist's fallacy."
It lists all human groupings as on the same level—the level of
coincidence or of conflict of interest. It discovers and classifies
churches, governments, mills, schools, golf clubs, homes, labor
unions, and the like. It finds each of these animated by some
driving force. Each has effects on the others and is affected by
them. And, that being true, the life of a society is seen as an
increasing struggle for power. It is that struggle upon which the
disorganic sociologist fixes his attention. As he views his collocation of externally related individuals and groups he follows their
coincidences and clashings. His only intelligible question is,

"How are the pressures working out?" In his vocabulary the word "ought" does not appear. He is not concerned with problems of morality and intelligence. He is a scientist. And, as such, he does not "judge" facts. He simply records and predicts them. As a seeker for knowledge he has nothing to do with wisdom.

The same disorganic attitude is adopted also in the description of individual behavior. Here it might be called "the psychologist's fallacy." The experiences of a single individual are given the same pressure-group explanation as are those of the society to which he belongs. Scientific inquiry discovers in human activity certain "drives" which it lists and classifies. Living is then described and interpreted as the interplay of those drives. As these are seen to wax and wane, to block and supplement each other, to win or lose mastery over that battlefield which is the human being, the story of a man's life is told.

Now the organic theory, either of the individual or of society, does not reject these "collocation" pictures of human behavior and its drives. It does not ignore the pressures of interest and of influence. No one in his senses can doubt that human activities are multifarious and conflicting. And yet, even for purposes of description, the disorganic theory misses the essential point. The figure of speech which regards a person or a society merely as a battlefield upon which active forces wage their conflicts is peculiarly abstract and partial. It belies and misconstrues that moral and intellectual activity with which education is chiefly concerned. Organic life organizes its drives. Consciously or unconsciously, it attempts to bring them into right relations with one another. Both individuals and societies are, in that sense, intelligent. And if we call intelligence itself a drive, it is not correlative with the other drives. It is not related to them as they are related to each other. It is a relation among them which the organism is attempting to establish. It adjusts them, judges them, organizes them. It does not claim to be stronger in pressure than they are. It claims to be superior in wisdom. Its words are "wise" and "foolish," or "ought to be" and "ought not to be." It plans and reasons.

If then we interpret Rousseau as saying that a society becomes a state in so far as it plans and reasons as a whole, in so far as it seeks to be intelligent in corporate action, the essential difference between his organic view and the disorganic view of Locke and Dewey becomes clear and explicit. Both types of theory are explaining "public" activities. But Locke and Dewey give to those public activities a secondary, derivate, and even accidental status by deriving them from "private" activities. For both of them it is "private" concerns which are primary. Rousseau, on the other hand, gives to public action a public explanation. For him the state is accounted for in its own field. Its roots are to be found in the sympathy and solidarity which are common to all individuals and to all groups. For Locke and Dewey government is the outgrowth of the multiplicities of self-interest. For Rousseau it springs from the unity of generosity and mutual understanding. For Locke and Dewey, political institutions are "interested." For Rousseau, they are "disinterested."

The significance of the opposition between the organic and the disorganic theories of society is nowhere more clearly seen than in the field of teaching. If a society is simply a collocation of separate individuals then the purpose of education must be stated in individualistic terms. The pupil must be taught to "live his own life" as a separate person. As we saw in Locke's *Thoughts Concerning Education*, the tutor has, then, two tasks. He must equip his student, first, for the saving of his own soul and, second, for the making of his own career. But, if we accept the organic theory, then a pupil should be taught, not as an isolated individual, but as a member of a fellowship, a state. He should learn to be sensitive, generous, intelligent, active, in his relations with his fellows. He will find his life, not by being apart from them, but by being one with them. If Rousseau is right, the state can teach. If Locke is right, the word "teach" has no reasonable meaning. What, then, is Rousseau's theory of human society?

2

Rousseau's analysis of the state as an agency of general intel-ligence is very incomplete. He was not a technical logician. He speaks much more easily about a general will than about a general mind. He himself was keenly aware of the inadequacy of his own work. The *Social Contract*, he tells us, was only a partial answer to a wider problem about which he had been puzzling for some twenty-two years before 1762. That answer left much to be done, much which has not yet been done. And still, he does go to the heart of the problem. He has an amazing capacity for defining an issue, for sensing an opposition.

The *Social Contract* offers two quite different descriptions of the political relationship between individuals and their state. As we try to follow our "cue" it will be necessary to see how those two descriptions correct and supplement each other.

In his first statement Rousseau tells us that, in so far as a state is constituted, its individual members give over to it all that they are, all that they have, whether of rights or of possessions, and that the state uses these for the good of all. The second state-ment says that individual men have neither rights nor possessions to give, except as these are bestowed upon them by the state.— If we can see, through the seeming contradictoriness of those two formulas, their identity of meaning we shall find a theory on which both modern society and modern education might be organized. We shall find, in human brotherhood, the social "cri-terion" which Dewey failed to give.

3

The first formula appears in the famous statement of the prob-lem of making a political society and the equally thrilling solu-tion of that problem. Rousseau faces squarely the paradox which has tormented political theory throughout the course of modern

Protestant-capitalism. How shall we combine the freedom of the individual with the authority, the organic unity, of the state? How shall we say that each citizen "owns by right" his own property and also that the state "owns by right" the property of all?

"The problem is," Rousseau tells us, in words already quoted, "to find a form of association which will defend and protect with the whole common force the person and goods of each associate and in which each, while uniting himself with all, may still obey himself alone, and remain as free as before?" The "whole common force" is to be in the hands of the state. But each individual is to be free. He is to "obey himself alone." To the problem of making that seemingly impossible combination, "the Social Contract finds a solution." It reads as follows: "Each of us puts his person and all his possessions in common under the supreme direction of the general will, and, in our corporate capacity, we receive each member as an indivisible[1] part of the whole."[2]—It is those two statements, giving the political problem and its political answer, which establish Rousseau as the first of the "moderns." He succeeds, or at least he points the way toward success, in formulating in secular terms the political relationship which, in the medieval era, had been defined by religion and theology. And the striking fact is that the meaning which that theology tried to express remains unchanged. The "Christian" tradition is maintained. The structure of civilization which that tradition had supported, still stands. "Whosoever will lose his life for my sake shall find it" was the old doctrine. It is now replaced by the assertion that each of us, in a well-organized society, yields to the state all that he is, all that he has, and that, in doing so, each of us becomes a free person. We give ourselves and our possessions "without reserve." And thereby we find our own persons, our own rights and goods, protected by the full force of the community. And, further, as

[1] This word should be, I think, "inseparable."
[2] Everyman's, 660, p. 15.

we share in the common will, the common devotion to the common welfare, each of us finds himself "obeying himself alone, and thus as free as he was before."[3]

Is that a valid account of the political relationship? The best way to test it is to confront it with such an explicit, conscious attitude as is taken by our people whenever the Constitution of the United States is accepted as the supreme law of the land. The Preamble to the Constitution reads, "We, the people of the United States, in order to form a more perfect union, estab- lish justice, insure domestic tranquillity, provide for the common defense, promote the general welfare, and secure the blessings of liberty to ourselves and our posterity, do ordain and establish this Constitution for the United States of America."—Does Rousseau express the meaning, the intention of that action? It seems to me that he does. By the adoption of the Constitution, every man who becomes a citizen of our government, agrees that he himself, his family, his possessions, his rights, shall be placed within the legal jurisdiction under the political authority, of the nation. And, further, he expects that, through that common agreement—and only through such an agreement—he and his fellows will win practical security and spiritual freedom. They will become free members of a self-governing society.

But there is a fighting point in this interpretation of the rela- tion between a state and its members. The fight rages round the use of the word "all" when the yielding up of possessions and rights is spoken of. Surely, we are told, some rights of person and of property are "reserved" by the individuals who enter the social contract. For example, the government, it is said, is for- bidden to interfere with the "free enterprise" of its businessmen. It is likewise forbidden to interfere with individual freedom of religion, of speech, of press, of assembly, and the like. How are these "reservations," these limitations of the action of govern- ment, to be reconciled with the sweeping declaration that, in so far as a state exists, all individual goods, all individual rights, all

[3] Rousseau should have said "free as he was not before."

individuals themselves, are surrendered to it, that there takes place, as Rousseau says, "the total alienation of each associate, together with all his rights, to the community"? The point at issue here is difficult and dialectical. And the difficulties have been sadly aggravated by the Lockian terminology in which our political fundamentals have been formulated. And yet, when the issue is clearly stated, there can be no doubt that Rousseau is right. Reservations, and limitations upon the action of government are not made by the individuals concerned. They are made by the government itself. Our Bill of Rights is a series of governmental enactments. It records the decisions of a body politic. It is a public, not a private, document. Its validity and authority are to be found, not in the separate demands of independent individuals, each fighting for his own rights and interests, but in the concerted wisdom and action of a political community.

The illusion which the Lockian system of politics has tended to fix upon the American mind is that the state is the enemy óf freedom. Liberty is taken to be only an individual matter. Governments, local and national, are said to have no concern with free enterprise, free speech, free press. On the contrary, these values are always to be defended by the individual from a state which is, as such, hostile to them. Freedom, for this view, is freedom "from" government. Is that the American theory? Certainly it is not. Our Constitution was adopted to "ensure the blessings of liberty to ourselves and our posterity"—not to destroy those blessings. When Jefferson and his colleagues insisted upon the adoption of the Bill of Rights they were not saying that the government of the United States has no concern with, no jurisdiction over, the intellectual and spiritual freedom of its people. They were demanding that the Constitution should express, in explicit, legal terms, the determination of that government to protect and cultivate the freedom of its citizens. They were not making the Lockian statement that individual freedom is an individual matter, to be cared for by the individual himself, and by him alone. They were expressing the passionate conviction of Rousseau that the primary business of a government is to see to it that its people are free. They did not mean that there should be no public provision for freedom. Rather they meant that the government should, in every way possible, protect and develop the independence of its citizens. The government, by its own action, forbade itself to "interfere" with speech and press. But, by the same motive, it went further than this. It undertook to see to it that no private individuals, no private groups, should interfere with these freedoms. But, even more than this, our governments have entered upon a positive program for the creation of intellectual freedom among their citizens. They have taken it as a primary task to establish an educational system which will create and develop in the community a freedom of mind to animate both speech and press and thus to make them free. The government not only defends freedom. It also creates it. To say, then, that the "reservations" of the Constitution mean that the government, as such, has no responsibility for, no jurisdiction over free enterprise, free speech, free press, is plain, unadulterated nonsense. The purpose of the Constitution, clearly stated in its Preamble, is "to secure the blessings of liberty to ourselves and to our posterity." American government has recognized the fact that individual freedom cannot be cared for by individuals themselves. It can be cared for only by the establishing and maintaining of a state. Into the jurisdiction of that state are taken all human rights, all human possessions, to be dealt with, in the interest of the common welfare, as that community, in its political capacity, may deem best. The state is not lacking in concern for freedom. It is justified to itself and to its citizens only as freedom is, by it, created and maintained.

4

It is, however, Rousseau's second formula which goes deeper into the presuppositions of a political society and which, therefore, brings us nearer to the basic principles of a system of education. The first statement had said that, when men form a state, they give everything into its hands. The second statement corrects this by saying that men have nothing to give, except as the state has already given it to them. Men have no rights: they have no property: they are not men, except as they are citizens of a politically organized community. That assertion seems to me to go to the very roots of a public system of education. If it is true, then we may be able to see how a government can plan and administer a teaching enterprise suitable to the life of a democratic community. The agency which creates the community may well undertake to teach what it is and does. The agency which is human reason in action may teach its members how to live reasonably.

We have already spoken briefly of the amazing Chapter VIII of the first book of the *Social Contract*. In that chapter Rousseau contrasts the nature and the life of man, as he would be, if there were no political institutions, with what man is and does in a politically organized society. If we imagine a group of men to pass over from the "state of nature" into a "civil state," Rousseau lists the changes which would take place in their behavior and condition. Justice, formerly unheard of, now comes into being. It replaces instinct, and thus morality, which before was inconceivable, is created. Beings who formerly were dominated by physical impulse and appetite are now "challenged" by "the voice of duty." Man "consults his reason" instead of merely "listening to his inclinations." The license of "natural liberty" is lost. But, in its place, men gain the order of "civil liberty." As a substitute for the "possession of goods," which are gained and held only "by force" or by "the right of the first occupier," the citizens of a civil state are guaranteed "proprietorship," founded on "a positive title." From control by the impulses of appetite, which is slavery, men rise to that obedience to law which is "moral liberty," the liberty which, by mutual agreement, we create for ourselves. In a word, "Although in this state, he deprives himself of some advantages he got from nature, he gains in return others so great, his faculties are so stimulated and developed, his ideas so extended, his feelings so ennobled, and his whole soul so uplifted, that, did not the abuses of this new condition often degrade him below that which he left, he would be bound to bless continually the happy moment which took him from it forever, and, instead of a stupid and unimaginative animal, made him an intelligent being and a man."[4]

It would take many volumes to develop the political, social, moral, and intellectual implications of those statements. That larger task we must pass by. But the fundamental implications for education are clear and inescapable. Rousseau says, first, that the institutions of property, of morality, of law, of justice, of freedom, of duty, of intelligence, of reason, with which teaching is concerned, are not "natural" in the Lockian sense. They are not conferred upon individual men in the "state of nature" by divine gift or decree. On the contrary, they are human conventions, human inventions. They grow with human society. Their growth is the growth of human society, or rather, of human societies. Right and wrong, good and bad, true and false, in all their forms and meanings are "conventional." They are made and remade as organized groups of human beings fashion and refashion their relations, one to another.

But Rousseau goes even further than this. The human conventions which establish the distinction between good and bad, true and false, mine and thine, just and unjust, are not merely social. They are also political. A group which constructs its life on the basis of those distinctions becomes not merely a community. It becomes also a state. The common life expresses an identity of purpose, a general will. And it is that organizing, reasoning, legislating, administrating will which marks the difference between a mechanical collocation of individuals and

---

[4] Everyman's, 660, pp. 18-19. That single sentence would seem to be a sufficient answer to those who interpret Rousseau's admiration of the "noble savage" as expressing a desire for a return to the "state of nature."

groups and that ordered, moralized, intellectualized, civilized fellowship which Rousseau speaks of as "the state."

5

Rousseau's theory of the relation between the state and its individual members seems to me valid. So far as I can see, it furnishes the only solid intellectual basis for a plan of democratic education. And yet, however strongly one believes them, it would be folly to ignore the fact that, to Anglo-Saxon ears, Rousseau's words sound absurd and even detestable. We have seen that Rousseau was "detested" by his contemporaries. And he is still detested. Protestants and capitalists find him, not only exasperating but also incomprehensible. What can a man mean who says that all that I have, all that I am, belongs to the state, that it is entrusted to me only so far as that higher authority may deem best for the good of all concerned?

This charge against Rousseau may be summed up in a single phrase. We individualistic democrats would call him a "Nazi." We would accuse him of "totalitarianism." And having thus overwhelmed him with our current undefined epithets, we would regard him as disposed of. But the truth is that Rousseau's democracy is so clear and unequivocal as to put our own to shame. No writer in European history is more bitterly opposed to tyranny, to despotism, in any form. The two goals by which every action of his "state" is judged are the freedom and equality of its individual citizens. For him the state and the citizen are not enemies. The state exists "to ensure the blessings of liberty to ourselves and to our posterity." It is nothing else than the concerted endeavor of all the people to accomplish that purpose. But we Protestant-capitalists are so obsessed by the fear of our own action as a unified people that even a mention of the common authority throws us into a terror which is both morbid and hysterical. We insist on license and call it freedom. And thus it has come about that, by a mental process which only a fundamental psychoanalysis could explain, we have avoided even the coining of a word which, in common usage, could express Rousseau's meaning. His "state" is not our "government." Nor is it "the community." What, then, shall we call that social institution to which we have given the responsibility of teaching but which we still regard with enmity and fear?

That Rousseau does not mean by "the state" what we mean by "the government" is clearly indicated by his classification of laws. His state is both moral and political. Governments, he tells us, make, for the state, three kinds of laws,—the basic, the civil, and the criminal. But the state has, in addition to these, a fourth class of laws, which are described as follows:

Along with these three kinds of law goes a fourth, most important of all, which is not graven on tablets of marble or brass, but on the hearts of the citizens. This forms the real constitution of the State; takes on every day new powers; when other laws decay or die out restores them or takes their place; keeps a people in the way it was meant to go; and insensibly replaces authority by the force of habit. I am speaking of morality, of custom, above all, of public opinion, a power unknown to political thinkers, on which none the less success in everything else depends. With this the great legislator concerns himself in secret, though he seems to confine himself to particular regulations; for these are only the arc of the arch, while manners and morals, slower to arise, form in the end its immovable keystone.[5]

The writer of those words was not blind to the distinction between morality and legislation. But he was irrevocably opposed to that separation of them into two independent regions which our Puritan individualism has established. For him laws are concerned with justice. And justice, in order to be effective, finds expression in laws. Morality is, for politics, "the immovable keystone of the arch." It is "the real constitution of the State." We who sunder the dictates of private conscience from the statutes enacted by a public will seem to him to have broken in

[5] Everyman's, 660, p. 48.

two the organic unity of human experience. He will have nothing to do with the moral duplicity of the Anglo-Saxon mind which that dualism has rendered both possible and inevitable. For Rousseau "the government" is not "the state." It is an agency of the state. The state is not "the party in power." It is all parties, whether in power or not. It is the whole body of the people. And government is the institutional servant of those moral and intellectual purposes which every genuine state finds "graven on the hearts of its citizens."

And, second, Rousseau's "state" differs from "the community." The two are equal in quantitative scope. Both include all the people. But the term "community" as we use it is affected by "the sociologist's fallacy." It is a mere collocation of individuals and groups. It has no life, no activity, as a unified whole. The state, on the other hand, is the whole body of the people, consciously or unconsciously taking direction over its own activities and those of its members. The state is "the people" *in action.* Whether it be in the form of traditional taboo, of accepted custom, of judicial decision, of administrative action, of formulated law, a state emerges whenever a local group assumes and exercises authority over itself. It establishes manners and customs. It builds roads, parks, hospitals, museums. It enacts statutes and enforces them. It issues currency. It makes war and peace. It sets up relations of collective bargaining between capital and labor. It conducts education. In all these, as in a multitude of other ways, the people, as "a state," are expressing and making effective a general will toward the general welfare. In a word, then, a community becomes a state in so far as it acts as a unified whole.

And, finally, though we have no single word which equals Rousseau's "the state," the Preamble to the Constitution of the United States provides a phrase which meets the need. In fact that Preamble as a whole might have been written by Rousseau. It speaks his mind both in its intentions and its way of realizing those intentions. The phrase "We, the people of the United

States" denotes the state, as Rousseau uses the term. It includes all the people. But it recognizes them as one unit, taking thought, taking action, toward a common end. "We, the people . . . do ordain and establish this Constitution." A state is a community which has become a sovereign people, governing itself.

Chapter 17. REASONABLENESS IS REASONABLE

WE HAVE been saying that the driving force of human civilization is the search for brotherhood. Men create a just and well-ordered society only as they recognize and deal with one another as fellows in a common cause.

But it is equally true that the aim of civilization is directed toward intelligence. When men seek for friendship they are thereby seeking for reasonableness. As a social contract is established it is agreed that conduct shall, as we say, be controlled "in accordance with principles." License gives way to law. Action upon caprice is replaced by action subject to reason.—We must now try to understand the assertion that friendship and reasonableness are two sides of the same human attempt to be civilized.

I

The demand that human behavior be reasonable goes down to the very foundations of Western culture. Throughout its career, that culture has drawn a contrast between "the appeal to reason" and "the resort to violence." Human beings, we have said, should learn to "reason together" about differences of opinion or of interest. They should not leave the settlement of problems to brutal, unscrupulous, irrational strife, which "proves" nothing. They should become civilized, that is, so related to each other that their thinking is a concerted attempt to reach common answers to common problems. They should practice a friendliness of the mind. Violence, we have said, is savagery. Civilization is reasonableness.

The depth of our commitment to this distinction is to be seen in our popular formulation of the issue between "dictatorship" and "democracy" in the present world conflict. The dictators, we like to say, are bent on destroying Western culture. We, on the other hand, seek to "preserve" it. We "appeal to reason." They "resort to violence." If we fight it is only because they have driven us into a corner from which no escape is possible except by fighting. But our basic purpose is to restore reasonableness to its proper place of control. As reasonable men we want a world from which fighting has been abolished.

These are brave words with which to stir men to defense of honor and country. And yet there is serious question whether we ourselves mean what we say. So strongly has our Protestant-capitalist civilization been affected by the "pressure-group" theory of human relations that a contemporary Anglo-Saxon world is no longer sure that there is an essential difference between reasoning and fighting. We can feel that difference in our blood. As I write these words on December 8, 1941, the American people is thrilling with passionate and instinctive condemnation of the "infamy" of the Japanese treachery at Pearl Harbor. But it has become exceedingly difficult for us to think the difference with our minds, to express it in the form of ideas. As one runs through the intellectual history of the Protestant-capitalist world nothing seems more obvious than that the principle of "the appeal to reason" has become vague, ambiguous, and even unavailable.

2

In our early chapters we spoke of Protestant culture as disintegrating. The basic beliefs and values which Comenius had accepted with simple faith were being sapped by the worldly wisdom for which John Locke spoke. In the despairing words of Matthew Arnold we were told how, in the strife of the "watchful jealousies" of the Protestant sects, "right reason" had been destroyed. And on the political and economic side, a like catastrophe had fallen upon the mind of England and America.

For purposes of business, men had devised a phrase which for sheer deceptive deviltry surpasses all other devices by which the human mind had ever led itself astray—the idea of "intelligent self-interest." That phrase can justify any crime. It can sanctify any sin. It can make respectable any disregard for the general welfare. The phrase is fruitful in all the bargaining tricks of self-deception and hypocrisy. A culture which prizes honesty because "honesty is the best policy" is not honest. It is shrewd. And shrewdness is violence become crafty. If we say that men "seeking their own advantage" are "led by an invisible hand" to promote the welfare of others which, however, "was no part of their intention," we are explaining human helpfulness in terms of human selfishness. Virtues are thus deduced from vices. Fairness has become a weapon which contending passions may use as they seek "to exhibit themselves as reasonable persuasions." And the distinction between reason and violence is gone. The civilizing of man is now seen to have been simply the taking on of a veneer. Laws, principles, rights, obligations— these are merely covers for the brutal fact of individual aggression. One need only scratch the skin of the saint to find beneath it the avid, craving flesh of what Huxley has called "the ape and the tiger" in mankind.

3

The question of the relation between the "appeal to reason" and the "resort to violence" is, I think, the most crucial political issue facing our contemporary culture. It would be madness to fight a succession of world wars in defense of reason against violence if the two are one. Do we still hold to the essential opposition between these two forms of behavior? Or have we, with our genius for compromise succeeded in amalgamating reason and violence, intelligence and self-interest? That achievement would reconcile God and the Devil. It would solve our problems by abolishing our scruples. Is that what we have done?

For the sake of our understanding of society and of education, no question is more urgent than that. Do we plan and teach for war or for peace—or are the two identical?

The issue of which we are speaking comes to focus in the opposition between the organic and disorganic theories of the state. Both theories ordinarily accept the notion of a social contract. But they give it sharply antagonistic meanings. For one of them, a contract is a bargain. For the other it is an agreement. And, for moral and intellectual purposes, this difference between bargains and agreements is as decisive as any human difference can be.

When men bargain they are traders. When men agree, they are friends. Bargainers, as such, do not "care for" each other. They use each other for profit. Each is seeking to advance his own interests. Each is calculating what he can afford to give up in order that he may get from the other something else which is more desirable. Each is asking, "What is there in it for me?" Bargainers are self-interested.

One of the best illustrations of bargaining as against agreeing is found in contemporary relations between capital and labor. Workers have at last learned from their employers the technique of trading. They have discovered how to mass their forces, how to take advantage of the weakness of their adversaries. They now know how to fight the devil with his own weapons. This is what we call "collective bargaining."

Now in this situation we commonly say that both sides should be "reasonable." What does that mean? In a competitive world it is taken to mean that the two sides should "get together round a table." They should "talk it over" rather than "fight it out." But nothing is more clear than that, in this case, talking is fighting. As they sit at the table, each side is exploring the strength and the weakness of the other. Each is asking, "At what point can I bring pressure to bear on him? How much can he stand? How much can I stand?" The motives which are at work in such conferences as this will come to light if the question be asked—as I have known it to be asked by employer of laborer, "How long will you keep this contract if we make it?" To that question only one bargaining answer is possible—the answer which was given in the case in question. "We will keep the bargain just as long as you would keep it in the same circumstances. We will keep it so long as it serves our interest. Then we will break it, just as you would break it, just as you have done." Bargainers do not agree. They fight, with their wits.

But the central contention of the organic theory is that human peace and understanding, human reasonableness and government, cannot be made out of bargains. They can be made only by agreements. The social contract expresses, not selfishness but sympathy, not hostility but friendship. It is a co-operative attempt to achieve a common purpose. And the disintegration which has come upon our Protestant-capitalist civilization is seen in the substitution which we have made of "bargains" for "agreements," in our descriptions of the social relations of men. That is what is meant when other peoples say that England and America are "nations of shopkeepers." We Anglo-Saxons have made bargains with God and bargains with men. So long as the external bargain with God was enforced by His punishments and rewards, it served as a controlling influence for the making and keeping of human bargains. Men could be counted on to be righteous so long as righteousness "paid." But with the slackening of the belief in God, economic and social arrangements are left with no effective support whatever. Men are traders. Their wisdom is "business" wisdom. And the organic theory says that to try to make a human society out of such wisdom is to weave ropes out of sand. It has no reasonableness in it, no disinterestedness, no friendship.

4

But the disintegration of "the appeal to reason" has gone beyond the unconscious duplicities of the business mind. It is now formulated as an explicit philosophical doctrine. Reason itself, we are commonly told, is unreasonable. The suggestion tentatively held, but also rejected, by Dewey, that reasoning about matters of conduct is only the rationalizing of our feelings is now clearly stated and strongly advocated.[1] If it is true, then the traditional foundations of our culture have been swept away.

The doctrine which thus discredits the appeal to reason is usually stated in terms of a contrast between the "method of knowledge" and "the method of intelligence." We are told that in thinking about matters of conduct one cannot maintain the impartiality, the objectivity, which are taken for granted when scientists investigate matters of fact. Relatively speaking, the attempt to "know facts" is disinterested. But the "assessment of values" is, of necessity, a private affair. It is self-interested.

The explanation of this difference between knowledge and intelligence is found in the assertion that scientists can "pool their facts," while seekers for wisdom are always dealing each with his own distinct set of facts. When scientists study it is understood that their data are common property. Information gained by any one of them is not his private possession. It belongs to all who are dealing with the same problem. The announcement of the results of an investigation is an invitation to all one's colleagues that they repeat the observations, use eyes and hands and wits and instruments in the same way and to the same intent. And if it should appear that the second observations do not tally with the first that discrepancy becomes a problem for both the investigators. Each man, in this way, is expected to "check" the work of his colleague. One of them may be in Java and the other in Kansas. One may have studied in the fourth century, B.C., while the other is working in the twentieth century, A.D. And yet their facts are "pooled." In this sense, they are reasonable with one another. Each is bound, and is eager, to consider what the other sees and says just as if he

[1] See the quotation from R. M. MacIver, pp. 160-161, note.

himself had seen and said it. Their co-operative enterprise, so far as they can control it, is dominated, not by individual prejudice or private information, but by a disinterested intention to discover and to interpret material which is open in the same sense, to every inquirer in the field.

But, as against this reasonable co-operation of scientific thinking the disorganic theories of human intelligence tell us that seekers for wisdom cannot "pool their facts." At the crucial point in a "practical" inquiry an emotional factor enters which makes such co-operation impossible. Each man lives his own life and can have no access to the life of another. Each has his own interests to further. And no one else can, in the same sense, "have" those interests. The difficulty is that, in the last resort, every man's practical thinking springs out of his own wants, and returns to them as its goal. No man can, therefore, "check" the wisdom of another. Men cannot be reasonable together in practical affairs because they are not dealing with the same facts and, hence, not with the same problem. So far as matters of conduct are concerned men think separately. A thinks A's welfare. B thinks B's welfare. Those separate thoughts may happen to lead to actions going in the same direction or they may lead to mutual conflict and frustration. But they can never take the form of reasonable co-operation. Reasoning about conduct is, as such, nonreasonable.

Now this argument calls attention to a feature of "practical" reasoning which must not be ignored. Into all questions of conduct a "value" element does enter. In practical situations men reason for the sake of interests, desires and needs. And the interests of one man are not those of another. My hunger is my own and no one else can feel it as I do. So too, my fears, my pride, my ambition, my longing—these belong to me. No one else can "have" them. This interest isolation of the separate individual is beyond question.

But upon this undoubted fact, disorganic theory builds the false conclusion that men cannot "pool their interests." It tells us that no human being can be interested in the interests of another as he is in his own. That inference does not follow. We are not saying that one person can "have" the value experiences of another.—It is equally true that no observer of fact can "have" the seeing of another.—But we are saying that, under certain conditions, one man can "care for" the interests of another. He can "pay regard" to them as if they were his own. When men are friends one of them can say to the other, "You have more need of food than I have, therefore you must take a larger share of our available stock than I do." And his fellow can agree that that is reasonable, even though it serves his own interest. If men are, in this sense, "brothers" they can plan together how to deal with a common problem. That problem concerns, not the interests of either taken separately, but the interests of both taken together. Friends can "pool their interests" in a way co-ordinate with that in which scientists can "pool their facts."

If, for example, two persons living in the same home have different tastes or needs as to temperature, there arises a problem which they can consider and deal with together. I like it hot. She likes it cold. In that situation, if people care for one another, they can co-operate. As each gives to the desires and needs of the other equal status with his own, each is concerned about two sets of pleasures, of comforts, of healths, as if they were both within his own experience. A family group is thus disinterested in the sense that when a desire or need is to be fulfilled or denied, the question with which all alike are concerned is not "Whose is it?" but, "How important is it?" And that question is common to all the members of the group. They can think about it together. They can come to a common decision by a common consideration of the facts and values involved. Each of the values, of course, belongs in a peculiar sense, to some one member of the group. But for the purposes of the common inquiry, that fact is irrelevant. In so far as a genuine family relationship has been established, each of the different persons involved is sensitive to the values of the others, and each is disinterested in the sense that all the values within the group are given equal status in his mind. He cares for them as if they were his own. That is what it means to be "reasonable" in a social situation. It means that people, having common values to measure, can engage together in the solution of a common problem of measurement. It means that men are friends. And, on the other hand, it means that, if men are not friends, to speak of reasonableness between them is to speak nonsense.

5

Now to this assertion that reasonableness implies fellowship there is an obvious retort. And hardheaded, double-minded, Anglo-American common sense will not hesitate to make it. "Look at the facts" we shall be told. Be reasonable about your reasonableness. If reasonableness is what you say it is, where do you find it in a contemporary society? After all, the human race is not a single family living in the same home. Mankind is a vast, multifarious collocation of nations, regions, towns, clubs, and so on, down to the separate individuals. And, on the whole, each of these is pursuing its own ends. These individuals and groups bargain and compromise. They yield to pressure. Each of them, it is true, will give up this or that specific interest in the hope of greater gains to come. You may even find, spotting the general map of human indifference or hostility, little regions where personal affection gives peace and kindness. But, on the whole, it is nonsense to say that in order "to be reasonable" one must give equal regard to the interests of all other men, whether one knows them or not—to Chinese, negroes, Russians, criminals, Englishmen, laborers, artists, employers, radio announcers —that he must give to the desires and needs of all these, equal status, equal value, with his own. Intelligent self-interest is not carried away by such sentimentality as that. Why not be realistic? Why not stick to the facts?

For the moment we need not challenge the cynicism of that retort. In December, 1941, it is a strange doctrine to hear from the same lips which are passionately exhorting young men by the millions to offer up their lives for the welfare of their country or of humanity. The "bargain" theory would tell us that those who do this exhorting do so "intelligently" for their own interest. Is that true? If so, here is another "infamy" more contemptible than that of Japan at Pearl Harbor. But, for our present argument, both retort and counter-retort are irrelevant. We are not just now asking, "How much reasonableness is there among men?" but rather, "What is reasonableness when, if ever, it occurs?" Let it be agreed that the human race does not act like a single family. But the question remains, "Would it be better if it did so act?" Let it be agreed that all men fall short of their duty. But we must still ask, "What is the duty of which they fall short?" And when that question is fairly faced I am willing to match the unconscious wisdom of the body of the race against the cynical confusion of a self-contradictory Protestant-capitalism. The moral individualism of England and America during the last three centuries is a mental aberration which is near to madness. We "intellectuals," with our lofty contempt for popular opinion, have regarded the principle of human brotherhood as a sentimental dogma, far removed from the methods and results of critical intelligence. But the truth is that that belief in human fellowship, stripped of its dogmatism, taken out of its mythological setting, is the basic principle of all "thinking" about society. Only "brothers" can "reason together."

6

In an earlier volume, published in 1935, the writer spoke of "the two most fruitful insights which Western civilization has known." He then continued, "For men who are forever asking what shall I be and do?" Socrates summed up his wisdom in, the phrase, "Be intelligent; act critically." And Jesus, likewise pondering, four centuries later, on human action, said to his fellows, "Be kind." And in terms of sheer domination over the mind of the Western world, no other pair of intellectual achievements can equal these two."[2]

That statement I should now like to correct by saying that these two insights are one. Jesus and Socrates, out of very different backgrounds, are saying the same thing. Intelligence is kindness. Kindness is intelligence. The fundamental quality, which the two terms suggest in different ways, may be found in varying degrees of conscious or unconscious acquaintance with itself. But it is the same quality on which all human civilization is built. We "Protestants" and "scientists" have over-mentalized human virtue. We have thought of "reasonableness" as an achievement of "the mind" in the narrow, non-feeling, sense of that term. We have assumed that the "goodness" of human nature was an external fact which science might discover. And, for that reason, the outcome of our scientific discovery has been that there is no goodness to be found. But, as against that skepticism and despair the truth lies in the fact that our minds and wills are engaged in the common task of creating a friendly society, a human fellowship. Science itself is a fruit of that fellowship. It is that fellowship which defines reasonableness, both in its intellectual and emotional aspects. That is why the two are fundamentally one. Reasonableness is kindness. And kindness seeks to be intelligent. For the establishing of a system of education we need both Jesus and Socrates. But, more than that, we need to recognize that their teachings are not two mutually irrelevant gospels. They are one gospel. Whoever would be a teacher must be both wise and kind. If either of these qualities be lacking, the other is under suspicion.

[2] *What Does America Mean?* Alexander Meiklejohn, Norton, 1935, p. 25.

Chapter 18. THE QUANTITY OF REASONABLENESS

~~~~~~

THE previous chapter suggested a question which must be faced before we can attempt to formulate our conclusion. It is a quantitative question. How much reasonableness is there in the universe? How much can there be? The teacher needs to know the limits of the field of his action.

At this point, the transition from a theological to a secular account of human experience takes on decisive significance. The theological view had found reasonableness pervading the universe. God, who had made the world was Himself a Divine reason. He had built into the very nature of things, moral and intellectual principles. He was kind and wise. He cared alike for all His creatures. And this gave to men assurance that, when they were disinterested, they could count on God's backing and support. Reasonableness was embedded in reality.

But with the advance of secular thinking, it becomes clear that, quantitatively speaking, disinterested intelligence plays a very small part in the world. Such reasoning is, as we have already said, a human invention. It finds both its origin and its validity in the unusual and peculiar behavior of men.

But even within human activity the quantitative scope of reasonableness is sharply limited. In the light of current studies of human behavior the old saying, "Man is a rational animal," smacks of absurdity. Men, it is true, have a capacity for being reasonable. But they have a much larger capacity for letting themselves go along lines of prejudice, of ignorance, of disloyalty to their own accepted principles. And, further, there are vast ranges of human experience in which the idea of reasonableness does not seem to apply. Here life is not merely unreasonable. It is nonreasonable. If, then, we are seeking for that quality of intelligence with which education has to deal we must look for it, not in the universe at large, not in the general nature of man, but in a special effort which men are making to transform themselves and their world. As judged by itself that effort is, at times, magnificent. But, as judged in terms of cosmic quantity, it is a slight and transitory thing.

I

What then is the scope of the attempt to live reasonably? Where and under what conditions, does it occur? Where does it not occur? The answer to that double question may throw needed light on what the teacher has to do.

Rousseau has told us that the relation of reasonableness or of unreasonableness can exist only between the members of an organized society, between citizens of the same state. Morality and intelligence are, he suggests, political inventions. And from this it follows that the education which attempts to cultivate those qualities is likewise political in scope and intention.

That suggestion we must now examine first in its negative and, second, in its positive aspects. If it should prove to be valid it gives us the intellectual basis which is needed for the founding of a tenable theory of society and of education. Such a theory we sorely need as the ideas of our Protestant-capitalist culture fall away into the bewilderment and chaos of a war-torn world.

What, then, is, in human experience, the difference between the state of nature and the civil state? To make this distinction we need not go back, in imagination, to some legendary, prepolitical, form of human association.[1] We need only examine, in our own daily living, our relations to the other objects with which we have to deal. Some of those relations are such that they are, or can be, "civilized." But there are others for which the laws

[1] This observation is beautifully made by Rousseau in his notes for an essay on "The State of War," which, unfortunately, was never fully written.

and customs of reasonableness have no meaning. We are asking, then, what are those areas of experience which of necessity, or through our own failures, are confined to a state of nature. They fall into several groups.

2

First, it would be quite impossible to "civilize" our dealings with "inanimate" objects. We can never be reasonable or unreasonable with them, nor they with us. Such things as sunshine and air, acids and metals, tornadoes and fires, have effects, for good or for evil, on human beings. And we, in turn, can in some measure affect them. We have, in fact, under the forms of technological invention, devised elaborate schemes for appropriating and using them. But we cannot reason with them. There are no common problems of behavior to reason about. We cannot do them justice or injustice. Nor can they be right or wrong in their dealing with us. We can reason with our neighbors about the use of inanimate objects. I may, for example, violate some civic principle by cutting down a tree or by starting a fire. But I do not transgress against the tree or the fire. My contacts with them are beneath good and evil. Those contacts lie forever in the state of nature.

3

The same naturalness is found in human dealings with a large class of animate things. Such living forms as typhoid germs, vitamins, mosquitoes, trees, cows, moths, tigers, have no "reasonable" relations with men. They contribute in varying ways to human health and happiness, or are destructive of them. And we, in turn, cultivate them as useful to us or, it may be, seek to destroy them as pests. But they do not deserve either our approval or our condemnation. I may, in furious anger, vow vengeance against a fly or a mosquito or a tiger, but I know that

238

I am talking nonsense when I do so. Since typhoid germs menace the health and life of human beings we join together in fixed determination to eliminate them from the process of the universe. But, in doing this, we sin against them just as little as they have sinned against us. These are situations in which moral terms simply do not apply. Our relations are, at this point, not open to reasoning. They are in the state of nature.

4

And the same limitation applies to many of our relations with our fellow men. Even here, morality exists only where we have created it. Men can "reason" only at the points at which they have made life "reasonable." Two areas which have not been touched by morality are pointed out by Rousseau, as he lays the foundations for the argument of the *Social Contract*.

There are no moral or reasonable relations, Rousseau tells us, between a slave and his owner. As between these two the word "just" is meaningless. The relation is one of violence on the one side and of subjection to violence on the other. The slave owes no allegiance to his master. He obeys him because, and only because, he must. But from that it follows that he need obey only so far and so long as he is weaker than his owner. An "agreement" between the two would be worthless because it is a forced agreement, and hence, not an "agreement" at all. If the slave can escape, if, by strength or guile, he can turn the tables and become master, there is no "moral reason" why he "ought not" to do so. And, on the other hand, the owner is under no obligation to his slaves. He will, of course, in his own interest, care for them as he cares for his cattle or his crops or his well. Slaves are an investment. Since they are for use, they must be kept as useful as possible, both in body and mind. But such care by the owner is not a duty to the slave. It is self-interest, which is dominant, making use of self-interest, which is subservient. And, as such, the relation is totally nonreasonable, nonmoral. Slavery, as such, cannot be civilized.

The statement just made is, of course, valid only if the "as such" is strongly emphasized. No human being is merely a slave, or merely an owner. In the case of slavery as in the other cases mentioned, the human beings concerned have civil relations with their fellow citizens. As already suggested, I cannot reason with a fire. But my neighbors may reason with me if I start a fire when the woods are dry and the wind is blowing. "They" may find my action unreasonable. So, too, a man may be detestable if he beats a slave. But, if so, he is detested, not as owner, but as member of a community whose principles are violated by his action. With that community he can reason. But with his slaves, as such, his relation is one of violence. It has nothing to do with those "rights" or "wrongs," with which reason concerns itself.

5

Rousseau's second nonreasonable social situation is that of war. War, he tells us, is in the state of nature. It cannot be civilized. Victory at arms decides no moral questions. It provides no principles of judgment. And, especially, it is impossible to establish political authority on a basis of military conquest. Right cannot be based on force. When one nation conquers another it is nonsense to talk of "a just peace." So far as war goes, the relation between victor and vanquished is that between any animal and its prey. When victory is won, one nation has been shown to be stronger than another, and nothing else has been shown. Such words as "ought" and "ought not" are as irrelevant between victor and vanquished as they are between spider and fly. Spiders and flies do not make agreements nor do they break them. Spiders are not cruel. Their acts are not unreasonable. They are natural. And in the same way, when conflict rages between the Germans and the English, the Chinese and the

Japanese, the Russians and the Finns, there is only one question which is being decided—which of the two is stronger and more crafty than the other. War, as such, cannot be civilized. Civilization is created only as war is abolished.

6

Our search for the limits of reasonableness has brought us face to face with the international crisis in dealing with which the choice between "the appeal to reason" and the "resort to violence" cannot be evaded. By which of these methods are disputes between nations to be adjudicated? By which method are the common interests of nations to be furthered? What is the relation between the many claims to "national sovereignty" and that "international law" which claims some kind of authority over them?

As I write these words in December, 1941, the United States has just entered upon war with Japan. We have done so with a sense of righteous indignation. Japan, we say, opened war treacherously. While peace negotiations were still going on in Washington, her forces, without the slightest warning, swooped down upon Pearl Harbor. So deep and passionate is our national resentment of that treachery that our body politic has cast aside all differences. As one man, we are ready to fight for the right, for justice, for fair play, for decency. Japan is guilty. And we will punish her.

But Rousseau would tell us that unless Japan and the United States have "reasonable" relations with one another, unless they are together members of an inclusive state whose government has authority over them both, such words as "right," "justice," "fair play," and "decency" can have no application to their conflicts. Is he talking nonsense? The doctrine of national sovereignty would seem to justify him. If we say that the political authority of each nation is ultimate, that no nation, except as specific bargains are made, has responsibility for any interests outside its own borders, what does it mean to accuse a nation of treachery toward other nations? If the doctrine of sovereignty is valid, nations at war do neither right nor wrong to one another. They win or lose, survive or perish. At this point, relations between states are radically different from relations within states. If, for example, within the national sovereignty of this country all the constituent states are subject to one federal authority, it means something when federal judgment is passed upon their actions. It means something when the Supreme Court rules that California may not debar indigents from crossing her borders. The Constitution says that she has no "right" to do so. That is an "agreement." It means something to say that coal miners have or have not a right to strike in time of desperate national emergency. Those are issues which, however difficult and debatable, are yet open to adjudication by civil process. But what does it mean when we say that Germany had no right to invade Poland, that Japan should have given notice before she launched her attack on Pearl Harbor? By what authority are those judgments made? What constitution do they violate? What law was broken by "the stab in the back"?

Now the intent of these questions is not to deny nor to excuse the sins of Germany and Japan. The intent is to understand them and thereby, perhaps, to understand our own. If we say that one nation has sinned against another that statement is a denial of the ultimacy of national sovereignty. It means that nations have obligations to one another, which may be kept or broken. And that means in turn that the nations belong to, are subject to, some social group which is wider and deeper than themselves. If we can reason about relations between states then those states are subject to a reasonable authority which is superior to their own. There is a supernational Reason to whose judgments appeal may be made. What is that "Reason"? Where is it? Tigers do not give notice as they descend upon their victims. Nor do we, except for the increasing of the pleasures of the hunt, send notice to them as we go out to slay them. We gladly give them the "stab in the back." No scruples of conscience disturb us as we launch our onslaughts upon the germs of disease and upon the living forms which transmit them. But, as against all this unscrupulous "natural" warfare, the nations of the earth do, at least, talk of scruples when dealing with each other. They have fashioned that shaky and equivocal structure which we call "international law." They have recognized a supernational law of reason which, while falling short of the domestic authority of a civil state, has yet some status, some claim to obedience by all civil states. What is that law which Japan has broken? Who wrote it? Why should it be obeyed?

7

At this point we must speak again of the belief in God and of the social effect of the weakening of that belief. Our culture has, with characteristic duplicity, found its basis for international laws, not in human reasonableness, but in the mind and will of God. Ruling over the separate sovereign states which men have made, we have asserted a law of nature which is, in turn, a law of reason which is, again, an expression of a Divine will. Like John Locke we have found even in the midst of the brutalities of the state of nature a "community of mankind" established not by men, but by God. It is under the laws of that community that "the stab in the back" is declared detestable. Each nation, taken by itself, knows only one law—that of self-preservation. If there are other laws than this, the God of all the Nations must make them and enforce them.

Now, for purposes of diplomacy, the essential duplicity of this view of the relations between nations is of enormous value. It enables us to answer both with a "yes" or a "no" the question, "Is there an international authority which is superior to that of the sovereign states?" On the one hand we can say that God has established laws of behavior which every nation should obey. We can be righteously indignant if we are wronged. But, on the other hand, we can say also, that international laws have no human authorization except as that is given by the "consciences" of the separate governments and by the "bargains" which they make with one another. And since each government is, under the doctrine of national sovereignty, concerned only with its own self-interest, the dictates of its "conscience" can be counted upon not to interfere very much with the requirements of its own policy. Out of the welter of sanctimoniousness and strife which has resulted from the setting up of such a pseudo superstate, two or three principles may be extracted.

First, the appeal to God gives evidence of a deep and persistent human conviction that relations between nations can be, and should be, civilized. The peoples of the earth are not, like spiders and flies, irrevocably doomed to the state of nature. When men say that God cares equally, reasonably for all nations, they are saying that the present bestial condition of international relations need not be permanent. They have, at least, hope for law and order, for peace and decency.

But, second, gains won by the theological myth in the international field, are pitifully small. The laws of God, it appears, do not forbid nations to murder one another. They require only that the murderer give notice in advance of what he intends to do. Reason authorizes killing by bullets or bombs or starvation. It forbids killing by gas, unless some desperate emergency should require it. Such lawmaking has all the quality of some preacher who would set up a pulpit in the jungle and would proclaim to the animals, as they go about their daily routine of mutual extermination, "So act that thy maxim might be made law universal," or "Thou shalt love thy neighbor as thyself."

But, third, with the fading away of belief in Divine authority, we can no longer make use of the duplicities of a bargaining internationalism. Our question must now be stated in human terms. If the reason of God does not establish control over the nations, what human reason takes its place? That is our contemporary, secular dilemma, a dilemma which, as yet, we seem unable to solve, unwilling to face. Out of the confusion of that dilemma has come the hysterical, but hypnotic, madness of a Hitler. Out of the same confusion came the cold-blooded, unscrupulous, stupid shrewdness of the treaty of Versailles. Peace will not come to the world until that dilemma has been squarely faced and reasonably resolved. Are the relations between nations of necessity in a state of nature? Or can they be civilized by the establishing of a superior authority? To answer that question is the primary political task of this generation.

8

Now it is the peculiar genius of a writer like Rousseau, that, when presenting such a dilemma as this, he lunges at his reader with both horns of it. And no one who really reads him, can escape either attack. Either there is a human distinction between right and wrong in the dealings of nations with one another, or there is not. Which do we choose? The philosophy for which the untutored, tormented mind of Adolf Hitler speaks, has made its choice. The nations, it says, are in the state of nature. Their relations are those of the jungle. They do not reason with one another, except for purposes of subterfuge and deception. All that happens in the jungle is that the strong and swift and crafty win mastery over the weak and slow and dull. These masters must, it is true, organize the jungle so that they shall not be forever disturbed by revolt and disaffection. But that organization is both created and maintained by force. Nations are eternally at war. They have nothing to do with reasonableness.

We "democrats," on the other hand, will not make Hitler's choice. We believe in civilization. We will, if need be, fight for it to the death. Will we, then, frankly take the other alternative? The present condition of the world is evidence of our unwillingness to do so. During the last century or two the developments of technology have been forcing the decision upon us.

In all external relations the world is now one world. It has been made one by science, by art, by communication, by commerce, by finance. Not only can it be dealt with as one unit but, also, unless men shut their eyes to what they are doing, it must be dealt with as one unit. But we Anglo-Saxons, who have been largely dominant during this time when men are thrust into closer relation with one another, have developed a special talent for evading such fundamental issues. We are Christians who say "but." We recognize that all men are brothers. But we value too highly the "independence" of men and of nations to put our Christianity into practice. We have therefore referred all basic moral problems to "the invisible hand of God." And since God is in charge of them, it has seemed unnecessary that we should deal with them. And the result of this moral disingenuousness has been to make the separate nations into so many "pressure groups," each seeking its own advantage. International policy has, therefore, been unable to rise higher than a balance of power regime by which each nation seeks to pit its enemies against each other. By such devices as this the masters of the jungle have tricked each other by words, have cemented eternal alliances and broken them the following year. But the scheming and bargaining of this disorganic pluralism does not mean that we have rejected the philosophy which Adolf Hitler follows. It means only that we have screened it with words. Our Hitlerism "would exhibit itself as a reasonable persuasion."

9

But the organic theory of international relations will not tolerate this Anglo-Saxon evasion and compromise. In an actual world men do not choose the right unless they so act as to make the right effective. In the world as it now stands the only possible evidence that men care for justice is that they establish and maintain courts of justice. The only evidence that men love their fellows is that they submit themselves to such institutions as are necessary for the furthering of the common welfare. The Puritan dualism which has allowed us to seek to the limit our own advantage and yet to keep for our own comfort the sense of personal and national righteousness has brought our civilization to the brink of disaster. At a time when the world, as a whole, is ready to be civilized it is idle for us to lay the blame for failure on those who resort openly to violence. That blame rests squarely on the shoulders of those who have refused to make honest and effective the appeal to reason. Justice, as Rousseau tells us, exists only among the members of a politically organized state. It is nonsense, then, to talk of "reasonableness" in the jungle, of "a community" in the state of nature. If nations are to have regard for one another they must have authoritative political institutions which enact and execute that regard. They must have a federal government which will give to them all equal status before the law. Within such a framework nations can reason together, can work together for a common end. Without it they are, and must be, beasts of prey. Do we, or do we not, prefer civilization to barbarism? If we do we will proceed with all our might to put an end to war. But the only alternative to war is government. Government is human reasonableness in action.

10

Our discussion of the scope of reasonableness has taken it far beyond the range of that family affection in relation to which, in an earlier chapter, we defined it. Reasonableness, as found in political institutions, exists between men who do not know each other. In the United States, for example, one hundred and thirty million people are bound together into a "Union" by the principles of the Constitution and their application to matters of daily life. These citizens do not "care for" each other in the "feeling" sense in which a mother loves her son or a husband his wife. But they do "have regard for" one another in the reasonable sense which gives meaning to the principles of freedom and equality. In these wider social reaches, the wisdom of the mind extends the wisdom of the body. Men act, as we say, on principle, rather than on feeling. But the fundamental motive is the same. Interests are pooled. The government acts for all alike and for all together. In this situation men will even give up their lives for the common cause. They do not, as our customary language suggests, die "for" principle. They die "on" principle or "according to" it. And the principle is that they care for others just as they care for themselves. It is their fellows "for" whom they are willing to die. It is the common interest which seems to each of them more important than his own private interest.

II

The question which we have been discussing, concerning the quantitative limits of reasonableness, is of primary importance to the American teacher. He is commissioned to teach reasonableness to his pupils. But how much of it does our country want taught? Shall we teach kindness, generosity, impartiality, intelligence within our own domestic economy? And shall we then reverse the process and give lessons in hatred, selfishness, prejudice and misunderstanding, so far as other nations are concerned? Much of our teaching of patriotism has that effect even though our words may try to conceal it. And, with the breakdown of theology, concealment is no longer possible. A younger generation distrusts an older one chiefly because the words of theology no longer have meaning for it.

Why should not the relations between China and Japan, between Germany and England, between the Soviet Union and the United States, be as reasonable as those between Rhode Island and Massachusetts, between California and Oregon? Why should we hold fast to barbarism when civilization is within our reach? That issue is now so clearly drawn that no one with any sense of fact can fail to see it. And our teachers

THE QUANTITY OF REASONABLENESS

must know on which side of it we wish them to take their stand. Do we wish them to teach half reason and half violence? If so, their proper answer is that it cannot be done. Lincoln's words with regard to halfway dealings with freedom and slavery are just as true with regard to the attempt to compromise between reason and unreason. Reason can be taught, because it is reasonable. But violence cannot be taught. It must be forced, impressed, driven home by every influence of deception and suppression. That is not work for teachers. And no one who is a teacher will do it.

Chapter 19. THE QUALITY OF REASONABLENESS

wwwwwwwwwwwwwwwwwwwwwwwwwwwwwwwwwwwwwwwwwwwwwwwwwwwwwwwwwwwwwwwwwww

WE HAVE been speaking of the quantity of reasonableness. We must now turn to its quality. We have found disinterested, intelligent living to be located in the universe like a small island in a vast and desolate sea. And yet that island is our home. Whatever of good men have created with their minds and bodies and wills can be summed up under the phrase, "reasonable living." Within the meaning of that phrase is to be found everything which a teacher may use as giving basis, theoretical or practical, for the work which is attempted in our schools and colleges.

Civilization, we have said, is fellowship. As men rise out of barbarism they "have regard" for one another. Their interests are pooled. They have agreements of common purpose and, hence, of mutual understanding. It is these agreements which provide content for education. We must try, therefore, to see what is their essential quality.

I

One of the best illustrations of the kind of agreement which creates a civilizing state is found in the human institution of language. Whatever may be said as to the origin of verbal communication, one thing is certain. The making and using of symbols is a co-operative enterprise. Consciously and unconsciously, men who use the same words, who employ and enlarge and refine and criticize the instruments of communication, are sharing in a common effort, are agreeing as to a common purpose. You and I cannot successfully use the word "red" unless we agree as to its reference and content. And "green" must have a different but related meaning. "Color" too, it is understood, must be so used as to include both "red" and "green" while excluding "hot" and "wise" and "heavy." With greater or less awareness of what we were doing we language makers have devised those forms of speech which, by later reflection, are called nouns, adjective, adverbs, verbs, conjunctions, and the like. We have made sentences, paragraphs, phrases, clauses, essays, books, exclamations. And, further, all this creative work is permeated by agreements which we are expected to keep. If a man says "green" when he means "red" there may be trouble at the crossroads. There are standards of speaking and hearing, of writing and reading. Any given use of words is good or bad, adequate or inadequate to its purpose. From this point of view, every language contains implicitly a dictionary and a grammar, a rhetoric and a logic. As we become conscious of the language which we have constructed, these manuals tell us how words "ought" to be used. They reveal to us our own principles which we have unconsciously adopted. Such formulations are, of course, open to question. But that very questioning illustrates, rather than denies, the basic fact that only by agreement can we achieve our common purpose of communication, of mutual understanding.

2

Modern studies of human behavior have made clear how essential is the agreement as to signs and symbols for the making and keeping of all the other agreements which, taken together, are the framework of civilized living. When men enter a social compact, when they pool their interests, such pooling obviously depends upon the conventions of language. One cannot share the interests of another unless one can learn what those interests are. I cannot love my neighbor as myself unless I know him as myself. And from this it follows that a primary task of the teacher is to make the members of a state better acquainted with one another. By every conceivable teaching device, the power of sympathetic imagination must be developed. Our schools must make their pupils sensitively aware of the interests, the conditions, the aspirations, the sufferings, the purposes, the hopes and despairs, the capacities, which are present throughout the human group to which they belong. They must learn, like Hudson's villagers, to respond to the experiences of others as if they were their own. But, unlike Hudson's secluded villagers, the pupils of a modern industrial society must gain such wisdom largely at second hand. They must get it, not only by personal contacts, but also by abstract ideas. By the use of words the wisdom of the mind thus extends and criticizes the wisdom of the body. Reason continues the work of feeling. The agreements of language are basic to all civilization. The attitude of "having regard for" other men depends upon the achievement of being in communication with them.

3

This instance of language throws light upon the general problem which, in our early chapters, we found to be basic to the theory of teaching. It is the problem of the relation between custom and intelligence, between belief and the criticism of belief. On the one hand, it appears that civilization, like language, is in every case, an achievement of some specific social group. Reasonableness is a meaningless term except as it describes a "way of life" which some assemblage of men has, consciously or unconsciously, established as its own. The demands of impartiality, justice, disinterestedness, fairness, do not come down out of the skies. They do not flourish in the mind of an isolated individual. They are not imposed upon men by "the nature of things." All our principles of behavior are expressions of the fact that some group of individuals to which we belong, is determined to act as a whole in some specific way. That wholeness of action, that organic unity of intention, is the one fundamental principle upon which all others depend. Each member of the group "cares for" what all the members, including himself, are doing. And this means that each group has its own specific and peculiar and limited code of reasonableness. There are as many such codes as there are groups.

For example, if we turn again to the illustration of language, it appears that the word "red" makes no direct demands upon the people of France or Germany or Rumania. Nor does it serve their needs. "Green" and "color" are likewise peculiar to the English-speaking group. That group has its own special agreements, its own prevailing standards, as to the use of words. And since every other language group is, in the same sense, peculiar, the human race, if it were not for an additional device which we call "translation," would be sundered into as many separate blocks as there are languages. Each of these would be as unintelligible to the others as are elephants to canaries. Such blocks, lacking common language, could have no common reasonableness, no common purposes, no pooling of interests.

But, in the field of language, translation does take place. The separate groups are so related, so agreed in cognitive and volitional process, that *red* and *roth* and *rouge* can be recognized as having the same reference and intent. And that means that indirectly and with difficulty an inclusive group can be formed within which communication does take place. The separate languages thus escape from the state of nature. They become civilized. Reasonableness and mutual understanding are made possible in wider human societies. And that widening may go on until it includes all beings who are capable of using symbols. So far as language is concerned, it seems possible that the enterprise of being reasonable together might become an enterprise of all humanity. We have no evidence on which to base the suggestion that it could go further than that.

4

The illustration of language has suggested that each social group has its own reasonableness. And that seems to mean that there are as many reasonablenesses as there are social groups.

But the fact of translation gives us a countersuggestion. In the human world, groups which "reason" are not isolated. They merge and fuse. Each separate society, it is true, has its own authoritative control over its own members. Each demands reasonable acceptance of that agreed-upon control. But, on the other hand, it is clear that separate groups are capable of combining, by voluntary agreement, into larger, more inclusive societies. And wherever this happens, the "reasoning" which is set up by the larger group is, in some sense, authoritative over the reasoning of its constituents. A wider reasonableness becomes the critic of narrower ones. It judges them. The range of the wider society is still specific and limited. Its voice is nothing else than the combined voices of a definite number of individuals. And yet it goes beyond its parts. It masters them just as they, in turn, have mastered their members.

Now this relation between social groups in virtue of which one of them becomes the critic of others is, as we have said, the basic fact in all social and educational theory. I propose that we examine it in a specific case, that we ask what are the "critical" relations of various groups within, for example, the structure of a state university.

If we look for the football team of the institution of learning we shall find on some playing field a squad of young men, together with their coaches, actively engaged in devising a scheme of reasonable procedure. The behavior of each player is, therefore, subject to criticism. As eleven men together plunge into the common attempt to advance the ball, one of them is chosen to "carry" it. The others are, by the same choice, made "blockers" to clear his way. If by a different decision, one of them "passes," the others become, by a carefully devised set of agreements, either "receivers" of the pass or protectors of passer and receiver. But, in either case, each player, as seen by the coach, as seen by his fellows and himself, is learning to play his part in a "reasonable" pattern of behavior. A good coach can tell his men not only what they should do but why they should do it. He can also assess what they have done, can make clear how what they did furthered the common cause or interfered with it. A common intention, made specific and concrete as a plan of action, thus gives basis for reasonable criticism.

But, next, there is a higher level on which both players and coaches are open to a different kind of assessment. The members of the team are not only football players. They are also students. As such they belong to the university, and that institution is commissioned by the commonwealth to advance scholarship as well as to advance footballs. It must train citizens in the use of the methods and results of scholarly work for the common good of the state. The university is an institution for creating knowledge and for transforming it into intelligence.

Now from this wider point of view the faculty and administration of the university are bound to question what the team is doing, to assess its value for an institution of learning. It is possible, of course, that the game is contributing to "intelligence." But it is also possible, as Woodrow Wilson once suggested, that the side shows are running away with the circus. The coach asks, "How can I get these boys to play better football?" But the teachers and president may well be wondering whether the students do not play too well, better than "students" ought to play. And this means that the authority of the institution as a whole claims a certain priority over that of any one of its parts. It criticizes their play, not as football, but as the football of students. And it has a right to expect their reasonable participation in its total enterprise, no matter what may be the cost to their own limited private achievements.

But again, our illustration will hardly be complete unless we take another step. Presidents and faculties are also open to criticism. They too have at times been accused of losing sight of the total enterprise. Scholarship for its own sake, is a game quite as fascinating as is football. And its motivations are not wholly different. Here, too, then, questioning is pertinent. What is the relation of the study of one science to the study of another? Do scholars play together as intelligently as do a runner and his blockers? What is the relation between the learning of the professor and the intelligence of his pupils, between the learning of the professor and his own intelligence? Such questions are not hostile in intent. The members of the football team, if they are intelligent about their playing, will gladly subject it to whatever criticism and control the general welfare of the university requires. That criticism is not "imposed" upon them. It springs from an agreement which they have voluntarily made. If they are disloyal to that agreement they have no proper place in the university. And the same observation applies to the work of the scholars. An intelligent scholar must know "why" he is studying and teaching. It is not enough that he merely play well the game of his own subject. A scholar who does that is as destructive of teaching values as are dozens of "ringers" who might interpret a university as an athletic club. The university, in every phase of its activity, has a part to play in the life of the society to which it belongs. And both scholarship and teaching are open to assessment in terms of their contribution, or failure of contribution, to that wider purpose. Such criticism comes upon the scholar not, as he sometimes assumes, from the stupid misunderstandings of a crass society. It comes from the social intelligence in which he shares, or ought to share. Is it unreasonable to expect that men who study cosmic rays should understand why cosmic rays should be studied? Perhaps it is. But, if so, it is equally unreasonable to entrust to unintelligent scholars the responsibility for guiding the activities of university life. Who, then, shall play the role of critic in our institutions of "higher learning"? Who shall see to it that not only is knowledge gained but also that it is used for the creating of intelligence in the life of the community? Who shall be the coach of the faculty and administration?

5

The illustration of the university again brings to light the fundamental issue which separates the organic and the disorganic theories of society. No one doubts that there is, in any given human situation, an indefinite multiplicity of social groupings, each of which, resting on an agreement, has its own code of reasonable behavior. No one doubts that, by voluntary agreements, consciously or unconsciously made, one group may be included within, may belong to another. And, when that happens the code of the lesser is, in some sense, subordinated to that of the greater. Football men ought to play like students. Scholars ought to think like human beings. And, in this way, as in the case of the university, there is set up an ascending scale of inclusiveness and, hence, of reasonableness. The principle here involved may be called that of the "hierarchy of intelligences or of criticisms."

But it is at this point that the conflict between pluralism and unity, between disorganization and organization, breaks out. If we follow any given series of ascending reasonableness how far does it go? Does it go without limit? If not, what is the limit? The issue here involved is decisive for the work of the teacher. Can we say that, in the end, all social groups belong to one single group which is authoritative over them all? Or, on the other hand, is pluralism right when it warns us against the abstract passion for unity? Is humanity one fellowship? Or is it eternally divided into many distinct groups among which there is no possibility of reasonable co-operation, of mutual understanding? Does the university, for example, serve only "the state"? Or must it have regard also for the interests of humanity? According as we answer that question we say either that there is one code of reasonableness by which all teaching efforts should be directed or we say that there are many mutually unintelligible codes of reasonableness which, in some way or other, a teacher must hold together, as he prepares his pupils for the chaos of human experience.

6

Now the organic theory of politics asserts that all social groups belong to one group, that the many reasonablenesses are all subject to one reasonableness. And, further, it finds the one all-inclusive group to be "the state." Our political institutions, it tells us, have the task of bringing all our manifold codes of behavior within the pattern of a single jurisdiction. The governing state is, as Dewey insists, unique among human associations. But it is unique, not as being secondary and negative and derivative, but as being primary among them all. It is the final, the supreme critic. The state is intelligence in action in its most inclusive form and, hence, at its highest level. It is the function of the state to organize, to harmonize, to make reasonable all the activities of its constituent groups and its individual members.

7

If the organic theory is true it is easy to see why, in the field of education, control of the development of intelligence should fall into the hands of the state as it slips from the hands of the church. In the theological era, all the social groups of humanity were made into one single group by a common relation to the mind of God. All men were His children. All their societies were responsible to Him. Through a common relationship to Him, all humanity was made one family. That belief was, as we have noted, a recognition in mythical form, of a profound conviction of the essential unity of mankind, so far as reasonableness is concerned. And the church, which was the spokesman for that fundamental reason, was therefore, the accredited teacher of mankind.

But in a secular era that belief in unity must find expression, if it is to be maintained at all, in some institution other than the church—an institution to which it belongs, not in myth, but in sober fact. That institution is the state. The state has the task of bringing into reasonable relation with one another all the activities, all the associations, which fall within its scope. In a secular world, the state replaces the church.

Does the state unify and organize all other associations? If anyone is inclined to doubt that description of the work of government I would ask him to examine what was happening in the life of the United States in January, 1942. We had just been told that the manufacture of automobiles must be stopped and that all the energies previously engaged in that field were to be turned into making the instruments of war. We were seeing millions of our young men withdrawn from their usual vocations in order that they might be sent out to fight. At least 10 per cent of each taxpayer's annual income was now to be taken from him and the number of those taxed was increased by 700,000. A censorship of public information was established. In these as in many other ways the whole nation was brought under authority. All the industrial, moral, and intellectual power of our people is being welded into one concerted attempt to grapple with a desperate emergency. What institution is issuing those orders, exercising that authority, carrying on those activities? The answer is clear enough. That is what a state does. It does it in peace as well as in war. It exercises control over all our activities according as its own judgment may deem best. A state is a sovereign people in action, seeking, by reasonable procedure, to promote the general welfare.

8

The inclusion of other groups within the state is found in two different dimensions. First, in any given locality, the society as a whole seeks to organize, to make reasonable, its varied activities. Whether it be as a village, a town, a country, a "state" in the

American sense, a nation, or a federation of nations, human groups do in some measure establish law and order. They become civilized in their domestic economy. That attempt is made not only by nations. It goes on wherever the sense of the whole is made effective as controlling and acting for its parts. A striking illustration of "a state," as we are using the term, is found in Hudson's Wiltshire village of which Dewey has told us. Unconsciously that village has devised and adopted a pattern of culture which both defines and promotes the general welfare. It has made arrangements for food and water and shelter, for communication and transportation, for manners and morals, for work and play and education. All this, Hudson tells us, it has done as "one organism, instinct with one life, moved by one mind." There are many families within the village. Presumably it has many other social groupings. But all these "belong" to the village. It governs them. It expresses the relation of reasonableness to which they are all alike expected to conform.

But, second, as localities fall within larger localities, so do states fall within larger states. The village belongs to the town, the town to the county, the county to the state, the state to the nation, the nation to—what? At each step in this progression a governing state finds itself governed. The lesser units are, by their own choice, bound together into a larger unit. No one of them, therefore, has more than a local sovereignty. The only sovereignty which could be unlimited would be that of a total group which includes in one organic, governing whole, all beings who are capable of joining in the common enterprise of living reasonably. To be reasonable at the highest level would be to live as a member of that all-inclusive state. If, following the suggestion which theology has given us, we assume that all normal human beings are fitted for membership in that fellowship of government then the task of civilization will be seen to be that of transforming all humanity into "a sovereign people." The human race is, in virtue of its intelligence, its kindness, a state in the making. Like all other manifestations of intelligence, the existence of a state is seen more vividly in its problems than in its answers, in the enterprises which lie before it than in the achievements which lie behind. And yet, wherever human intelligence is at work, consciously or unconsciously, the attempt at self-direction goes on. Political institutions think and speak and act for the whole body of the people. They are the whole body of the people thinking and speaking and acting for itself, making out of its manifold activities a reasonable and unified enterprise of living. As that enterprise advances, as humanity becomes more widely and deeply reasonable, it becomes a world-state, taking charge of its own destiny.

Chapter 20. THE STATE AND THE INDIVIDUAL

wwwwwwwwwwwwwwwwwwwwwwwwwwwwwwwwwwwwwwwwwwwwwwwwwwwwwwwwwwwwwwwwwww

WE HAVE now defined, in principle, the road which human intelligence seeks to travel. It leads from the state of nature toward the state of civilization. Its signposts say, "The Appeal to Reason." The direction of that road gives direction to education. Our schools and colleges are successful according as their pupils escape from confusion and violence and equip themselves for reasonable living in peace and order.

Before we apply our findings to the interpretation of teaching we must try to clear away some misunderstandings. As already noted Anglo-Saxon political thinking is steeped in ambiguity. The pressure-group theories of society have so fashioned our minds that the description of men as seeking peace and fellowship seems to us visionary and sentimental, if not alien and disloyal. It would be quite impossible to deal with all the attacks which the dominant pluralism would make upon our argument. Two of these, however, must be mentioned, and a third must be carefully examined and squarely met.

I

First, this book has so strongly stressed the claims of unity and reason that we shall be accused of ignoring the multiplicity, the chaos, the conflict in human experience. That charge is valuable as a warning, but it does not seem to me valid in fact. If it be true that the task of human intelligence is to bring order out of disorder, then at every step in that process there must be full and detailed recognition of the disorder with which we are dealing. To ignore it would be worse than madness. It would be idiocy. And yet it would be equally idiotic, for a "reasonable" person, to deny that there is, in human experience, a striving for fellowship, for understanding, for reasonableness. It is no longer possible for us to personalize those two sets of facts. We can no longer attribute them to the universe by calling them God and the Devil. But the stubborn facts still remain. The life of man, so far as it has value at all is, at every point, a struggle of wisdom against folly, of generosity against selfishness, of objectivity against prejudice, of civilization against barbarism. That struggle may be a losing one. Chaos may be too intractable for our vagrant and fitful attempts at thinking. And yet that struggle is the only thing which gives dignity and worth to human living. Our task is to create a fellowship in which all reasonable beings may live on equal terms, with equal status, with mutual regard, one for another. No one who really faces the agony, the meanness, the misunderstandings, the self-righteous brutalities of the modern world, will think that task an easy one, will fail to see the desperate difficulties that stand in its way.

2

Essentially the same charge will be made in another form. Human society, we shall be told, does not find its origin in reason. It is the result of the forces which play upon human beings from within and from without. The sun in the sky, the moisture in the air, the minerals in the ground, the growth of plants, the blind surges of human feeling—these are the factors which, without any intention of doing so, fix the nature of human association. Let any one of them change radically and the whole structure of civilization would be transformed or destroyed. Reason itself would disappear if these forces should vary from their normal courses.

Now, here again, the facts alleged are not to be denied. But they must be thought about. No one supposes that human reasoning creates civilization in a vacuum. The human task is to take the world as it is and to make of it, so far as possible, what we wish it to be. And when that task is faced, the fundamental distinction which was long ago drawn by Epictetus still holds good. "Some things," he tells us, "are in our power; other things are not." We cannot decide whether or not there shall be a sun in the sky or minerals in the ground. We have not made that relation between physical bodies which we call "gravitation." Such facts are "given." They are not "in our power." But what is, to some extent, within our power is the enterprise of knowledge and intelligence. We can study the forces, measure them, learn how to predict their action in this case and that. And since we have, at our command, bodies of our own, we can use those forces for the making of a civilized society, if we choose to do so. That is what reasonableness is trying to do. Reason is not a substitute for the powers of nature. It does not try to abolish them. On the contrary, it tries to so know them that, by means of them, a human fellowship may be created and maintained. It takes both forces and reason to make a civilized state.

3

But our argument is open to a third attack which is more deadly than these formal warnings. We shall be accused of exalting the state at the expense of the individual. It will be said that we have lost sight of personal rights and liberties, that we have denied man's dignity, his moral and intellectual independence. In a word, we shall be called Nazi or Fascist or totalitarian. And, further, we shall be told, such totalitarianism is peculiarly fatal to the cause of education. The teacher deals with individuals. It is individuals who learn, individuals who are taught, individuals who are reasonable or unreasonable. Where, then, in all this piling up of the town on the villages, the county on the towns, the state on the counties, the nation on the states, the supernation on the nations—where is the individual pupil whom you propose to teach? Is he at the bottom of the pile? Can you find the "free spirit" of man beneath this huge weight of controls and authorities and organizations?

This charge of totalitarianism is not to be evaded. It brings to its sharpest focus the issue which is at stake in the World War, the issue which lies at the heart of any theory of teaching. We Anglo-Saxons say that we are fighting to destroy totalitarianism. But what does that statement mean? We have already, in 1919, lost one war which we had "won," because we did not know what at bottom we were fighting for. And there is desperate danger that we will do it again—if we win again. What is the totalitarianism which we are determined to root out of the political life of mankind?

4

When men say that the exaltation of the state is hostile to the dignity and freedom of the individual they are making an assumption. They are assuming that the state and the individual are enemies. They are taking it for granted that what the state gains the individual loses, and vice versa. But those assumptions are false. Government by the consent of the governed is not hostile to the governed. Government of the people, for the people, by the people is not intended to destroy the dignity and freedom of the people. Democratic government cannot be too strong. It is the weakness of our democratic governments which is chiefly responsible for the chaos and disaster which have come upon ourselves and, through us, upon all the nations of the earth. Civilization is not a burden. It is an opportunity. No man loses dignity by accepting wider responsibilities, by taking into his mind wider reaches of interest. The cure for bad government is not no government or weak government. It is strong, intelligent, responsible, good government. "Only by becoming civilised"— may I again quote Rousseau at this point?—does one "cease from being a stupid and unimaginative animal, does one become an intelligent being and a man." We Anglo-Saxons loudly protest our passion for freedom and equality. But we have persistently blocked the concerted political efforts of men to establish and maintain freedom and equality, both at home and abroad. As between law and license, where our interests are safe, we have preferred license. And we have called it "freedom" because we wished to "exhibit it as a reasonable persuasion."

What then, is totalitarianism? As interpreted by Adolf Hitler or Benito Mussolini it makes two assertions. First, the state must be strong and powerful, eager and able to achieve its purposes against all opposition from within and without. Second, the state can be strong and powerful only if it becomes a dictatorship, only if one man, with his abject subordinates, rules ruthlessly over the many.

What is our democratic reply to those assertions? Shall we deny them both? If we do so, we are doomed. The first assertion is true. Only a strong state can maintain freedom and equality in any nation, or in the world as a whole. No collocation of individuals, in which each individual assumes responsibility for the guarding of his own freedom and equality, can succeed in the attempt at democracy. As Rousseau tells us, the "whole common force" of our human association must be brought to bear wherever the issue of freedom arises. Whenever the general welfare and some individual good are incompatible with one another, the former must prevail. So far as the question of authority alone is concerned, a democracy must be a totality in action. We must rise as one man in the furtherance of freedom. The state which is the guardian of our liberties must be exalted.

But it is the second assertion which is false, which must be shown to be false. The task now facing our democracies is to show that a free people does not need a "dictator" to make it strong. It can govern itself strongly, efficiently, wisely. That would be the real victory over Nazism. We must show it in war by being more efficient in war. But it is even more important, in the long run, that we show it in peace. The human will to freedom and equality must be so strongly expressed in the agencies of government that no selfishness of individuals or groups can prevail against it. Can human intelligence create and maintain a political organization which is adequate to that task? I think it can. But the first requisite is that we recognize our own previous errors and failures. We Anglo-Saxons have loved, and do love, human freedom. But at the same time, our minds have been too lazy and inept to protect freedom against our own individual aggressiveness. Gangsterism is not peculiar to Germany and Italy. It flourishes wherever men doubt the efficacy of reasonableness and intelligence. In the face of it, freedom and equality can be maintained only by a strong, an intelligent, an authoritative, democracy.

5

The charge that the exaltation of the state is hostile to the dignity and freedom of the individual attacks directly the interpretation of teaching for which, from beginning to end, this book has been fighting. As a reply to that charge our argument can be summed up in a single assertion. If that assertion is true, the argument stands. If it is false, the argument falls.

The assertion to which I refer is this—all the activities which give a man dignity are done "for the state." And, vice versa, the test of any government is found in the dignity and freedom, the equality and independence, of its citizens. It exists through and for them, just as they exist through and for it.

6

The principle just formulated can be understood only if we make a distinction which the political theorizing of our Protestant-capitalist culture has perversely obscured. Every citizen of a democratic state has two different relations to his government. In a government which is carried on by the consent of the governed every citizen is both governor and governed. He is both ruler and ruled. As ruler, he shares in the making and administering of political decisions. As ruled, he is subject to the decisions which are made. But these two roles of the individual are radically different in kind. And the error of the individualistic theory of society is that it confuses them. It demands for men as governed rights which belong to them only as governors. It denies to men as rulers, a dignity which can be denied them only in so far as they are subjects. If we can clear away that confusion, our social principle will be ready for application in the field of education.

Now, if this distinction is made it becomes clear that men have dignity only in so far as they are rulers, only in so far as they share in the attempt to advance the common welfare. And, further, only as rulers have men a right to liberty. When a man is using his mind and will in dealing with matters of public policy, that mind and will must be kept free. The public welfare requires it. That is what is intended by the magnificent first sentence of the Bill of Rights in which the government itself declares that not even the government shall limit the liberty of religion or speech or press or assembly or petition. When, on the other hand, a man is pursuing his own private interests, when, therefore, he is one of the governed, there is no reason why his activity should be free from regulation. On the contrary, it is of the very essence of government that "private" activities should be regulated and controlled as the public interest may require. That distinction between the citizen, as ruler, who is promoting the general welfare and the same citizen, as ruled, since he is carrying on his own business, is essential to any clear understanding of what we mean by "liberties" and "rights" in a democratic society.

The two roles of which we are speaking will be seen to fall apart if we imagine a young man of military age voting on a public decision between war and peace. In terms of private interest, he can see that a declaration of war may cost him his life or may leave him maimed and disabled. It threatens both his family affections and his career. Does that settle the issue for him? Is he free to vote "No" on the grounds of private interest alone? Certainly not. The question which, as a ruler, he faces at the polls, is not "What is good for me?" but "What is good for the country?" If his vote answers that question in terms of his own interest, that vote is a lie. He has answered, as one of the governed, a question which was asked him as one of the governors. He has lost all proper sense of human dignity, of the freedom and responsibility of a sovereign citizen of a free society.

When men talk of human dignity it is essential that we ask in what that dignity consists. A man does not acquire personal dignity by owning a million or a hundred million dollars. He may still be utterly contemptible. Nor is dignity won by shrewdly protecting one's possessions to see that no one else takes them away. So far as possessions are concerned men are worthy of "recognition" only in so far as those possessions are used by them for the common good. The value of a man, we commonly say, rests not in what he has but in what he is. And the judgment of what a man is, is an assessment of his attitude toward the total enterprise of his people. Is he sensitive to interests other than his own? Is he impartial and just in objective measurement of those wider interests? Is he courageous and self-forgetful in his devotion to the common cause? Those are the characteristics that give a man dignity. They are the qualities of a ruler. It may perhaps make them more vivid if we describe them in terms of one of Rousseau's most paradoxical phrases.

7

A state is, Rousseau says, "a moral person." To our individualistic ears that phrase sounds absurd. How can a hundred and thirty million people be one "person"? And yet, here as always, Rousseau is slashing his way through our Anglo-Saxon duplicities. He sees where human dignity is, and is not, to be found.

If I understand Rousseau he is saying that every government, local, national, or supernational has to deal with moral questions. The state has a purpose—the discovering and advancing of the common good. It gathers information bearing on that purpose. It interprets facts. It plans. It decides. It executes its decisions. And in the carrying on of these activities of intelligence, the state does well or ill. It is often dilatory and dull and negligent. It commits crimes. But, also, it has virtues. It shows courage and wisdom and loyalty to principles. It is both reasonable and unreasonable, admirable and detestable. For example, during the period of the Industrial Revolution, England has, in this sense, acted as "a moral person." Not only has she created an empire but also, in spite of her protestations to the contrary, she has had more or less awareness of what she was doing. She is responsible both for her virtues and for her crimes. Rousseau's phrase has usable meaning when one thinks of England's role in the making of the contemporary world.

If one wishes evidence of this statement, one need only read such a book as *The Rise of Modern Industry*, written by the Hammonds. I know no story of an individual career which reveals with greater dramatic power the experiences of moral decision and action. As one reads it, one sees how England surpassed her neighbors in grasp of the industrial process. She became avid for power, eager for wealth. She saw how the black people of Africa could be used for profit. And so she built up the trade in slaves. Later she also led the way in abolishing that traffic. She saw how her own people could be industrialized. And so she created the manufacturing towns of the middle counties. These she has not yet abolished She took command of the seas and of finance. She loved literature and science and games. Her life was filled with a peculiar quality of devotion, of sportsmanship, of comradeship, which, in every emergency has, in some way or other, seen her through. Who then, will deny that, in some genuine sense, England has been and is, a moral—and immoral—person?

But if we say that England thinks and acts as a moral person that statement must be matched by another which is equally significant for an understanding of human dignity. If England thinks, that thinking can take place only in the minds of her individual members. There is no "social mind" apart from the separate minds of separate persons. As history records the criminal blunder at Munich, it will record also the journeyings of a man with an umbrella. It will tell too of those other Englishmen who kept him in office. If England was magnificent at Dunkirk and after it, that quality has some peculiar relation to Winston Churchill, as well as to the great body of the population who, individual by individual, discovered that they "could take it" rather than submit to foreign violence. States can think, can will, can plan, can decide, can execute, can be great or small in spirit, magnificent or contemptible in action, only through the activities of their members. A state is its members, ruling themselves, obeying themselves in accordance with a general mind, a general will, which is their mind, their will.

8

Now the point which I am making is that if we wish to understand human dignity, freedom, and independence we must see men acting as rulers of the state. That state rests upon a social agreement that life shall be made reasonable. But such reasonableness can be created only by individuals who act for the state, rather than for themselves. It is that spiritual achievement which gives men dignity, which reveals their freedom and independence. What Englishmen did achieve greatness, as individuals, during the Industrial Revolution? Was it those who piled up possessions for themselves or who held fast to wealth and power handed down to them by their ancestors? If one thinks that, let him read again the words in which Matthew Arnold describes the "Barbarians" of the upper classes. These men, he tells us, were, in their idealessness, "forever asleep." But the men and women who have been magnificent through all the ghastly horrors of the transition from an agricultural to an industrial economy were persons who "lost themselves" in public causes. Bright and Cobden, Carlyle and Mill, Florence Nightingale and John Henry Newman—these were thinking, not of themselves but of England and, in their higher moments, of a human society wider than England. And, in our own day, side by side with the courage and audacity of a Churchill, one may place the brilliant studies of John Maynard Keynes or the scholarly and magnanimous insights of Richard Henry Tawney. These men and women have dignity because they are thinking and acting "for the state," identifying themselves with it. They plan for the war and for the peace of their people. They analyze the financial and industrial and social influences of their people. They grapple with the intellectual and moral problems of their people. They are rulers. They are disinterested. In so far as that is true, the state is not their enemy. It is themselves.

9

The relation between an individual and his government can be seen in another light if we turn from the question of dignity to that of freedom. The right to freedom raises the traditional political problem of our culture. "We hold these truths to be self-evident. That all men are created equal; that they are endowed by their Creator with certain inalienable rights; that among these are life, liberty, and the pursuit of happiness. . . ." So speaks the Declaration of Independence.

Are life, liberty, and the pursuit of happiness "inalienable rights" under our government, as we think it and practice it? To answer that question we need only return to the young voter who faces military service if his country goes to war. What inalienable rights has he in that situation? Can he say, "I have a right to my life; therefore you, the government, have no right to send me to war." Can he, on the basis of his claim to liberty

272

and happiness refuse to take his place in the ranks? Obviously not—on that basis.[1] These are his private concerns. With respect to them, therefore, he is governed and regulated and controlled. With respect to them he is not free to act as he himself desires or thinks best. He must obey the general decision. In sober earnest, in spite of the impassioned eloquence of the Declaration of Independence, we Americans are bound to recognize that the members of a civilized state have no unqualified right to life, liberty, and the pursuit of happiness. In the field of human possessions our "rights" are limited and regulated as the public judgment may deem best.

In what respect, then is our young soldier free, as he goes out to risk his life, his liberty, his happiness, in the service of his country? He is free in so far as he is a ruler. His freedom lies in the fact that he himself has joined in the making of the decision that sends him into danger. The only right he can claim in that situation is that the decision shall have been freely and fairly made in accordance with the social agreement. He can demand assurance that the country has not been tricked into fighting, that private interests are not using the public welfare as a cover for their own devices and plots. If, in the democratic sense, every man has had a chance to make up his mind with fair and open access to the facts; if, directly or through his representatives, his judgment has been recorded and counted, then he has no complaint to make. He can claim freedom to participate on equal status, in the making of common decisions. He cannot claim freedom to disobey those decisions when they have been made, no matter what their effect upon his own life, liberty, or happiness. The "interests" of individuals have no right to freedom.

But freedom, as Henry Wallace has recently reminded us, is much more clearly seen when viewed as a duty than when claimed as a right. It is the duty of every ruler of a state to par-

[1] The "right of the conscientious objector" rests, not on his "interests," but on his "beliefs" about the public welfare.

ticipate freely in those activities of intelligence by which the common life is guided and controlled. The intellectual task of creating a free society is an infinitely difficult one. The state needs knowledge which is both specific and general. It needs wisdom in the use of that knowledge for the enhancement of human living. And those needs of the state can be met only by the minds of its citizens. They must think; they must inquire and reflect, and confer, and decide, and administer. The ruling upon which the life of a free society depends can be done only by the participation of all its members, each according to his capacity, in the common enterprise of intelligence. It is a duty, as well as a privilege, to have a free mind, and to use it for the common good. It is the "rulers" of the state who have a right to freedom.

10

It follows from what has been said that the only unequivocal freedom of an individual citizen is freedom of thought, freedom to participate in the forming of public policy. The First Amendment to the Constitution seems to give assurance that Congress will make no laws interfering with speech or press or assembly or petition. And yet Congress does, and must make such laws. It is only with the speech, press, assembly, and petition of men as governors that these activities are guaranteed freedom from interference. If speech and assembly are being used for private ends, it is essential that they be subject to regulation. Libelous speech cannot be permitted. A press controlled by interest or by faction is a public menace. A radio used for advertising is an insult to public taste and integrity so revolting that it should at once be abolished. The only freedom which any state can guarantee and demand is freedom to act for the general welfare. The state needs, as the essential condition of its existence, the free minds of its people. That is why the reasonable thinking of all men must be kept free. That is the only possible basis for our civil liberties.

We have been saying that "freedom" belongs to men only in so far as they are using their intelligence for the promoting of the general welfare. This is the field of what we call "civil liberties." We have been saying, also, that, in so far as they are pursuing their private interests, men can claim, not "freedom from regulation" but only "justice" and "equality" in the imposing of regulations. This is the field of what we call "civil rights." It is at this point that the Fifth and Fourteenth Amendments differ so sharply from the First. Those statutes do not declare that "life, liberty, and the pursuit of happiness are inalienable rights." They assure only the justice and equality with which the regulation of private interests shall be conducted. They demand that "due process" be observed. Possessions are not inalienable. But justice is.[2]

There is, however, an American tradition that business enterprise should have, not only equality, but also freedom. It would be idle to deny the presence or the power of that tradition. But the time has now come when we can see how ill-founded and misleading are its claims, as they are commonly derived from the Declaration of Independence. The demand that business enterprise should be kept free from governmental interference was based upon the belief that "the laws of the market place" are more wise than is the mind of any group of men. The best way, the only way, to promote the general welfare is, therefore, to let each man seek his own welfare. The common good is furthered,

[2] As we discuss issues of public policy it is dangerous to correlate "liberties" and "rights," as if they were essentially alike. For example, in our current American planning for a post-war world, one hears much about the four freedoms which must be preserved. But it is obvious to anyone who examines the words thus used that "freedom" is ambiguous and shifting in meaning. Freedom with respect to religion and to speech is not the same as freedom with respect to want and to fear. We plan that, so far as possible, men shall be free "from" want and "from" fear. We do not intend that they shall be free "from" religion and "from" speech. And the ambiguity involved in the correlation of these different meanings under a single term is so serious that it might even wreck the thinking process by which a peaceful human society is, we hope, to be initiated and sustained. We will not get or give freedom until we know what it is.

not by the intelligent planning of the government but by the competitive play of private enterprise.

If that is true, it follows that private enterprise must be left free from regulation. In that case the attempt at public intelligence is a nuisance. It is not only ineffectual, it also interferes with the beneficent free play of the laws of nature. "Thinking" about economic problems is not then to be encouraged. It is to be condemned and prohibited. The public welfare depends upon the freedom of business. The common good has no other means of realization. The businessman must, therefore, be turned loose to go without hindrance wherever the hope of profit may lead him. The general will gives him the right to be free.

But, today, that laissez-faire belief has broken down. In the world as we now face it, social forces, if left alone, do not further the common good. They have given us starvation in the midst of plenty, conflict where co-operation might prevail, meanness and cruelty in place of fellowship and peace. If we wish to have wisdom with respect to our relations to one another, we cannot trust to the forces of the market place to provide it. We must make that wisdom by our own co-operative intelligence. And, with the departure of laissez-faire the whole illusory structure of private "liberties" falls to pieces. Freedom and dignity belong to men not as subjects but as rulers. They are not private. They are public. Men win them, not as they seek, each his own life, liberty, and happiness, but as they participate in the common attempt to further the common welfare. Men must have dignity to deserve to be free. And the dignity of the human spirit is found, and found only, in the intelligence, the imagination, the sympathy, the courage, the justice with which one participates in the reasonable fellowship of a free society. A democratic state is not the enemy of human dignity and freedom. It is the co-operative enterprise of a group of individuals who regard dignity and freedom as the supreme values of their experience.

Chapter 21. THE GENERAL THEORY OF EDUCATION

THE human road, we have said, leads from barbarism to civilization. So far as they are intelligent, men seek to establish reasonable relations with their fellows. Such relations are not possible with mosquitoes or tornadoes or trees. But they are possible with normal human beings. And the human task, so far as men are moral and intellectual, is that of extending the scope of reasonable co-operation to its widest and deepest limits. The final goal of that attempt would be the creation of a world-state, in which the appeal to reason would have replaced the resort to violence in the relations of all men to one another.

I

If we accept for humanity the goal which our argument has suggested, the ruling motive of education becomes clear. Learning is not merely the acquiring of mastery over intellectual subject matter. It is, first of all, initiation into many social groups and, ultimately, into one social group. The teacher leads his pupil into active membership in a fraternity to which he himself belongs. The motive force of that fraternity is found in a common devotion to a common, co-operative enterprise. Just as, in the home, each child learns, or should learn, to play his part in the family circle, so, in our schools and colleges, every citizen of the world should become "at home" in the human "state." He should acquire a sense of what humanity is trying to do, and a will to join in doing it.

The calling of the teacher, as so defined, is one of infinite difficulty. But it's also infinitely significant. He is commissioned to form and fashion both human society as a whole and the individuals of whom that society consists. He acts for the state with a completeness of responsibility which is equaled by no other official.

As he engages in his task, the teacher needs two kinds of equipment. He must acquire command, both of method and of content. On the one hand, he must be expert in the technique of his art. To this end he must know human nature just as any artist knows his materials. He must have considered the principles and practices which are propounded in Rousseau's *Emile*. He must understand how intelligence grows and is kept from growing. In each specific case he must assess capacities and incapacities, powers and impediments. He must discover how to cultivate powers and to remove impediments. Like Comenius he must seek to provide for the plants which he is cultivating, good soil in which to grow, a sunny place whose warmth will stimulate their powers to action. Unlike Comenius, the modern teacher will find his sun, not in the mind and will of God, but in the human fellowship which, against frightful odds, mankind is trying to establish.

2

We have said that a teacher should read Rousseau's *Emile*. But it is far more important that he read, and study, and read again, the *Social Contract*. One of the greatest failures of our contemporary training of teachers is that they become mere technicians. They learn the tricks and devices of the classroom. But they do not learn the beliefs and motives and values of the human fellowship for the sake of which the classroom exists. The primary question of teaching theory and practice is one of purpose. Why do we teach? What should we teach? For whom do we teach? What is our goal, and what is the source of its authority over us? Those are the questions which must be answered if our teachers are to be themselves members of the fraternity into which they seek to initiate their pupils. Only as those questions find solution do our schools and colleges understand what they are doing.

3

The argument of this book has centered around the contention suggested by Rousseau that education is, and must be, carried on under the authority of some social group. It is an expression of the will of some social "organism, instinct with one life, moved by one mind." Teacher and pupil are not isolated individuals. They are both agents of the state. They are called upon to go about the business of learning. And, as they do so, the truth, beauty, and goodness with which they deal, come to them, not from some foreign source, not from their own separate experiences, but from the "state" of which they are members. The content of teaching is found in the modes of behavior, the "patterns of culture," which are approved, and criticized, by the fellowship for which the teaching is done. And, that being true, it is clear that the fundamental question with regard to any system of education is, "By what social group is it given; what are the purposes of that group; why does it will that its members be educated?"

4

In the course of our argument we have touched upon four different answers to this basic question. And these four answers give as many "general theories of education."

First, the answer which Comenius gave to the question of authority and purpose was direct and unequivocal. His pupils were the children of God. His teachers were servants of God. Schools and colleges were, therefore, commissioned to follow after the mind and will of God. The Divine purpose was directed toward the making of a human community. It required peace rather than violence, reasonableness rather than selfishness, intelligence rather than stupidity. The "world-state" was established by the Divine will. And a common citizenship in that state prescribed a common curriculum of wisdom and piety for all mankind.

But, with the weakening of theological beliefs and sanctions, our culture has faced the task of providing a "secular" authorization for the purposes of teaching. We moderns have, therefore, tried to describe, in "scientific" terms, the relation between an individual, whether pupil or teacher, and a social consciousness which is wider and deeper than his own. These scientific accounts of human behavior have followed three lines. They suggest, therefore, three different types of educational theory which are now competing for our acceptance.

5

The disorganic theory, in its most extreme form, finds an individual life to be related to the conscious life around it as a drop of water in a stream is related to the current which carries it along. In this figurative description, the total stream of consciousness, as it flows, has no intention of doing so. It does not choose its course. It may, at points, become aware of its own process. But that awareness is merely cognitive. It is a recognition of conditions and their consequences as mere facts. Each individual drop of consciousness, therefore, as it is swept along, may feel what is happening to itself and to others. It may even recognize the influence of this set of conditions or that as determining the course of events. But it cannot participate in the purpose of controlling that course, for the simple reason that there is no such purpose in which to participate.

When we say that this "scientific" account of human relations can never provide a basis for a theory of education, we are not denying its validity as "science." We are saying that knowledge, as such, does not express purpose. It describes happenings. Knowledge of conditions and consequence is necessary for the directing of education. But it is not sufficient. It is only as knowledge, being used for the purposes of human brotherhood, becomes intelligence, that it serves the purposes of the teacher. Pupils must learn, not only what they are and how they act, but also what they have to do and be. They must see themselves as participating in enterprises which have a right to their allegiance.

6

A second, less extreme form of disorganic theory, does not exclude purposes from the stream of events. But it finds them to be scattered, multifarious, episodic. They occur on specific occasions. They appear and disappear as individuals and groups are stirred to "adjust" themselves to their situation, to adjust their situation to themselves. This is the point of view which Dewey expresses when he describes the "conscious" activities of men as dealing with a "plurality of problematic situations." Each of these situations requires purposive action. But each is dealt with separately as the specific conditions may require. They do not fuse into a single situation. It is true that a number of individuals may become a social group, that their many enterprises may become one enterprise. But these groupings also, are separate and episodic. At the best, they give us only a multiplicity of conflicting pressure groups, each going its own way. The stream of events is marked here and there by eddies or currents of conscious purpose. But, in its general flow, it remains merely a stream which rushes along with no conscious control of what it is doing.

This view of human behavior is, likewise, inadequate as a basis for a theory of education. As already noted, it gives us, not one human education, but a vast multiplicity of separate and unrelated educations. It finds in the circumstances and interests of each individual life the materials and the needs which prescribe a peculiar and distinctive plan of teaching. But it does not express that general will of the state, that devotion to the common good, which is required if the members of a social group are to be properly prepared for reasonable co-operation in the life of the community.

7

As against extreme naturalism or partial pluralism, this book has insisted upon a continuous purpose which runs through the course of human experience. We have not said that that purpose dominates the total course of events. But we have said that it seeks such domination, so far as it is humanly possible. The race of man has before it the possibility of being civilized. And it is that possibility which defines the course of education. All women and children and men may become intelligent, loyal members of a single social group. And it is for that group that teaching should be done. Teaching itself should be intelligent and loyal. It should recognize that the will to reasonableness has critical authority over all individuals and all groups which are found in the ranks of humanity.

It follows from what has been said that all human beings should have the same essential education. This assertion does not deny that they should have different educations as well. The drummer and the violinist have different techniques to acquire. But they must also learn to play together. It would be disastrous if, in the midst of a symphony, either drummer or violinist were found unable to make his instrument play. But it would be at least equally disastrous if either of them should play with vigor and efficiency but with no regard for the score which had been placed before his eyes.

Humanity has, I insist, one intelligence. That intelligence, it is true, is only "in the making." Its making is a difficult and precarious venture. It may at any time collapse. And yet, the statement that all men may share in a common enterprise is both true and significant. It tells us, in part, what the world is. It tells us, in part, what men are. And it is upon that basis of fact that any proper plan of human education must be based. It is the lack of that basis of fact which has made our current theories of teaching so negative, so lacking in positive direction. There is a fellowship of civilizing intelligence into which every human being, so far as he is capable of it, must be initiated. Each of us must have loyalty to that company. As pupils, we must turn aside from the resort to violence. We must acquire skill in the appeal to reason. We must become citizens of the world. Education is the fitting of people, young and old, for the responsibilities and opportunities of that citizenship.

8

If we accept the belief that the whole world of human behavior can be dealt with as a single enterprise which a single co-operative human intelligence is trying to direct, and if we regard all lesser enterprises as finding their basic justification and criticism as participants in this all-inclusive attempt, some general conclusions concerning education seem to follow.

First, governments, local, provincial, national, and supernational, are equipped to teach. The handing over of the control of education from the church to the state has not been a fatal blunder. The state is not Moloch. It is not "nothing but your worst, nothing but the worst of us, lifted up." On the contrary, the state is the best of us, trying to control and to elevate the worst of us. It is ourselves seeking to be reasonable, to live in justice and freedom with one another. Man, at his best, is a political animal. His wisdom creates manners and morals. The same wisdom, when institutionalized, creates laws, roads, hospitals, parks, pensions, peace, schools. But these two expressions of wisdom are not hostile to one another. They are one in purpose, one in idea and value. And since that is true, education by the government is radically sound in principle. As our culture now stands, no other institution can equal the state as the representative of those purposes and beliefs which are the fruits of human reasonableness. We do not understand what a state is unless we see that it is both a student and a teacher. We belie its essential nature when we regard it as a policeman.

The statement just made does not mean that "private schools" may not do good teaching. After all, the thinking of the race is done by individuals. And groups of individuals who are disinterested, who are moved to teach, not by private interest or party bias, but by zeal for public intelligence—such groups may teach successfully. On the whole, however, the drift of circumstance is against them. Under current economic conditions private schools and colleges are, almost inevitably, agencies of special privilege. They give to a few advantages which are denied to the many. And that very inequality is destructive of education in reasonableness. It is hard to teach justice when the selection of the students must be recognized as unjust. Inequality of educational opportunity does not conduce to the inculcation of a zest for equality. Actions teach more effectively than words. And for this reason the role of private education seems sure to be a dwindling one.

At this point it may be objected that schools, when conducted by a government, are, of necessity, "plunged into politics," that they are used by "the party in power" for the furthering of its own selfish purposes. And that objection will hold good so long, and so far, as we Americans can see in political life, only the strife of contending pressure groups. That prevailing social philosophy has done enormous damage to our schools. But, on the other hand, that philosophy is false. And our actual social practice rises, at some points, far above it. In the organization of the state university, for example, our governments have devised a system of administration which combines, with amazing success, the independence of the teacher, and the responsibility of the institution to the public as a whole. The essence of that system of administration is found in the belief that men who are qualified to study and teach can be trusted to do so in the public interest. As against this, in other fields of political action, we Americans have dealt with our public servants on the theory that they cannot be trusted. We have assumed that they need to be watched, to be kept under constant pressure by us. And the inevitable result is that we have had as public officials the kind of person who needs to be watched, who responds to pressure. Every teacher knows, that suspicion breeds trickiness and guile. Persons who are not trusted become unworthy of being trusted. That "pressure" philosophy will never give us a democracy. It must be abandoned. Mutual confidence is the prerequisite of freedom. Unless men can trust each other, there is no hope of reasonableness between them. I do not mean that a democracy should give up control over its representatives. But I do mean that such control should not be degrading and hence self-defeating. Our national and state legislatures give constant illustration of that degradation and self-defeat. They represent, not democracy, but a crude and stupid individualistic falsification of it which, while keeping the forms of freedom, has made men themselves unfit to be free.

As we attempt the sadly needed revision of our processes of government, we may find valuable suggestions in the structure and procedure of our state universities. We have, in those institutions, men who, in the public interest, are seeking for the truth. They are, in the best sense of the term, "responsible public servants." And yet, it would, on the whole, be meaningless to "subject them to pressure," to send telegrams telling them what truth to find, as we do with the members of our legislatures. The public servant of a free society must himself be free. That fact our pressure-group philosophy has disastrously obscured.

9

Our first conclusion has been that teaching should be a government activity. But, second, which of our governments shall take charge of it? Shall it be the village or the town or the county or the state or the nation or the world-nation? Each of these "states" represents a level of reasonableness. Each of them has its own "pattern of culture." And the choice among them is, in effect, the choice of the subject matter of our teaching. Shall we teach young people to live in a village or in a nation or in the world? The answer to that question must not be oversimplified. Every human being needs to learn how to live in all the social groupings to which he "belongs." And yet, if our argument is valid, one principle emerges from it which is of primary importance. Fundamentally education belongs to the world-state. The reasonableness of that institution includes and criticizes all the lesser reasonablenesses of our experience. Every human being, young or old, should be taught, first of all, to be a citizen of the world, a member of the human fellowship. All other lessons are derivatives of that primary lesson.

The statement just made branches out in two different directions. It tells us, first, that all education should be given "for" the world-state. It tells us, second, that all education should be given "by" the world-state. If we can explain those two assertions, our attempt at a theory of teaching will have reached its goal.

10

The need of so transforming our plans of education that our pupils will learn to participate in the total human enterprise is thrust upon us as we see the dictatorships of Germany, Italy, and Japan at work in the field of teaching. They have built and are running educational machines which torture and twist the minds of their people out of all resemblance to the forms of human reasonableness. Those nations are guilty of many crimes. But the deepest and blackest of all their offenses are committed against their schools. It is not true, however, that they are the only sinners. The democracies, too, in more subtle ways are likewise guilty. Our localisms and provincialisms do not so obviously and brutally undertake to root out of our minds the appeal to reason. But they are, nevertheless, effective in doing so. It is not enough today to teach a young person to play his part in the life of Indiana or Boston or the South. It is not enough to make him a loyal Pole or Japanese or Canadian or Brazilian. The world is in crisis. There has come upon us all the necessity, as well as the opportunity, of creating a world-state, of making reasonableness prevail for all humanity. And we must have schools which will serve that purpose.

As I write these words my mind goes back to Comenius and to the Christian faith which was for him the basis of education. He saw *all* young people as the children of God. He saw them all, therefore, as having the same life to live. He, therefore, wished to provide for all alike, rich and poor, girls and boys, noble and ignoble, the same lessons in the same scheme of instruction. And that insight, in the new setting which the advance of secularism has brought upon us, still holds good. If we are to have an effective human fellowship, the pupils in every corner of the earth will have the same basic lessons to learn. They need to know each other. They must become aware of the humanity of which they are members. They must become acquainted with that whole human undertaking which we sum up under the phrase, "the attempt at civilization." Only by having that common knowledge, can they become reasonable in their relations to one another. "The proper study of mankind is Man."

II

The second implication of our principle is that the control of education, its planning and basic administration should be in the hands of the world-state. It is, I think, obvious as we plan for the future, that the nation which is to include all the nations and rule over them must have military force sufficient to give it mastery over its members. It must have a legislature and an executive. It must have courts of justice. It must have an equitable and stable system of finance and trade. But more pressing than any of these is the need for a universal scheme of instruction, whose driving force shall be the purpose that all men shall live together in peace and freedom, with reasonable regard for one another. First of all, the world-state like any other state must be a teacher. If it cannot teach, it will do nothing else successfully.

I have spoken of the desperate urgency of the need that people be educated as citizens of the world. But not even that urgency must be allowed to lead us into the illusion that changes have been made when they have been written on paper or even when they have been voted by legislatures. No teaching can go far beyond the actual living, the prevailing pattern of culture of the group by which it is given. Schools, like churches, are too often used as mechanisms of compensation. We live by one code which, in our hearts, we condemn. And we try to restore the balance by having another code taught to our children. But that procedure in education is just as futile and disastrous as was, in an earlier day, Sunday preaching which was balanced by Monday practice. We cannot teach world fellowship unless we believe in it, unless we put it into action by the creation of a political organization which shall take charge of the fortunes and the virtues of humanity. To attempt it would be like trying to teach Shakespeare to young people in whose homes the only reading is found in the pulp magazines. It is not easy to teach children to despise their parents. Nor is it, perhaps, desirable.

12

At this point, our argument returns to the principle from which, at the suggestion of Rousseau, it took its start. Education is, and must be, an activity carried on by a social group. It is initiation into an existing "pattern of culture." And, as such, it depends upon the support and the authority of the group to which both the pattern and the pupil belong. But that means that we cannot teach world reasonableness unless there is a reasonable world. We cannot teach citizenship in a world-state unless a world-state exists. Are we Anglo-Saxons willing to recognize that implication and to act accordingly? Are we willing to put aside the hypocritical superiorities of the "White Man's Burden"? Are we able to stop the brutal pretense of giving "justice" to the "lesser breeds without the law," and to join with them as fellows in creating a law which shall be equal for all mankind? There is a curiously vital connection between teaching and the truth. If we practice justice and freedom we can teach them. If we do not practice them our words are like "the crackling of thorns under a pot."

13

If we are to have a world-state and to teach its lessons it is clear that the most difficult, as well as the most essential, education must be given, not to children but to men and women. As the new world takes form, the minds of children of every race and country will accept it as easily, more easily, than the chaotic, confusing, self-contradictory scheme of behavior which we now present to them. But that is not true of the grownups. We elders are caught in fear, in habit, in custom, in prejudice, in prudence, in common sense. It is we, therefore, who resist the education or re-education which we need. If we are to have the moral and intellectual reconstruction which are implied in the making of a world-state, the prime essential is an adequate process of adult education. Our minds will have to be refashioned. And we ourselves must do it. There is no one else to teach us. We, members of a common humanity, acting together as one sovereign people, must teach ourselves to do and to be what our common citizenship offers us to do and be. We must learn to so know and care for all our fellow men that we can participate with them in the one common cause. That task of human self-education our generation is called upon to begin. But it will be only a beginning. The road to reasonableness goes on and on.

289

From church to state! From myth to fact!—Can our culture make that transition? There can be little doubt, as Matthew Arnold has told us, that an old world is "dead." And for a long time now the new world has seemed "powerless to be born." And the essential guilt of "the three great democracies," Britain, France, and the United States, as well as of lesser democracies, has been their holding back in the face of the vast and terrifying possibility of a new birth. All over the world the new expression of the human spirit has been striving to break loose, to enter upon its career.

In China, so long abused and mistreated and contemned, there is new hope, new resolution, new achievement. The ancient wisdom is making contact with the modern world. In Russia, a new and relatively untried wisdom has come into action. And the magnificent loyalty and endurance and efficiency of the Russian people, in the face of overwhelming odds, give some suggestion of the power and majesty which a creative program might bring to us. India, too, is stirring. Her demand for justice and freedom will not be denied. She will not remain a subject people. Even the hysterical madness of the Germans and Italians and Japanese springs from the conviction that, the present chaos being intolerable, something better can be devised to take its place. The words of Adolf Hitler are madness. And yet that madness, as a power which threatens the peace and freedom of the modern world, does not spring primarily from the mind of Hitler. It is the madness of a civilization which has denied its own faith, which has been untrue to its own principles. If we believe in democracy we must practice it between nations as well as within our own nation. If we believe in freedom we cannot be content that other peoples shall be enslaved. If we believe in law and order we must join in establishing them for all mankind. If we believe in equality we cannot defend so desperately our own "higher standard of living." If we believe in reasonableness we must follow wherever reason may lead.

In the midst of all our agonies and uncertainties the new world is being born. It is that new world which gives meaning to education. Every pupil must be learning for it. Every teacher must be teaching for it. Every scholar must be thinking for it. Humanity is reasonable as well as unreasonable. It is the struggle between these two which defines the course of education. We know what teaching is only as we see and feel what the free spirit of man is trying to do and to be.

INDEX

293

Brotherhood of man (*see also* World-state): as basic belief of our culture, 203; and education, 205-207; as an hypothesis, not dogma, 204-205; implications of, in reasonableness, 233-235; state, not church, as primary institution of, 210; validity of, as a fact, 207-209

Cannon, Walter B., 106
Capital and labor, relations between, 228
Capitalism, meaning of, viii
Carlyle, Thomas, 134-135, 185
China, modern, 298; and Japanese tradition, conflict between, 115-117
"Christian" tradition maintained by Rousseau, 215
Christianity as a theory of education (*see also* Church), 21-22
Church: consent of, in transfer of power to state, 7; Comenius' accounts of, truest, 21; purposes of, in teaching, 4-5; replacing of, by state, in teaching, 3-10, 258-259; school's transfer from, to state, 53, 67-68; state substituted for, as brotherhood institution, 210; as teacher, reason for, 258
Churchill, Winston, 271
Citizen (*see* Individual)
Civil liberties (*see also* Liberties, Rights), 274
Civil state (*see* State)
Civilization (*see also* Culture): aim of, 225; meaning of, 250; as reasonableness, 225
Comenius, John Amos, 11, 13-25, 278; and Dewey compared, 124; educational theory of, 279-280; insight of, tenable today, 287; and Locke, compared as to concepts on toleration, 56-60; and Locke, differences in attitudes of, 14-18; rebellion of, against scholastic formalism, 14; on rights and authority, 82; schools of, 19-20; teaching methods of, 16-17; on toleration, 57-60
Communist Manifesto, 36, 54
Community, 9 n

Community: as God-established, 205-206; life in, principles of, 193, 208; school as expression of, 86; without a state, 174-175; and state, different, 223
Conscientious objector, right of, 273 n
Constitution of the United States, 223-224; Amendments to, differences among, 275; and Rousseau, 216-218
Consumer, the, in economic planning, 179-180
"Content" of teaching, 17-18; Comenius on, 19; desirable, according to Arnold, 50-52; useful, according to Locke, 30
Critical intelligence (*see* Intelligence, critical)
Criticism (*see also* Intelligence, Intelligence, critical, Reasonableness): Dewey on, 167-170; hierarchy of, 257; meaning of, 17, 169; method of, lost, 199; nature of, 209; philosophy as, 163; reasonable, of behavior, in social groups, 254-256; social, 171, 187-195
Cultural authority (*see also* Culture), expression of, as purpose of teaching, 9, 92
Cultural codes (*see also* Culture, pattern of), effects of, on teacher, 102-108
Cultural conflicts, reactions to, 103-108
Cultural groups, kinds of, 96-101
"Cultural lag," 139-140, 142
Culture (*see also* Culture, pattern of): basic beliefs of, 203; contradictoriness of Anglo-Saxon, 7-11
Culture and Anarchy, 39
Culture, patterns of (*see also* Behavior, Culture, General Will): as authority source, 97-99; among business men, 98-99; congruity of, 89-90; as criticism of behavior, 90-91; education and, 288; meaning of, 87-89; among scholars, 97-98; shifting of, 99-100

account of, ambiguous, 128-129; "disinterested," meaning of, 116-117; not a "drive," 212-213; function of, 139-140; and government (*see* Government); hierarchy of, 257; in judging, 170, 171; as kindness, 234-235; meaning of, new, needed, 199; and knowledge (*see* Intelligence and knowledge); methods of, search for, 163-164; nature of, as a procedure, 167-168; nature and function of, 117-119; origin of, 199; single, 282-283; state as, in action, 258, 260-261; and wisdom of God, dissimilar, 206

Intelligence, critical (*see also* Intelligence): as an authority, 105-108; as master of teacher, 108

Intelligence and custom (*see also* Custom, Intelligence): relation between, 252; relation between in teachers, 109-119

Intelligence and knowledge (*see also* Intelligence, Knowledge): Dewey's confusion concerning relation between, 166-167; relation between, 126-127, 150-168

"Intelligent self-interest," 227

"Interest" theory of education, 199

Interests, pooling of, 231-233, 248

International law (*see also* International relations), 242-243

International relations, 240-249; organic theory of, 246-247; teaching of, 248-249

Isolationism, moral, in education, 62

Italy (*see also* Dictatorship, Totalitarianism), technology's influence on, 186

Japan (*see also* Dictatorship, Totalitarianism): technology's influence on, 186; tradition of, in conflict with China's "unison," 115-117; United States at war with, 241-243

James, William, 93

Jesus, 234-235

John Dewey, an Intellectual Portrait, 182, 185

Kant, Immanuel, 81 n

Kindness as intelligence and reasonableness, 234-235

"Knowing" (*see also* Knowledge), 150, 153, 156, 166

Knowledge (*see also* Knowledge and intelligence): nature of, 280-281; unity of, 18-21; useful, 30; useless, nature of, 142-145; and wisdom, distinction between, 151-152, 167

Knowledge and intelligence (*see also* Intelligence, Knowledge): Dewey's confusion between, 166-167; Dewey's theories concerning, criticized, 194; difference between, 230-233; relation between, 126-127, 150-168

Labor and capital, relations between, 228

Laissez faire, belief in, broken down, 275-276

Language as an illustration of civilizing agreements, 250-253

Laurie, S. S., 14

Law, international (*see also* International law, International relations), and national sovereignty, relation between, 241-243

Law of self-preservation among nations, 243

Laws of classification, Rousseau's, 222

Learning (*see also* Education, Teaching): Comenius and Locke on, comparison of, 30; freedom in, 86-87; function of, equivocal, 66-68; meaning of, 277; as component of teaching, 27

Leisure class (*see also* Upper class), education of, 142-145

Liberalism: "dilemma" of, 112-119; as a pattern of culture, 112-114

Liberalism and Social Action, 178

"Liberties," private (*see also* Rights), 274-276

Locke, John, 11, 14, 18, 24, 26-34, 55, 205-206; atomism of, 60-62; and Barbarians, 43-44; and Comenius,

298

compared, 26-34, 57-60; community of mankind, 243; contradictoriness of, 56-57, and Dewey, comparison of, on the state, 173-174; on freedom, 217-218; moral dualism of, 66-68; on morality, 66; political theory of, 211, 213; and Rousseau, compared, 71-72; social theory of, 79-80; state, concept of, 173-174; on toleration, 57-60; on the upper class, 43-44; and "working schools," 38
Logic, The Theory of Inquiry, 162

MacIver, Robert, 9 n, 160-161 n
Mankind (*see also* Brotherhood), Comenius on, 20-21
Marx, Karl, 36-37, 48, 135
Method (*see also* Teaching): from "content," 17-18; experimental, in government, 190-191; of teaching, Rousseau on, 73-74
"Method of consequence," inadequacy of, 186-187
"Middle class," Arnold on teaching the, 39-40
Mind (*see also* Intelligence, Reason): as integral part of organism, 143-144; as "trouble-shooter," 129-130
Monism and pluralism, conflict between, 257-258
Morality (*see also* Reasonableness): non-existence of, in certain areas of experience, 239-240; origin of, 219-220; and prudence, 83; Rousseau on, 222
Morris, William, 135
Munich, blunder at, 271
Mussolini (*see* Italy)

National sovereignty and international law, relation between, 241-245
"Natural Rights," (*see* Rights)
Natural state (*see* State of nature)
Naturalism, 48, 124
Nazi state (*see also* Dictatorship, Totalitarianism), democratic state's influence on, 94-95

Need for a Recovery of Philosophy, The, 164
New Learning, 13-14, 18, 33

"Occasional Thoughts," 26
"Organic" theory (*see* also Disorganic theory, Political theory): in education, 258; of international relations, 246-247; of politics, 258; of society and individual, 211-213
Organization of teaching, Comenius on, 19-20
Origin of Species, 48

Pansophic Institute, 23
Peace, "just," impossible, 240
Philistines of middle class, Arnold on, 43-46
Philosophic thinking, Dewey on, 163
Philosophy: as criticism, 163; of education (*see* Arnold, Comenius, Dewey, Locke, Pragmatism); multiplicity of, 157-158; "pressure," and teacher, 285; and sciences, distinction between, 151-154; social, Dewey on, 157-158
"Philosophy and Democracy," 155, 157, 164
Philosophy of John Dewey, 166
Planning, economic, "pressure-group" attitude's effect on, 179-180
Plato, 12
Pluralism and monism, conflict between, 257-258, 262-265
Political institutions (*see* State)
Political theory, conflicting types of, 211, 258
Populace, Arnold on, 43-44, 54
Pragmatism (*see also* Dewey): general features of, 123-136; an influence for good, 134-135; negative ideas of, 193-195; outmoding of, 148-149; as a philosophy, 132-134; slogans of, 136, 138; social criticism, adopted by, 187-195; as social reform movement, 132; theories of, concerning democracy, 188-195; traditional beliefs attacked by, 139-142; and Victorianism as enemies,

299

INDEX

seau as enemy of, 83; toleration in, 56-60

Rights (*see also* Bill of Rights, Liberties), 205-206; and authority, origins of, Rousseau on, 83-84; civil, 275; Comenius on, 82; in a democratic society, meaning of, 268; dual functioning of, 133-134; "inalienable," questioned, 272-273; individual, according to Locke, 80, 82; individual, according to Rousseau, 80-84; and liberties, unlike, 275 n; origin of, 82-84

Rise of Modern Industry, The, 270

Rousseau, Jean Jacques, 12, 71-84, 180, 265; democracy of, 221-224; detested, reasons for, 76, 83-84; "duty" element in teaching of, 73-75; educational theory's cue from, 210-224; on freedom, 84, 94-95, 266; on human dignity, 266-270; and Locke, compared, 71-72; and national sovereignty, 241-242; as a naturalist, 75-76; as a "Nazi," 221; on non-reasonableness of social situations, 239-241; paradoxes of, 73-74; political theory of, 211, 213; on reasonableness, 237, 239-241; on social-group authority over education, 279; social theory, 79, 81-85, 213-224; state, concept of, 210, 213

Russia: technology's influence on, 186; wisdom in action in, 290

School (*see also* Education, Learning, Teacher, Teaching): Comenius' concept of, 19-21; dangers of, according to Locke, 31-32; as expression of community, 86; private, 284; purpose of, 127; social authority asserted by, 93; success of, criterion for, 262; transfer of, from church to state, 3-10, 53, 67-68 (*see also* Church, Education, State)

Sciences: Dewey's concept of, 151; and philosophy, distinction between, 154

Segregation in American education, 146

Self-preservation, law of, among nations, 243

Slavery, reasonableness lacking in conditions of, 239-240

Social authority (*see* Authority, Culture)

Social beliefs of Arnold, 42-46

Social change, need for, according to Arnold, 52-55

Social classes, Arnold's classification of, 43-46, 49-50

Social contract: expressions of, 229; freedom under, 215, 218; organic and disorganic theories concerning, 228; as origin of the state, 79; of Rousseau, 215 (*see also* Social Contract); theory of the state, 63-68

Social Contract, 72, 79, 214, 219, 239, 278

Social criticism, 187-195

Social groups (*see also* Culture, State): Arnold's classification of, 43-46, 49-50; congruity of, 89-90; relations between, in social and education theories, 253-256

Social philosophy (*see also* Philosophy), Dewey on, 157-158

Social science, "rationalization" in, 159-160

Society (*see also* Culture, pattern of, Government, Social groups, State): atomistic view of, 61; Comenius on, 22; Dewey discussion of, 183; and individual, relations between, 76-79; laws of, separate from laws of nature, 209; organization of, as evaluation criterion, 191-193; political, theories of, 211-224; rights in, 77-78 (*see also* Rights); Rousseau's theory of, 213-224; study of education essential for understanding, viii; two-class, in America, 146

"Sociologist's fallacy," 211-212

Specialization, dangers of, as seen by Comenius, 18-19

State, the (*see also* Government, World-state): authority of, 259;

301

Thinking (*see also* Intelligence, Mind, Reasoning): abstract, 134; as man-made, 200; philosophic, Dewey on, 163; practical, 130-134; process of, according to Darwin and Dewey, 125-126; scientific, reasonableness in, 230-231 (*see also* Reasonableness, Reasoning); social, contrasted with sciences, 159-160; as "trouble-shooter," 177
Thoughts Concerning Education, 14, 29, 31, 213
Toleration, 57-60
Totalitarianism (*see also* Dictatorship, Hitler): nature of, 265-267; in state-controlled education, charge of, 264-265
Tradition (*see* Culture, Culture, patterns of, Custom)
Treatise of Civil Government, 79

United States (*see also* Anglo-Saxon, Democracy), culture of, Arnold on, 46
Unity: Comenius on, 18-22; of intention, as principle of behavior, 252-253; of mankind, 258-259 (*see also* Brotherhood of man); in religious beliefs, 58; of understanding, intelligence as motivator of, 105-106
University (*see also* School): function of, 255-256; as illustration of relations of groups, 254-256
"Unwisdom," 107 n
Upper class (*see also* Barbarians, Leisure class): Anglo-Saxon, 142-143; education of, Comenius on, 29-32

Value experiences (*see also* Values), 231-233
Values: beliefs about, Dewey on, 162-163; evaluation of, Dewey's, 162-163; evaluation of, methods for, 188; and facts, relation between, 151 (*see also* Knowledge

and intelligence); of freedom, 193; human, depicted in Bible, 202; in intelligence functioning, 151; judgments of, 152; relativity of, 139-140; source of, 154
Veblen, Thorstein, 100
Versailles, Treaty of, 245
Victorianism: as aristocratic, 145-146; and Arnold, 47-50; as a disintegrating pattern of culture, 134-135; as an enemy of pragmatism, 132, 134-136, 142-148; revolt against, by Dewey, 183
Violence (*see also* Reasonableness and violence, War), teaching of, 248-249

Wallace, Henry, 73
War (*see also* Great War, World War): as nonreasonable social situation, 240-241; and peace, distinction between, 227-228
Western culture (*see* Anglo-Saxon, Democracy, Protestant-capitalism)
What Does America Mean?, 234-235
Will (*see also* General will): of pupil and teacher secondary, 86-87; of society, 183
"Wills" vs. General will, 87
Wisdom: expressions of, 283; and knowledge, distinction between, 151-152, 167; of the body, 106, 125-126; of the mind, 107, 125-126; negative, of Dewey, 188-191
Working class, education of, 143
World-state (*see also* State), 260-261; education belongs to, 286; Divine-will establishment of, 279-280; education for and by, 286-291; as goal of reasonable co-operation, 277
World War (*see also* Great War, War): reason for fighting, obscure, 265; "rights" as basic issue of, 78